IMAGINING COLUMBUS
THE LITERARY VOYAGE

Twayne's

LITERATURE
&
SOCIETY
SERIES

Leo Marx, General Editor
Massachusetts Institute of Technology

Previously Published

Epidemics in the Modern World
Joann P. Krieg

Tales of the Working Girl:
Wage-Earning Women in American Literature, 1890–1925
Laura Hapke

Vietnam in American Literature
Philip H. Melling

IMAGINING COLUMBUS

THE LITERARY VOYAGE

Ilan Stavans

Twayne Publishers • *New York*

MAXWELL MACMILLAN CANADA • TORONTO

MAXWELL MACMILLAN INTERNATIONAL • NEW YORK OXFORD SINGAPORE SYDNEY

Twayne's Literature & Society Series No. 4

Imagining Columbus: The Literary Voyage

Ilan Stavans

Twayne Publishers
Macmillan Publishing Company
866 Third Avenue
New York, New York 10022

Maxwell Macmillan Canada, Inc.
1200 Eglinton Avenue East
Suite 200
Don Mills, Ontario M3C 3N1

Library of Congress Cataloging-in-Publication Data

Stavans, Ilan.
    Imagining Columbus : the literary voyage / Ilan Stavans.
        p.   cm. — (Twayne's literature & society series : no. 4)
    Includes bibliographical references and index.
    ISBN 0-8057-8851-4 (alk. paper)
    1. Columbus, Christopher, in fiction, drama, poetry, etc.
2. Literature—History and criticism.   I. Title.   II. Series.
PN57.C6S7   1993
809'.93351—dc20   92-24431
                                                                          CIP

The paper used in this publication meets the minimum requirements
of American National Standard for Information Sciences—Permanence
of Paper for Printed Library Materials. ANSI Z3948-1984. ∞™

10 9 8 7 6 5 4 3 2 1 (hc)

Printed in the United States of America

To
Miriam Slomianski
(1909–1991)

CONTENTS

FOREWORD

Each volume in the Literature and Society Series examines the interplay between a body of writing and a historical event. By "event" we mean a circumscribable episode, located in a specific time and place; it may be an election, a royal reign, a presidency, a war, a revolution, a voyage of discovery, a trial, an engineering project, a scientific innovation, a social movement, an invention, a law, or an epidemic. But it must have given rise to a substantial corpus of interpretive writing.

The idea of elucidating the relations between writing and its historical context is not new. In the past, however, those relations too often have been treated as merely ancillary, static, or unidirectional. Historians have drawn on literary works chiefly in order to illustrate, corroborate, or enliven an essentially socioeconomic or political narrative; or, by the same token, literary scholars have introduced a summary of extraliterary events chiefly in order to provide a historical setting—a kind of theatrical "backdrop"—for their discussions of a body of writing.

In this series, however, the aim is to demonstrate how knowledge of events and an understanding of what has been written about them enhance each other. Each is more meaningful in the presence of the other. Just as history can be created only by acts of interpretation, so any written work invariably bears the marks of the historical circumstances in which it was composed. The controlling principle of the Literature and Society Series is the reciprocal relation between our conception of events and the writing they may be said to have provoked.

Leo Marx

The practice of literature sometimes fosters the ambition to construct an absolute book, a book of books that includes all the others like a Platonic archetype, an object whose virtue is not lessened by the years.

—Jorge Luis Borges,
"Note on Walt Whitman" (1947)

He cried in a whisper at some image, at some vision—he cried out twice, a cry that was no more than a breath—"The horror! The horror!"

—Joseph Conrad,
"Heart of Darkness" (1902)

        Paradise anew
Shall flourish, by no second Adam lost . . .
    A Canaan here,
Another Canaan shall excel the old.

—Philip Freneau,
"The Pictures of Columbus:
The Genoese" (1788)

PREFACE

I have been fascinated by Christopher Columbus since I was a little boy. The legend of his Sephardic blood, the vision of him as either the traitor or the savior of the oppressed, the coincidence of his arrival in the Bahamas in 1492, Spain's annus mirabilis—the year of the final unification of Castile and Granada by the Catholic kings and of the official edict proclaiming the expulsion of the Jews from the Iberian peninsula—these historical facts and ancestral rumors were enthusiastically promoted by my part-Russian, part-Mexican grandmother, a descendant of a globe-trotting family with previous incarnations in Eastern Europe, Palestine, and South America. Our delightful afternoon conversations, which took place regularly during a period of almost a decade in her old-fashioned living room, transformed her opinions into stimulating fantasies that haunted me for a long time and left stamped indelibly on my mind a sense of the heroic and the futile.

She was intentionally ambiguous. Often she would portray the admiral as disoriented, uneducated, and dumb; on other occasions, however, she would bestow upon him a kind of celestial power, turning him into a sort of

messiah ready to embark on an enterprise that seemed beyond the scope of
most of his contemporaries but that for him appeared an easy task. Two facets
then, two dimensions—two masks. If I was never sure how to understand
his legacy and behavior, it was clear without a margin of doubt that in my
grandmother's eyes the Genoese had possessed the talents of a superior
individual, that he was a man like no other. This aura of excellence, this
unique, magnanimous, poetic quality, was one reason for my fascination. I
soon understood that the admiral she fantasized about was nothing but an
invention she would joyfully create to make Columbus concrete, to feel close
to him, to make him part of herself. Always waiting for the apocalypse and
the redemption of God's world, she would distort the facts to accommodate
the biographical data (she had learned a lot about him in newspapers, magazines, and pseudoscientific books) to her own set frame of mind. He was a
savior because she wanted him to be one, because she needed a figure who
could have rescued thousands of Jews from the terrible fate that awaited
them in the torture chambers of Tomás de Torquemada's Inquisition. Or she
perceived him as a traitor because, having had some influential power over
Queen Isabella (she was sure they had been passionate lovers), he never did
enough to save his doomed fellow Jews and other foreigners in Spain. By the
time I grew up to become a bookish adolescent, I looked for the truth and
found it, but only partially. I read everything that fell into my hands. Wondering why my grandmother could never make up her mind about Columbus, I
was ultimately forced to understand the profound subjectivity and contin-
gency with which history has approached this gigantic figure. And I embraced
a kind of antihistoric stance because I came to understand that Columbus is,
for the most part, whatever people want him to be.

The mariner's adventure, I also concluded, had been from the very beginning a literary event. Fully conscious of his role, Columbus, a terrible speller
and perhaps speaker, kept a journal that was later lost and then found,
rewritten, and edited by the Spanish priest and historian Fray Bartolomé de
Las Casas. The text is full of suggestive descriptions of his Iberian environment and of what he saw on this side of the Atlantic. Having a good sense of
the power of the written word, he would occasionally send ravishing if inaccurate letters to friends and patrons in Spain, and when hard times darkened
his future he even dropped a line or two to the Vatican. As a reader, one
Roland Barthes would have liked, he wrote down his own thoughts and
impulsive comments in the margins of book pages, as he did with Marco
Polo's account of his voyages to the Orient.

Besides his own writing, pamphlets big and small began to be published
in Europe, from Venice to Lisbon, from Marseilles to Seville, immediately
after his first and second voyages. They conveyed rumors about his Jewish
origin, conflicting reports about his mysterious friendship with an unknown
Icelandic pilot, unconnected ideas about the unexplained death of his wife
and his affair with Beatriz Enríquez de Arana, and other infamous stories.
By the time he died in 1506, at the age of 55, penniless and not knowing the

true scope of his success, the lands across the Atlantic Ocean were attracting other travelers and serving as a source of inspiration for the collective imagination—and his life was being recounted already as an epic adventure.

Since then innumerable creative and historical writings, both fictional and nonfictional, have been produced. Every author, it is clear, has his own agenda: Columbus has proved to be as malleable a historic figure as one could find, a shapeless stone waiting for the sculptor. But time has shown that objectivity about him is also attainable. Empirical evidence, in the Maimonidean (and Popperian) sense, tells us that even if we cannot positively prove many details of the admiral's life, we can at least dispel falsifiable claims, as indeed some researchers have done. The verifiable facts are on file, and although full knowledge of Columbus's life is impossible, much of the history of his life is perfectly distinguishable from fiction. The mysterious fate of a handful of essential manuscripts—for instance, his journals (most of the narrative material we have about Columbus was transcribed by Las Casas)—the loss of a crown, the loss of a decisive map, these possibilities have encouraged detective novelists to compose thrillers in the tradition of Umberto Eco's *The Name of the Rose* (1981). In these scholastic plots the discovery of a missing link would change forever our fragile perception of reality. Nevertheless, in addition to the overcrowded flow of fiction, numerous scholarly articles and books on aspects of the admiral's life have appeared at an incredible rate every year, as if repeating his biography, searching his past, is a form of therapy in our quest to find the origin of modernity. The stuff of literature is everywhere to be found in his complex legend—his obscure childhood, his struggle to raise enough money to accomplish his project, the poverty he suffered with his son Diego after becoming a widower, the mutinies by both his Spanish crew and the Taino natives before that crucial 12 October and after. Fiction writers have played with Columbus's biographical data ad infinitum to invent plausible endings to unfinished stories or to revamp those that already end conclusively.

There are at least 20 valuable, if controversial, biographies of Columbus available in English, including those by Washington Irving, Salvador de Madariaga, Simon Wiesenthal, John Noble Wilford, and Samuel Eliot Morison. More than 100 novels, plays, oratorios, and poems were written between the nineteenth and twentieth centuries alone, most of them by Iberians and North and South Americans but a good many of them also by Greeks, French, Italians, and other Europeans. The tone and content are constantly changing: the Genoese is canonized or crucified and is depicted as an illuminated mystic, a prophet, a businessman, a courageous freedom fighter, a devoted Christian, and a messiah. For the most part, writers south of the Rio Grande have attempted to show his villainous face, while those in the North and in Europe prefer to perceive him as the inaugurator of an illustrious historical destiny.

Take, for instance, Washington Irving's biography, which heavily borrows from the scholarship of the Spanish scholar Martín Fernández de Navarrete. Irving, who became fluent in Spanish, was invited by Alexander Everett, then the U.S. ambassador in Madrid, to do a quick translating job of the Navarrete research on Columbus. Depressed, anxious, in a middle-age crisis about his struggle to become a well-known writer, and ready to leave England, the creator of "Rip Van Winkle" (1819) happily accepted the offer. But when he saw the dryness of the material he decided it needed embellishing. The result was a four-volume narrative account of the life and times of the Genoese, published in London in 1828, that mixed truth and fiction. Since Irving felt the division in his own identity between his European ancestry and his childhood and education in the United States, his mariner is a bridge between the old and new civilizations, a link between the two continents. In a way, that was precisely how Washington Irving wanted to be perceived by his contemporaries. Hence, Columbus's face reflected Irving's—a mirror.

A completely different view is offered by Alejo Carpentier, the baroque Cuban novelist and music critic who wrote the novel *The Harp and the Shadow* (1979). His conception of Columbus is that of a gold-thirsty explorer, a liar and charlatan who, after getting Queen Isabella's attention and love, described the Americas in a magical, surrealistic fashion, distorting reality, corrupting it. In fact, what Carpentier wants to prove is that the so-called magical realism movement (*lo real maravilloso*) subscribed to by South American writers such as Gabriel García Márquez and himself embodies nothing new: it reaches back to the sixteenth century, when the admiral talked about rivers of gold and exotic, chimerical animal beings. His mariner is very much the usurper of a whole native tradition, a victimizer, the metaphorical source of all the suffering for 500 long years by Hispanic America. Carpentier, it should be said, was a participant, albeit not a fully committed one, in Fidel Castro's 1959 socialist revolution. He was also a devoted scholar of Cuban music and folklore who spent part of his lifetime in exile for opposing repressive regimes. Thus, his view of the mariner is furiously negative: he attacks Columbus as a wrongdoer and debunks his glorified stature. Columbus, his face symbolizing evil, acquires the metaphysical appearance of Carpentier's own enemy.

Others who have drawn portraits of the Genoese include Joel Barlow, Walt Whitman, William Carlos Williams, Rubén Darío, Abel Posse, Carlos Fuentes, Paul Claudel, Friedrich Nietzsche, and James Fenimore Cooper. Each inserted his own message in his portrait; each advertised the qualities he liked the most and hid or deformed those he detested. As the admiral was lying on his deathbed in Seville, a myth was being born: Christopher Columbus the literary character, a narrative entity with a thousand different countenances, a man of resemblances, a chimera.

Most of the first literary texts describing his voyage were poems, including those by the seventeenth-century Mexican nun Sor Juana Inés de la Cruz and the Revolutionary-era American poet Philip Freneau. But that generic predilection soon changed. After 1792, and especially after the publication of Washington Irving's life account, there was an explosive production of novels, for two simple reasons, one historical and the other literary. First, the Geno-ese's life and legacy had come to be used for nationalistic purposes as the past was slowly made fully conscious in the Americas. The emergence of Columbus as a full-scale historic figure reached an apex only with the consoli-dation of the United States as an international power and with the economi-cally and politically unstable rise of the South American republics. As Kirkpatrick Sale claims in *The Conquest of Paradise* (1990) during the years immediately after his death the mariner was in a complete shadow. Nobody cared for him, and his contribution was largely ignored. But soon the popula-tion of the Americas increased considerably, and literature acquired a crucial role in the soul-searching process of exploring the collective past. Intellectuals and artists defined themselves by finding historic figures who legitimated their shared ancestry. If in 1692 the centennial of his so-called discovery was not celebrated in the new territories, by the time of the tricentennial in 1892 Columbus had become a legendary figure. Academic institutions, such as Columbia University, formerly King's College, were named after him, as were towns, squares, public monuments, and artistic events everywhere north and south of the Rio Grande. Through this transformation, Columbus acquired larger-than-life features.

The second reason for the nineteenth-century plethora of novels about the Genoese has to do with aesthetic and generic artistic trends in Europe and the Americas. The rise of the novel as a literary genre is fairly recent compared with poetry and drama. Only after Cervantes' *Don Quixote* (1605), Daniel Defoe's *Robinson Crusoe* (1719), and Jonathan Swift's *Gulliver's Trav-els* (1726) left a mark on the seventeenth and eighteenth centuries with their lucid, imaginative prose did Europe witness a marked increase in novelistic adventures. Immediately after 1492 other literary genres prevailed, but by the eighteenth century this new literary form had captivated the contempo-rary mind more than any other and had acquired an unparalleled popular status. The rapid development of sophisticated printing and book manufactur-ing techniques during the first part of the twentieth century has pushed the genre even further. More historical and fantasy novels have been published since World War I than in any other period of literary history. And Columbus has been a favorite novelistic character.

My grandmother's embellishments of the admiral's talents were but one more item on a long and inexhaustible list of such inventions. Today, some 15 years later and far from Mexico, a country my imagination has turned into a fantasy, what attracts me to Christopher Columbus is the notion that he is nothing but a collection of multiple disguises assembled around a set of historical facts. Thus, I am much less interested in what really happened in and around 1492 than in what did not but could have.

My purpose here is to revisit, to investigate, to play with the asymmetrical geometries of the admiral's literary adventures in the human imagination. This book is a huge tapestry in which the collective rumors and fabrications my grandmother narrated to me, and others I myself found later, are interwoven with my personal interests. I am interested in fiction, not in history, in literature, not in verifiable information. I hope that readers, each and every one who by chance or intention encounters these pages, will be able to create another individual version of the life and times of this essential discoverer, a unique perspective to be added to the eternal flux of inventions of our free, fecund collective mind. Certainly such contributions would be as provocative and needed as any other recorded or formulated to date. Ralph Waldo Emerson once wrote: "I am very much struck in literature by the appearance that one person wrote all the books; as if the editor of a journal planted his body of reporters in different parts of the field of action, and relieved some by others from time to time; but there is such equality and identity both of judgment and point of view in the narrative that it is plainly the work of one all-seeing, all-hearing gentleman."[1] Why not pretend, then, that the unreal, the fabulous, the collected, literary Genoese is a product of an all-seeing, all-hearing reader?

In the journey laid out in the following pages, two essential facts should be kept in mind. First, although I have tried to be as inclusive as possible, not even a third of the world literature about Columbus is discussed in this book. I refer to most of the well-known poems, novels, short stories, and dramas, but I have been careful to comment only on those that have left a mark. My selection is personal: I have chosen to discuss texts that I find compelling. In other words, my tastes as a reader have had a major influence on the shaping of my book. It could not have been otherwise. As Jorge Luis Borges, the Argentine fabulist and author of *The Aleph and Other Stories* (1948), claims, the "practice of literature" often engenders the need to create a "book of books," a text that is like a "Platonic achetype" in that it includes all others. All the texts written about Columbus over the last 500 years are chapters in one of those archetypal volumes. I have attempted to anthologize only those that belong to *my* book of books, which I have titled *Imagining Columbus: The Literary Voyage* so as to elaborate on the idea of a fifth and final triumphant trip of the Genoese that began once his last breath expired.

Second, I do not intend to be chronological. Great books, unlike scientific or technological discoveries, live alongside each other in a sort of eternal library. If one pays enough attention to the social and literary context that surrounds any of them, it is not necessary to read them in sequence. These are books of fiction, not history. One is likely to get a more fascinating, although somewhat chaotic, understanding of the human mind if, instead of following writers from the past to the present, one chooses certain thematic lines along which to navigate back and forth in time. And that is precisely what I have done in this archetypal voyage of mine. I intend to examine the following three characterizations of the admiral: a prophet or messiah; an ambitious gold-seeker; and a conventional man, equal to all others and not particularly remarkable. I will try to show how these three images have traveled chaotically through history, turning the admiral into a three-faceted metaphor. They have appeared spontaneously in different epochs, and together they offer a vision of how the imagination approaches Columbus.

Chapter 1, "Discovery or Encounter?" is a prelude to the unmasking of the many literary identities of Columbus. It thoroughly discusses the two opposing views of the celebration of the Columbian quincentennial and includes comments by Tzvetan Todorov, Edmundo O'Gorman, and Germán Arciniegas. Chapter 2, "Biographical Sketches," is a critical parade of the most notable biographies of the admiral. Although I focus on the contributions of Washington Irving and Samuel Eliot Morison, I've also included the views of Ferdinand Columbus, Fray Bartolomé de Las Casas, Salvador de Madariaga, Cecil Roth, Simon Wiesenthal, Kirkpatrick Sale, and John Noble Wilford, as well as the insightful historical, philosophical, and literary analysis of Pedro Henríquez Ureña, Alfonso Reyes, and Mario Vargas Llosa. While suggesting that the past is inherently unrecoverable, I offer in chapter 3, "Facts on File," the necessary, unchallengeable data about the mariner's life and achievements against which the plots of fiction will and should be judged.

Part 2, "Lives of a Literary Character," the core of my book, is divided into four chapters. Chapter 4, "Masquerade," is an attempt to explain how, with the help of Columbus, literature has shaped the collective identity of the Americas. It discusses the geographic and historic development of the admiral as a narrative figure in poetry, drama, short stories, and novels throughout the romantic, realist, naturalist, modernist, and post-modernist movements in literature. It also offers a view of the different masks—not only concrete but metaphorical (translations, revisions of long-lost manuscripts, and so forth)—worn by the Genoese in literary texts. Chapter 5, "The Man," includes commentaries on the works of Philip Freneau, Walt Whitman, James Fenimore Cooper, and Stephen Marlowe and lists those authors who have written about the mundane side of Columbus. In Chapter 6, "The Villain," I discuss the works of Alejo Carpentier, Rubén Darío, Abel Posse, and Michael Dorris and Louise Erdrich, all of whom believe the mariner to be a satan of sorts. Examining the works of Joel Barlow, William Carlos Williams, Friedich Nietzsche, Paul Claudel, Nikos Kazantzakis, and Carlos Fuentes, chapter 6, "The Symbol," gathers texts that tend to enlarge, shrink, or simply allegorize the admiral's life and achievements.

Chapter 8, "In Search of the Future," serves as the volume's conclusion and has a special place in my heart. If in the previous pages I discuss those works written about Columbus from 1492 to the present, here I foresee what the future might bring. My goal in this chapter is to describe some of the unwritten books on the mariner, the apocryphal titles that are likely to be published in the next 100 years in various countries and languages and for different audiences. With the end of the twentieth century around the corner, reaching outer space and conquering—if that is the term to use, knowing its horrendous contemporary connotations—new planets may become our own liberating experience, one similar to the experience Columbus offered fifteenth-century Europe. It remains to be seen whether in expanding our horizons beyond the conventional frontiers we have learned from past mistakes. The Genoese is our mentor but also an antimodel. He personifies courage and glory but also death and destruction. The imaginary titles I analyze, inspired by Stanlislaw Lem, Borges, Italo Calvino, and Ursula K. Le Guin, at times deal with past events, but their content is shaped by unseen circumstances, by a reality that is still intangible to us.

In his remarkable 1963 novel *Hopscotch*, Julio Cortázar, an extraordinary Argentine essayist and fiction writer, states that there are two types of readers: the active reader who jumps back and forth while digesting the text, thus establishing his own sequence and reinventing the author's creation; and the reader who passively follows the text from cover to cover without rebellion. Although this book certainly is not an experimental work of nonfiction, while producing it I had in mind a nonpartisan, strong-willed reader who could begin with the chronology and end with this preface. That approach corresponds to my own structural approach, as well as to my view of fiction as an autonomous universe *sub specie aeternitatis*.

To distinguish between the narratives written in the United States and those of the Southern Hemisphere, I use the terms North and South America—that is, I refrain from describing U.S. writers as "American." The terminology may sound bizarre to some, but after all, we are talking about one and the same reality, one divided into at least three different linguistic zones (including Portuguese). Nowhere do I offer new speculative information on Columbus's ethnic or religious origin, his true purpose in sailing across the Atlantic Ocean, his possession of a map of Vinland before he sailed from Palos, or his love affairs or lack of them. My ultimate task is to interpret literary narratives in the light of real historical events, not to add another theory to the already overcrowded pantheon of historical views on the mariner. The purpose of the following pages, therefore, is to examine the tremendous potential of human imagination when devoted to demolishing, rebuilding, and rediscovering a life that had turned commonplace.

ACKNOWLEDGMENTS

Perhaps the best way to experiment with ideas is to actively review current books. Many segments of this book originally appeared as essays on recent titles, native or translated into English. I wish to acknowledge the following editors: Alida Becker and Eva Hoffman of the *New York Times Book Review*, for allowing me to examine in their pages the work of Alejo Carpentier and others from Spain and Hispanic America; Mihàly Des of *El Observador* in Barcelona; Bart Schneider of *Hungry Mind* in Minnesota; René Avilés Fabila of *Excélsior* in Mexico; César Antonio Molina, Benjamín Pardo, and Amalia Iglesias of *Diario 16* in Madrid; Paco Ignacio Taibo and Eduardo "Gordo" Mendoza of *El Universal* in Mexico, two cosmopolitan journalists in what at times seems to be a wasted land; Pedro Pablo Alonso of *La Nueva España* in Oviedo; James L. W. West III of *Review* at Pennsylvania State University; Paul Baumann of *Commonweal* in New York City, whose devotion to providing space for criticism on Hispanic–North American letters will one day be remembered; María Beatríz Medina of *El Nacional* in Caracas, Venezuela, whom I have never met but whose face I have often seen in dreams; Mary S. Vásquez of *Letras Peninsulares* at Michigan State University; Jaime Alazraki, Gonzalo Sobejano, and Susana Redondo of *Revista Hispánica Moderna* in New York City; and Tom Auer and Leighton W. Klein, a devotee of the intonations of the Portuguese poet Fernando Pessoa, of the *Bloomsbury Review* in Denver. Thanks to all for offering me a space to invent and polemicize.

My gratitude also goes to the School of Liberal Arts and Sciences at Baruch College of the City University of New York for the financial help and the intellectual encouragement; to the staffs of the New York Public Library and Butler Library at my alma mater Columbia University, for helping me find lost, dusty, and forgotten volumes; to Liz Fowler, my former editor at Twayne in Boston, for her advice and support, and to my present editor at

Twayne in New York, Mark Zadrozny, for his dedication, patience, and a persistence expressed through polite and encouraging phone calls; to my friend Alfred J. MacAdam at Barnard College, for revising some translations from the Spanish, in particular the poem "To Columbus" by the Nicaraguan *modernista* of the late nineteenth century, Rubén Darío; and to Cindy Buck, who did a masterful job in copyediting the manuscript. Harold Augenbraum, director of the Mercantile Library in New York City, embarked with me on a journey into the brightness of Hispanic letters (written in English) in the United States, a voyage of discovery in which I confirmed how essentially different the two cultures are north and south of the Rio Grande and realized that Christopher Columbus is but a broken vessel, a link in the forking, disparate paths of these two cultures. Finally, Leo Marx, the William R. Kenan, Jr., Professor Emeritus of American Cultural History at the Massachusetts Institute of Technology and the general editor of the Literature and Society Series, gave me his wise advice and encouraging comments, without which this book would have certainly become a labyrinth. A grant from the National Endowment for the Humanities provided me with the funds to proceed with this manuscript and with other intellectual and creative endeavors.

PART I

Mapmaking

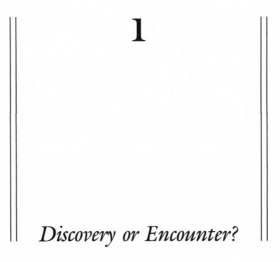

1

Discovery or Encounter?

BERTRAND RUSSELL ONCE FORCEFULLY ARGUED THAT IF some 100 men had been removed from European history, we would still be groping through the labyrinths of the Middle Ages. It's a persuasive idea. Perhaps for some the absence of Christopher Columbus from the history of North and South America, and for that matter from world history, would not mean much. After all, if he had not opened up a new geographical dimension across the Atlantic, somebody else would have, as indeed Amerigo Vespucci and other sailors and voyagers succeeded in doing during and after the fifteenth century.

In fact, there is little doubt that the Vikings, among them Leif Eriksson and Thorfinn Karlsefni, all great shipbuilders and courageous warriors, did it before that crucial, memorable year of 1492. By the eleventh century, more or less while the Normans were conquering England and the Crusaders were embarking on the bloody recovery of the Holy Land from the Muslims, these Scandinavians had already settled in Germany, France, and Spain. And around the year 1000 they founded a colony in the region of New England.

The reasons for their territorial outreach included overpopulation, quest for trade, internal dissension, and a passion for adventure. Yet the Vikings, we know, ultimately vanished and their legacy evaporated when Christianity was introduced into Scandinavia, thus giving rise to the emergence of strong, self-protecting kingdoms in Norway, Denmark, and Sweden. And since history is nothing but the version of past human events as perceived and recorded by the winners, not the losers, today Eric the Red and his itinerant followers are not considered the "official" discoverers of the so-called New World. Columbus has that honor.

But what if Russell's playful supposition were actually true?[1] What if the admiral never existed? What if he is only an invention of the human imagination which likes to play tricks, is fond of dreams, magic, and unreality, and gets lost in physical and intellectual labyrinths? If so, in almost no other case have our imaginings been so vivid, so exuberant, so prolific. With the probable exceptions of Jesus Christ, the prophet Muhammad, and William Shakespeare, no other individual has ever awakened as much passion and controversy, generated as many rumors surrounding his life and achievements, and inspired as prolific an imaginative effort to darken or enlighten his endeavors. If Christopher Columbus is indeed an invention, humankind certainly has to be congratulated for its fertile, everlasting creativity.

= Armageddon =

The end of a millennium always brings nightmare prophecies of doom and apocalypse, as well as ambitious reconsiderations. Already, as our restless, violent twentieth century is coming to its conclusion, the ominous scriptural visions of disaster, of ecological collapse and socioeconomic Armageddon, are cropping up everywhere. Even as the irrevocable collapse of Marxism has inspired the rebirth of messianic, democratic hopes for a new global ideology that could save the whole of humankind, witch-hunting and secret ritualistic organizations are working to alter people's views and influence religious beliefs. The year 1984, the date George Orwell suggested would be representative of the totalitarian Stalinist state, has been replaced with the year 2000.

What will the new century bring us? Will our overpopulated, intoxicated planet be able to survive? Can we ever escape fraternal blood spills and ancestral ethnic rivalries? Are humans meant to become robots? Will art as we know it today be part of our collective future? In Spain exactly 500 years ago, in 1492, similar speculations were in vogue.[2] The battles to reconquer Andalusia from the Moors had been successful. Just as Antonio de Nebrija was compiling his grammar of the Castilian language in Salamanca, Isabella and Ferdinand, the Catholic monarchs, decided to reinvigorate the kingdom by getting married and joining forces, uniting Granada and Aragon. It was also during that year that the Jews were expelled from the Iberian peninsula, thus eliminating, or at least dismantling, all foreign power inside the proud new nation. Catholicism was unanimously revealed as the one and only religion, and the Church conducted the inquisition—the dreadful search for chastity and *la pureza de sangre* (cleanness of blood).

Not all was vanity and glory. The empire's finances were actually stumbling: citizens were refusing to pay the taxes randomly collected, and institutions like the army were devouring mammoth amounts of money. Overexpenditure was also the result of lavish government parties and the lack of administrative planning. All these factors contributed to a xenophobic atmosphere and an unhappy population. To balance the budget, the state had to find new capital through viable financial alternatives that would decrease social unrest without threatening the grandiose life-style of the court and aristocracy. To make things worse, commercial routes to Africa and the Indies in Asia were under a blockade by the Turks, endangering the economic stability of Spain as well as Portugal. A new trade line had to be found—that, at least, appeared to be the best solution. On this volatile, potentially explosive stage, Columbus made his entrance.

An unknown Italian mariner, he had been seeking support from Portuguese and Spanish government officials, as well as from private entrepreneurs, to try out his idea that the only way to find a new trade route was to sail westward from the Canary Islands. He had been trying to raise funds for several years and was disheartened by the poor results. But suddenly his luck changed. With the support of Queen Isabella, the money finally came through, mainly from the pockets of rich *marranos*, or crypto-Jews. And a courageous adventure was set in motion, one that eventually proved to be a liberating, ecstatic experience.

= A New Era of Distant Neighbors =

The mariner's true motives are in dispute. If indeed he was looking for a viable commercial route to the Indies to reinvigorate the Spanish kingdom, he seems to have been a disoriented oceanographer with little knowledge of sailing techniques, a fortunate fellow at the right time and place. His marine calculations were often mistaken, and his data frequently incomplete and wrong. Artists, historians, and intellectuals, among them the Argentine novelist Abel Posse, argue that Columbus's admiration for Marco Polo, the Venetian who had set foot in Cathay (China) in 1266 and reached the court of Kublai Khan, transformed his passion for sailing from an adolescent infatuation into a lifelong career. In the Genoese's eyes, this enterprising, spirited Italian was the true role model: he had been looking for Cipangu (Japan), a legendarily wealthy island, half-paradise, half-reality, full of gold, located on the map some 30° to the east of Cathay. Columbus wanted to duplicate Marco Polo's success by attempting a similar voyage by another path.

But a handful of academics and independent scholars, such as the Oxford professor Salvador de Madariaga and the Nazi hunter Simon Wiesenthal, have argued that during his first voyage from Palos to the Bahamas Columbus had a hidden agenda: sailing westward across the Atlantic, with money raised from wealthy Jewish businessmen, was secretly a plan to look for a new land where the *conversos*—Jews who because of the torture and merciless persecutions of the Inquisition had openly converted to the Christian faith but in truth remained loyal to their ancient Hebrew heritage—could freely practice their original belief.

Whatever the actual facts, the Spanish empire, in financial trouble and facing social unrest, needed a gold mine to balance its budget and was lucky enough to find it in the Americas. Thus Columbus became a sort of messiah, an economic wizard.

Perhaps there is at least partial truth in each of these views: it was a search for a new trade route, a quest for money and richness, fueled by fear of an apocalypse and anxiety about things to come in the imminent new century. All of these ingredients helped Columbus to shape his loyalties, to justify his navigations, and to get people around him to make his dreams become a reality. When the admiral first reached Guanahaní (Watlings Island) and later on Juana (Cuba), Hispaniola (Haiti and the Dominican Republic) and San Juan Bautista (Puerto Rico), a new era had begun.

It was not a very happy era, however, and it was one that could tolerate both success and disaster. After Columbus reached the New World—according to some, not before stealing important maps and information from an Icelandic pilot—the fruits of his success were savored by almost everybody except him. Others who were perhaps as uncompassionate and ambitious but no doubt more bloodthirsty immediately took advantage of his precarious position and left him poor and forgotten. Having been named sole governor of all new territories beforehand, his titles and properties were revoked or taken away by old friends and loyalists. After Queen Isabella's death, even King Ferdinand, instead of fulfilling his official promises, hurried to repossess the mariner's legacy. There was nothing new, I should add, in this opportunism; after all, intrigue and disloyalty have always crowned grandiose human enterprises. The mariner's successors, among them conquistadores such as Francisco Pizarro and Hernán Cortés, with their respective armies in Mexico and Peru, were cruelly barbaric toward the native population, although some missionaries tried to stop their atrocities by acting as the voice of morality. Hispanic America eventually became a wasteland. In contrast, the United States ended up a triumph of progress and civility. Why? One of the many reasons is that the vast territory of the North was not settled by sophisticated native empires like the Aztec and Inca that had to be ousted. The British colonists, although abusive and entrenched, didn't need to dismantle a powerful civilization, but scattered tribes without a solid and well-equiped army.

Could Columbus foresee the outcome of his 1492 trip and the three that followed? Some say he could, and that he should be held accountable for his crimes against humanity and those of his successors. Others perceive him on the other hand, as an unwitting product of an imperialist, violent epoch.

Shortly after that decisive year of 1492, two very distinct, almost antagonistic realities emerged north and south of the Rio Grande. The passengers on the *Mayflower* were inheritors of the Puritan tradition. Their dream was to begin anew far away from England, to create an improved version of their motherland based on the manners, laws, and reason of their forefathers. Not only were these Calvinists fortunate enough not to find a huge Indian empire ready to oppose them, but their contact with another race did not extend to miscegenation; their ethnic ancestry remained pure and their Protestant religion was left intact. They were motivated to work hard and to make progress, giving birth to the myth of a new Israel, the chosen people of the New World.[3] Their dream became a success. But Cortés, Pizarro, and the other conquistadores came with a different attitude: they arrived to destroy, to proselytize, to exploit, to rape, to kill. Moctezuma II and Cuauhtémoc, the last two Aztec emperors, confused them with Quetzalcoatl and other divine entities; instead of battling them, the Aztecs sent jewelry, gold, and exotic gifts to greet them. Immediately afterwards, the Church began baptizing "infidels," treating the Indians[4] in an ambiguous, two-faced fashion: priests like Fray Bartolomé de Las Casas, a champion of Indian rights in colonial times and one of Columbus's biographers, had a benevolent, philanthropic attitude toward the native environment, both human and natural; but others—the majority, unfortunately—supported the cruel laws enacted by the Spanish crown and perpetuated in the Americas by the viceroyships. The conquerors, whether sexually abusing or simply "buying" native females, fathered bastard mestizo children of mixed ethnic background—half-Spanish, half-native. In the words of José Vasconcelos, a nineteenth-century Mexican philosopher who became minister of education, *la raza de bronce* (the bronze race) was born.[5] Yet pitiless plagues and other natural disasters quickly took a toll, killing a high percentage of that new race. As a result, Hispanic American civilization has been marked by violence, chaos, and repression. Octavio Paz claims in his psychological and intellectual study *The Labyrinth of Solitude* (1950) that the collective identity of Hispanic America is obtuse, introspective, and full of fears and tremors.[6] While the nations of North America became successful new societies, Mexico, Peru, Argentina, the Caribbean nations, and other parts of the region were unable to find political, military, and financial stability. Theirs is the legacy of what Las Casas called the "black legend," his account of the disasters and massacres perpetrated by the Spaniards in the newly explored lands.[7] Probably nowhere in the world do two civilizations as dissonant and contrasting live side by side, divided only by the muddy flow of the Rio Grande. Distant neighbors, indeed.[8]

A book that attempts to explain why the Europeans were cruel, merciless, and deceiving in Hispanic America is *The Conquest of America*, published in French in 1982 and written by the renowned French literary critic of Russian descent, Tzvetan Todorov. His thesis, phenomenological in nature, is that when making a discovery, an immature self most often finds what it is looking for, not the true reality surrounding it. "We can discover the other in ourselves," he argues, "realize we are not a homogeneous substance, radically alien to whatever is not us: as Rimbaud said, *Je est un autre*. But *others* are also "*I*"s: subjects just as I am, whom only my point of view—according to which all of them are *out there* and I alone am *in here*—separates and authentically distinguishes from myself" (3). As a product of his time, Columbus, who was not a particularly avant-garde individual but was full of energy and had a talent for overcoming obstacles, was incapable of understanding the environmental and aboriginal treasures he found in the Americas. With a set frame of mind, he interpreted what he saw according to his own dogmatic weltanschauung. More than an itinerant voyager, he was a tourist interested only in a segment, not the whole complexity, of reality. He failed both in communicating with the Indians and in realizing the vastness of his enterprise because, according to Todorov, he was always the dupe of his illusions (14–33). But not only Columbus is to blame: the European travelers, especially the Iberian ones, arriving in the New World were representatives of an unripe civilization incapable of accepting or living in peace with other cultures. The "civilized man" was self-righteous and individualistic, an egomaniac. Recognizing the Aztecs and Incas as humans, as equals, would have entailed dialogue. But the Genoese and his successors traveled across the Atlantic to find wealth and, perhaps, to discover another facet of themselves, though not a self different from their own. They massacred, destroyed, and burned because power could not be shared. Had they acknowledged the inherent difference between Europe and the Americas, their attitude, claims the French critic, would have been totally different. But it could not have been: in 1492 feudalism still prevailed in Aragon and Castile; the principles of *liberté, egalité, et fraternité* and the growth of the bourgeoisie, already apparent in England, France, and Germany, were still in embryonic form in the Iberian peninsula and would take centuries to fully germinate.

= Black-and-White in Color =

Thus, we have two viewpoints on Columbus's achievement. According to one, the 1492 discovery of the Americas was a benign event, a true beginning, that enlarged the material and spiritual resources of humankind. The opposing view, that Columbus opened the door to tragedy, is more pessimistic. Disastrous yet foreseeable consequences unfolded that far surpassed any other tragedy in history up until then and perhaps ever since. More people died in plagues (according to some estimates, close to 7,000,000), wars, and religious conversions because of the confrontation between these two civilizations—the European and the native—than in World Wars I and II, the Vietnam War, the Crusades, the U.S. Civil War, the French Revolution, and all other battles that have ever occurred.

Amplifications of these two views are always at hand. Proponents of the first view refer to Columbus's reaching the Americas as a *discovery*: in the second view, it was only an *encounter*, since you can only discover that which you don't know but already exists.[9] The "discovery" group argues that it was a glorious moment in history that should be celebrated with an annual holiday and centennials; the "encounter" group believes that it should be remembered only by a moment of mournful silence. Two opposing portraits of the Genoese emerge: hero and villain, saint and scoundrel.

In 1992 the governments and cultural institutions of the Southern Hemisphere—where the castastrophe has been felt far more than in the United States—supported the encounter thesis when it came to celebrating the quincentennial.[10] In Madrid, Rome, Hollywood, London, and Washington, D.C., however, there was a readiness to celebrate and money to spend. The supporters of the discovery thesis planned innumerable fiestas full of color and fireworks, museum exhibits, operas, films, public television programs, outer-space projects, diplomatic gatherings, and the publication of some 35 commemorative books.[11] With as much energy, the opponents—among the most important was the Alliance for Cultural Democracy in Minneapolis— sabotaged the occasion; they claimed their campaign reached back to Fray Bartolomé de Las Casas and his accusation of European atrocities.

The year 1892, it should be noted, saw a big Columbus party as well, although not quite as generous and polemical as the 1992 fete. Rubén Darío, the most famous Hispanic American poet of the time, traveled to Spain under the sponsorship of several South American governments, but instead of delivering a congratulatory sonnet, he read a confrontational poem accusing Columbus of rape and holocaust. His voice, nevertheless, was not loud. The admiral was honored north and south, east and west. A memorial to the mariner was unveiled at the southwest corner of Central Park in Manhattan, and in Chicago, a city consumed by fire in 1871 but rebuilt with magnificent skyscrapers, there were colorful festivities. The Czech composer Antonín Dvořák wrote his symphony *From the New World* (1893) for one of the celebrations. That same year, the World's Fair held near Chicago was known as the World's Columbian Exposition.[12] By then, of course, France and North America had well-established, democratic, constitutional governments, and some Hispanic American nations, among them Mexico and Argentina, were tentatively independent.

In 1992 the polemic turned sour and the celebration revealed the hypocrisy in Columbus's position. The novels and poems produced before and during the yearlong happening, including *The Dogs of Paradise* (1985) by Abel Posse and *Christopher Unborn* (1987) by Carlos Fuentes, were full of candor and criticism, reflecting a new multicultural global order and the reshaping of the collective identity. With the end of World War II, countries in Africa, Oceania, Asia, and Hispanic America sought their independence. The end of colonialism gave rise to the idea of internationally recognized human rights. With time, that worldview has matured. "Multiculturalism is not a plot of some left-wing professors in the U.S.," claims Garry Wills. "It is the most obvious of global facts, in a world where the 'natives' are telling Columbus how to behave, rather than the reverse. That, oddly, is a cause for celebration. The next century will not be [North] America's to call its own— or any other single nation's. We are all in a boat together, and Columbus must travel with us now as a fellow passenger, no longer the skipper" (61).[13] At the end of the twentieth century the world believes that history can no longer be written by Europeans alone. New artistic and intellectual centers have emerged in what was once the periphery of culture—Buenos Aires, Johannesburg, Tel Aviv, Mexico City, Cairo, and Tokyo—as has the sense of an integrated planet, what the Canadian mass-media analyst Marshall McLuhan calls "the global village." Since the late 1950s and 1960s, writers such as Gabriel García Márquez, Milan Kundera, Nadine Gordimer, Chinua Achebe, and Mario Vargas Llosa have been promoting a different, multilingual, multiethnic order.

The attempt to make a villain out of the mariner has particularly angered a handful of intellectuals and more than a few conservatives in the Anglo-Saxon world. If we remember the victims of the Holocaust perpetrated by Adolf Hitler, claim some, why gather in joyful parties on an occasion that also marks the massive killings of millions of Indians in the Southern Hemisphere? To respond, Karl Meyer, an editor of the *New York Times*, wrote a brief essay in 1991 entitled "Columbus Was Not Eichmann." He argues, not without logic, that living as we do in a self-righteous age, the arguments against the sailor tell more about us than about him. The conquistadores were not war criminals, he claims, at least not like the deranged, machinelike commanders and soldiers who served Hitler and his merciless army. Although the violence perpetrated by the Spaniards was far beyond any reasonable limit, "what needs to be added is that cruelty was the common currency of power among Europeans, and indeed among less-than-noble high Indian civilizations." Meyer offers a passage from Sir Walter Raleigh in which the British courtier and man of letters depicts life in the *evil* Spanish empire; Meyer then writes: "The colonizers had much to answer for. But to ignore their achievements travesties history. Europeans passed judgment on themselves, thus nurturing the very universal norms that enable people today to throw mudballs at their ancestors."[14] Indeed, Meyer has a point. After the 1863 abolition by Abraham Lincoln of slavery, with its endless repercussions, after World War II, after the civil rights movement of the 1960s, we now live in an aggressive age that professes little tolerance for cruelty. To identify with the victim has become a fashionable ideological stand. A revised view of 1492 forcefully argues that blood was the ink with which the conquerors wrote their signature. Yet history is nothing but the need of the present to comprehend and find meaning in the past. And each epoch colors the past with tones that legitimize its own moral and spiritual values.

Looking at Columbus as a treacherous saboteur may be nothing but a mirage in which we are trying to find the victim we always wanted to be. Thomas Aquinas is said to have argued that God has power over everything but the past. Although history is unchangeable and we are forced to live with both its happy and horrendous consequences, our interpretation of past events can vary. Perhaps the best way to approach a controversy of this magnitude is with some degree of humor. Finding the humorous side has always been the job of Russell Baker, a newspaper columnist and the celebrated author of *Growing Up (1982)*. "Listening to these charges," Baker argues in a hilarious article, "you get the impression if it hadn't been for Columbus there'd be no air pollution, no grim Interstate highways or ugly housing developments marring the continent's beauty, no mountains of burning tires or reeking gasoline refineries blighting the landscape." He goes on to say that the perfect paradise that the Americas could have been if the admiral had not arrived also has its *serious* disadvantages. If the Genoese had not discovered the new territories, some other traveler, perhaps in the nineteenth or early twentieth century, would have, and money would have begun to flow in, eventually turning the newfound lands into an amusement tourist park, a Disneyland of sorts. "The trouble is, though, that once the tourist dollars start flowing, residents of the new-found continents are going to be under heavy pressure to make a mess of Paradise. I don't know about you, for instance, but I'm not going to be in a hurry to go until they build some decent highways and motels and a few places where you can get a cheeseburger at 3 o'clock in the morning." Baker finishes by admitting that, indeed, Columbus opened the door to a long list of maladies: "slavery, capitalist exploitation, cultural arrogance, racism, sexism, ethnic jokes and steroids. . . . Such things always happen when two utterly alien cultures encounter each other for the first time. That's why I'm against sending earth people to other planets."[15] His clear conclusion is that the mariner has become an all too easy target, a villain in a heroless universe.

= Imago Mundi =

Two of the most fascinating scholarly books that preceded this controversy were written by an important Mexican historian and philosopher, Edmundo O'Gorman, and by the Colombian Germán Arciniegas. Originally published in 1958 and still a best-seller in Hispanic America—particularly in Mexico, where it has had enormous influence on intellectuals and artists, such as Octavio Paz—O'Gorman's *The Invention of America* went through many revisions and additions and appeared in somewhat different form in English in 1961. (The book is based on lectures delivered at Indiana University). Philosophical in nature and Aristotelian in method, it is divided into four parts. The first, "History and Critique of the idea of the Discovery of the Americas," uses systemic logic and the related game of syllogisms to prove that in order for us to accept the idea that the lands across the Atlantic were indeed "discovered," Europe needed to have had some sort of intuition about its possible existence, a premonition, or an ideal picture. O'Gorman argues that there are no real accidents in history: all events can be seen as consequences preceded by immediate causes. Thus, for the New World to be discovered, it had to be waiting for a visitor, it had to be ready for an unmasking. Does that mean that for a gold mine to be discovered, it has to be waiting to be discovered? Yes, because the discoverer of a gold mine needs to have an appreciation for the value of gold as a metal that society deems precious. Otherwise, society would ignore the discover's finding.

The second part, "The Historical Horizon," explores the prevailing myths about the extra-European reality before 1492, from Christian theology to Marco Polo and Roger Bacon. The third part, "The Process of Inventing America," again using systemic logic, discusses the reaction to and aftershocks from Columbus's achievements. And the fourth part, "The Structure of Self in America and the Meaning of American History," investigates how the New World reshaped the ancient concepts of time, space, and humankind.

O'Gorman's nonfiction narrative, although at times convoluted and opaque, has one objective: to show that America is a creation of Europe.[16] Thus, his central thesis is that the New World is nothing but fantasy, a utopia like those imagined by Jonathan Swift, Charles Fourier, Edward Bellamy, and Ray Bradbury—an imaginary reality. (Saint Augustine, in "The City of God" [413–27], is brave enough to give the Greek meaning of *utopia*: "There's no such place.")

The same argument is developed in Arciniegas's *America in Europe*, a book originally published in 1975 and translated into English in 1986. "When Columbus steers his three caravels westward," claims Arciniegas,

> he is not heading for the uttermost unknown. He is moving toward a magical reality. He sets out to locate a land already occupied: those populous regions, conquered already by fable. Medieval man, to whose society the admiral belongs, is more likely to believe in the fancifully elaborated than in the real and tangible. The giants and pygmies of fictional jungles exist for the learned and the ignorant alike with the same certainty as the folk they jostle in the marketplace or greet in the town square, see in church or pass on the highway to and from the countryside. The islands and the mainland of the other hemisphere have got to be the home of Cyclopses, of a whole race of big-eared people, of dog-faced tribes, of Amazons.[17]

An essayist born in 1900 and the author of some 30 books, including *Latin America: A Cultural History (1965)* and a study of the chivalrous search for El Dorado, Arciniegas is bewildered by the fact that Western historians have emphasized the European perspective on what went on in and after 1492. He asks, What would our global reality be today without the New World? He goes one step further than O'Gorman: his goal is to rewrite the history of the world in reverse, to explain how during the sixteenth century and afterwards the New World reformed, transformed, and deformed the Old.

Divided into 12 chapters, *America in Europe* was not written for the specialist but for the lay reader interested in historiography. Unchronological in format, it uses rhetorical suppositions, anecdotes, and myths to set forth its convincing and solid ideas. Arciniegas discusses just about everything: the political agenda of Denis Diderot's *Encyclopedia*, the theological motifs behind the Inquisition, the so-called utopian science fiction of Plato and other Greek thinkers, the slave trade from Africa to Brazil, the Caribbean islands and North America, the foundations of the Industrial Revolution, the biological theses of Charles Darwin, even the military intervention of the United States in World War II. His conclusion is that France, Spain, England, Germany, and Italy have drastically changed their distinctive diet, art, philosophy, literature, morality, and politics since the admiral first set foot on Watlings Island. Instead of looking down on the Americas as virginal and inexperienced, we must reorganize our vision of history if we are to fully understand the profound transformation wrought by the event—a (re)discovery of the ancient by means of the new and invented.

= The Key to Modernity =

Columbus died poor, forgotten, neglected. His life story is that of a journey from poverty to fame and back to invisibility. Yet for over 100 years we have regularly celebrated his enterprise. In Hispanic America, 12 October, the date he set foot on non-European soil, is called Día de la Raza (Day of the Race); in the United States, it is known as Columbus Day. There is a marked difference between the two names: the first commemorates the ethnic line formed as a consequence of his voyages, the birth of an entire civilization; the second glorifies not a collectivity but the mariner himself. The moment the mariner left this earth in 1506, rumors and speculations began to spread about his true identity, the secret of his success, his posterity. His metamorphosis into a mythical figure was instantaneous. People began imagining his origins, his loyalties, his true character. Was he a villain or a messiah?

Winifred Sackville Stoner, Jr., a North American, wrote in 1919: "In fourteen-hundred and ninety-two, Columbus sailed the ocean blue."[18] In spite of the controversy over whether the admiral made an encounter or a discovery, one thing is certain: the Genoese is a key to modernity. Utopia—an earthly paradise, a fresh beginning—had been conquered. Only 50 years after the annus mirabilis, in 1543, Copernicus laid the foundations of modern astronomy by disproving the ancient conception of our planet as the center of the universe. More or less simultaneously, one of the supreme examples of Renaissance genius, Leonardo da Vinci, with his attraction to the infinite and passion for the architectural life of bodily things, made tremendous contributions to engineering, medicine, drawing, and music. And in 1516

Thomas More placed his own idea of utopia, presided over by an ideal government founded in reason, in the lands named after Amerigo Vespucci.[19] After
1492 the vast globe was changed forever and with it, the limits of the Western
imagination. Novelty became a craze: *new* fauna and flora, *new* patterns
of culture, *new* idioms were incorporated into the catalog of the human
adventure.[20] Science and technology developed and religious dogmas gave
way to liberalism and progress.

Bertrand Russell surely was right: if Columbus had not existed, somebody else would have done the job. While it is true that the Vikings landed
in New England first, the admiral was the lucky one: applying a useful
metaphor, he was there when the photographer was at hand. And for that
alone he deserves credit.

2

Biographical Sketches

Plagiarize,
Let no one else's work evade your eyes,
Remember why the Lord made your eyes,
So don't shade your eyes,
But plagiarize, plagiarize, plagiarize—
Only be sure always to call it please "research."
—Tom Lehrer,
Lobachevsky (1981)

"WRITING LIVES," VIRGINIA WOOLF BELIEVED, "IS THE DEVIL."[1]
As a nonfiction genre, biographies are dangerous in that they enlarge or
shrink the natural size, talents, and defects of their object of study. Leon
Edel, the Pulitzer Prize–winning biographer of Henry James and Willa
Cather, claims that to compose a narrative account of a person's life, an author
must not be genealogically or sentimentally related to him or her; impartiality
could be threatened. Data are always malleable and subject to interpretation.

15

Patience, distance, perspective, a love and respect for the subject, these ingredients are critical to the accuracy of the project. Every biographer adapts, revises, and invents, and in the end the text is an indirect account of the author's mental associations and affinities.[2]

Each biography of Christopher Columbus plays more or less with the same information, from his obscure birth in Genoa, Italy, to his miserable death in Valladolid, Spain. Some writers even seem to plagiarize others, though they are all careful enough to always call their research innovative and original. My intention here is to look behind the veil, to look for the biographer in his biography. Most life accounts of Columbus have been produced by writers in the United States and Europe—Italians, British, Austrians, Spaniards, or Portuguese—all mature males in their forties.[3] Their accent is always on the masculine qualities of the mariner, on his wisdom or foolishness, on his courage and struggle for power or on his sensibility and loving care for family and friends.

= Ferdinand, or, The Ambiguities =

"It is one thing to write like a poet, and another thing to write like an historian," says the character Samson in *Don Quixote*. "The poet can tell or sing of things, not as they were but as they ought to have been, whereas the historian must describe them, not as they ought to have been but as they were, without exaggerating or suppressing the truth in any particular."[4] This wise epigraph introduces *Admiral of the Ocean Sea* (1942), a magisterial account of the mariner by Samuel Eliot Morison, a Harvard professor interested in oceanography who in order to write the book sailed, in 1940 and before, the course of the first and second voyages, from the San Salvador landfall through the Bahamas to Cuba, the Virgin Islands, and Puerto Rico (xv–xx). No other biography has been so systematic, so ambitious in capturing the whole scope of Columbus's adventures. Subsequent researchers, consciously or not, use it as a model. Yet Morison's was hardly the first biography of its kind.

Many previous biographies were important documents that illuminated the admiral's life, although, as exercises in historical recording, one has to handle each and every one of them very carefully. One of the first was written by Ferdinand Columbus (Don Hernando Colón), the illegitimate son of the mariner and his lover Beatríz Enríquez de Arana. Ferdinand was a Renaissance man of letters who, after accompanying his father on the fourth voyage (May 1502 to November 1504) and living for a while on the island of Hispaniola, traveled extensively throughout Italy, France, and other European countries. He died in 1539 in Seville, where he had accumulated a huge library of over 15,000 volumes.

When the Catholic kings revoked the privileges previously granted to his father, limiting them in 1511 to the viceroyship of the Antilles, Ferdinand defended his family heritage and in particular the memory of his father. That defensive attitude permeates his biography, which is never free of subjectivity—a sin, one should recognize, that Ferdinand is the first to openly confess. Apparently worried that history might not include Columbus in its eternal pantheon of decisive historical figures, the biographer improves, embellishes, and glorifies his subject at every opportunity, turning his work into a larger-than-life portrait *pro vita sua*. The result is a subjective, biased text full of private agendas.

The title of his volume is *Histoire*.[5] Its date of composition is uncertain. Although the currently available text is slim, Ferdinand claimed to have taken almost five decades in composing it. The first thing the reader should remember is that *Histoire* was not written by a professional historian or chronicler but by a direct descendant of the navigator. Ferdinand was a bastard son who was discriminated against and not as favored as his half-brother Diego, the child of Columbus and his only wife, Felipa Perestrello e Moniz. A banquet of envies, of rivalries between the siblings, thus permeates his work. Ferdinand's two objectives in writing the biography were to restore his father's reputation and to promote his own image as his father's legitimate heir. He pursued both almost without scruple. Often Ferdinand adds fictitious data or reshapes a scene or circumstance. He tells us, for instance, that Columbus attended the University of Pavia. According to Morison, Paolo Emilio Taviani, Wilford, and other scholars, the assertion has no basis in reality: the records of the institution show no sign of Columbus ever having matriculated. The son also informs us that his father came from an illustrious family, when actually his genealogical origins were humble, stigmatized by poverty.

Beyond its lack of objectivity and its transformation of lies into certainties, the text suffers from another problem, one Cervantes himself and his purported Arabic friend Cide Hamete Benegueli would have found intriguing: Ferdinand's original manuscript was lost, and the only surviving version is the Italian translation, by one Alfonso Ulloa, published in Venice in 1569 and 1571, some 30 years after Ferdinand's death. Those aware of the perils and tricks of the art of translation know that when transposing a text from one language into another, a translator adapts and revises. But Ulloa did something more: his translation is unconvincingly done. His version, one guesses, is but a shadow of the original. Most probably, he exercised some sort of censorship, either for personal reasons or under somebody's influence. And since the biographical content does not come directly from Ferdinand's pen, some critics—among them, José Torre Revello and Ramón Iglesia, the noted historian at the University of Wisconsin[6]—have claimed that the textual errors are not to be blamed only on Ferdinand but may also be attributable to the foreign, antagonistic translator. Ferdinand was not alive when his biography was published in Italy; much damage could have been done in his absence. The fact that *Histoire* was not published in Spain might well reflect resistance in financial, political, and intellectual circles to the instant elevation of Columbus into any kind of immortality.[7]

Histoire is divided into 58 chapters, most of them only a few pages long or less. The style is uncomplicated, the narrative straightforward but sketchy. It begins with a discussion of Columbus's family name and origin and ends with Queen Isabella's death and that of the admiral. (In a final note, Ulloa claims that the mariner's remains were deposited in the Cathedral of Seville.) Controversial, infamous rumors of the time—such as the one about the navigator's knowledge of Vinland, an Icelandic, quasi-mythical colony across the Atlantic, and his contact with an unknown pilot from Greenland who could have handed him maps of a huge, mysterious continent—are ignored. Specific details of the ocean voyage and the Genoese's insatiable passion for gold also go unmentioned. The resulting portrait is too benevolent, even caricaturish.

Still, Ferdinand is not without supporters. Washington Irving claimed that he was a man of probity, discernment, and admirable judgment who wrote more dispassionately than could have been expected about the honor, interests, and happiness of his own father. That opinion is validated by others who believe that, although *Histoire* should be handled with caution, it is a helpful resource to researchers in that much of its information comes firsthand from a relative's mouth, whatever the level of censorship the text underwent before it reached print. One can even think of the errors as symptomatic: if one approaches the book with a critical eye, looking for the clues hidden between the lines, Ferdinand's silences, secret messages, and mysteries can be illuminating.

= Defender of the Faith =

Along with *Histoire*, three other early biographies deserve mention: *Of the New World* (1511) by Peter Martyr d'Anghiera, an Italian who helped spread the word of Columbus's discovery, and *A General and Natural History of the Indies* (1535) by Gonzalo Fernández de Oviedo y Valdés, a Spanish *hidalgo* who traveled to the Americas in 1513 and stayed in the Caribbean for 34 years. Perceived by Ferdinand and other Columbus family members as an enemy, Oviedo proclaimed that the Americas had already been Spain's property from time immemorial, thus making the admiral a dispensable player in the historical game.

The third and perhaps most relevant to the dissemination of the legend of Columbus, *History of the Indies*, was written by the first priest ever to be ordained in the colonies (in 1510), Fray Bartolomé de Las Casas.[8] Although planned as a six-volume enterprise, each covering a decade, the final work is an ambitious, encyclopedic, three-volume panoramic overview of the New World. Volume 1 spans the period 1492–1502, volume 2 1502–12, and volume 3 1512–22. Las Casas began writing sometime around 1527, and the book was published in 1575, nine years after his death in 1566.

A missionary and prolific writer born in 1474 in Seville, Las Casas lived in the Dominican Republic and Cuba and witnessed the European cruelties in the Americas.[9] The experience turned him into an activist. He visited Spain before 1542 and again some four or five times to urge government action to protect all humans, regardless of color. (He finally settled in Spain in 1547.) His fame is due to his passionate devotion to defending the rights of the aborigines in the Americas—hence his nickname, the Father or the Defender of the Indians. His tireless writing, including his most critical book, *Very Brief Account of the Destruction of the Indies*, published in 1552 and immediately translated into five European languages, were ardent calls for justice. Europeans saw him as a bad omen, an unwelcome advocate in diplomatic and intellectual circles. (In *Of the New World* Martyr also describes some atrocities by the Spaniards, but without Las Casas's acrimony.) Critics attacked him as distorting, even malevolent. In fact, his books had a very small circulation up until the nineteenth century because of political repression. Eventually he became known for promoting the "black legend"—a consciousness of guilt, rape, and cruelty in the Iberian spirit. He instated the humanitarian code known as the New Laws, adopted in 1542 to protect the Indians in the colonies. But the legislation proved to be ineffective. And even if the missionary's voice was loud and clear, little changed in the Americas.

Las Casas finished *History of the Indies* in the Dominican College of San Gregorio in Valladolid. Deeply immersed in the teachings of the Bible, he was interested in narrating the rise of the colonies not as perceived by a fragile, ephemeral eye but from the point of view of an omniscient divine power. With the book of Genesis in mind, he starts virtually with the creation of the world, his goal being to locate the Indies on center stage in universal history, as if God had always perceived the islands as equal, not inferior to, the Old World. His minutae on Columbus's four voyages and on the establishment of the system of *encomienda*[10] is invaluable to modern researchers as unequivocal proof of the collective pain of early native Americans. His motto was, "The future shall know the truth" (7).

Las Casas had two relatives, one his father, who traveled with Columbus on his second voyage. His biography of the navigator amounts to only about one-third of the text: it begins in chapter 3 of volume 1 and ends at chapter 39 of volume 2. Patiently describing Columbus's origins, his personal aspirations, his theory that the earth was round, Las Casas portrays a humble, self-assured, honest mariner, a pious individual with a celestial mission. Most of his data seem to have been taken from other biographies (he had a copy of *Histoire*) and from the accounts of friends and acquaintances of the mariner. Describing his hero's vulnerability and toughness, his dogmatic character and his role as a leader, Las Casas praises his personality at some length and recalls the few occasions on which he met Columbus face to face. The missionary also refers to the admiral's illegitimate love affairs and bastard children, his intense desire for fame, his battles with his crew and the mutinies in the three caravels, his encounter with the Indians, his problems with the Catholic kings, and his death. As a historian, he pretends to be objective, but between the lines one can read his true political message—an attack on the rape of one civilization by another. Unlike Ferdinand, Las Casas does not overlook or revise valuable information about the darker aspects of Columbus's life but discusses such topics in full.

It is well known that most of Columbus's journals and letters have been lost. Yet for some mysterious reason, Las Casas had some of the mariner's papers at hand in the Dominican Republic when he was putting together *History of the Indies*. (He even edited Columbus's diary of the first voyage, and the only copy we have today is the one adapted by him [Wilford, 37].)[11] His historical account quotes the navigator here and there, but the words are very much his own. Some scholars have, of course, promoted the idea that, in quoting some paragraphs from Columbus's diaries and ignoring others, Las Casas distorted the admiral's intended message, adjusting it to his own ideological agenda. Since he often made factual mistakes, such as interchanging oceanic orientations, the claim is that he was an irresponsible scrivener. After intensive scrutiny, Morison disagrees: "[I] say that nobody, not a seaman, and no seaman who did not follow Columbus's route, could possibly have faked this document, so accurate are the bearings, the courses and the observations; and any such navigator would have needed the aid of the cleverest of literary forgers to complete the work, so closely are woven into it Columbus's ardent quest for the Indies, and the wonder and surprise are completely new experiences" (156).

Las Casas has relevance today because of his activism. He chose the side of the victims in 1514 and gave up his role in the *encomienda* system. In *History of the Indies* he offers a benevolent, positive portrait of the navigator. Being careful enough to avoid confusion about his target, he accuses Spain, not the admiral, of crimes against humanity. The distinction, I should add, is very important: in the priest's eyes, Columbus had discovered new wonders in the universe. But the conquerors were quick to destroy them.

= An American in Spain =

Each century has a new take on the Columbus story. Ferdinand Columbus, Gonzalo Fernández de Oviedo y Valdés, Peter Martyr d'Anghiera, and Fray Bartolomé de Las Casas wrote the most valuable life accounts of the Genoese during the sixteenth century. Washington Irving wrote his mega-account some 200 years later with the advantage of that much more perspective. He also had at his disposal most of the previously known historical material and used his literary talents masterfully to embellish the story. The result is by far the most popular and pleasurable biography—or I should say *narrative* biography—of the admiral ever published, although it is perhaps not the most accurate.

Born in 1783 in New York City, the author of "Rip Van Winkle" was to some the first true North American writer and is mostly remembered for *The Sketch Book*, published first in installment form in 1819 and in its final version in England in 1820, when Irving was 37 years old. It includes many celebrated stories, among them, "The Spectre Bridegroom: A Traveler's Tale" and "The Legend of Sleepy Hollow." Irving used a pseudonym—Geoffrey Crayon—for *The Sketch Book* because being a fiction writer in the early days of the Republic was not looked upon kindly as a career or aspiration. Ironically, he is the first U.S. writer to have supported himself through his art. Many of his successors, among them Mark Twain, looked to him for inspiration, but some twentieth-century critics, including Alfred Kazin and Edmund Wilson, have held him in very low esteem.

In his early twenties, Irving—who was named Washington after the nation's first president—wrote satires about New York personalities and gathered them into two volumes, *Salmagundi* (1807–08) and *A History of New York* (1809), also written under a pseudonym, Diedrich Knickerbocker. His humor made many uncomfortable, and he become known as a dangerous, not to be trusted fellow. This reputation and some financial setbacks forced him into exile. He left for Europe in May 1815 and remained there for over 20 years, until he acquired a large literary following and was able to return home with pomp and fanfare. After *The Sketch Book*, which was a big success, he produced another collection of stories in London, *Tales of a Traveller* (1825), which received terribly depressing, discouraging reviews. He came to believe that the problem with his short stories was that they were lies and fables. People needed the truth. This shift from fables to historical fiction was the origin of *The Life and Voyages of Christopher Columbus* (1828).[12]

By then Irving had already been living in England for nine years. He felt he needed to write "a truly American work."[13] His income was just enough to support himself, but at times he underwent economic penuries.[14] So he was looking for a topic to captivate his audience and earn him money. In his journals he pondered several possibilities, but, none of them seemed sharp enough to be tested. Still unhappy but wanting to keep his mind healthy, he gave up his many obligations in December 1824 and began an intensive study of Spanish. Six months later he met in Paris Alexander H. Everett, the U.S. ambassador to Spain. Perhaps the diplomat tried to persuade Irving to join the Foreign Service, although it is not clear. What is certain is that the writer was invited to travel to Spain to undertake the translation of a newly discovered manuscript originally written by Columbus himself and abridged by Las Casas, *The Book of First Navigation*, which at the time was in the hands of Martín Fernández de Navarrete, a famous bibliographer, a retired navy officer, and the secretary of the Royal Academy of History in Madrid.[15] With nothing else at hand, Irving accepted.

He planned to enjoy the trip, to perfect his Spanish, and to keep his mind busy finding a good narrative project. It sounded as if he could finish the job in a few months. In February 1826 he traveled to Spain. Immediately upon consulting Navarrete's text, he discovered that the material was too dry, too unappealing. But instead of giving up, he embarked on a full-scale biography of the Genoese. Written during the next three years, Irving relied heavily on Navarrete's documents but also, as he claims in his preface, on other volumes in the library of the American consul, Obediah Rich. He sent the finished manuscript to a publisher in London who agreed to bring it out following all the writer's instructions. The book was a hit, more so than any other title by Irving before or after. He wrote in December 1828, "Thus ends the year— tranquility. . . . The literary success of the *History of Columbus* has been greater than I anticipated and gives me hopes that I have executed something which may have greater duration than I anticipate for my works of mere imagination."[16]

No other biography of the mariner was available for the English-speaking reader at the time, and Irving certainly touched a sensitive nerve. After the War of Independence, the United States seemed to need heroes, mythological figures to legitimize its past. Columbus was one of them; he was the source, the missing link, between the old European order and the new reality. Irving was so overwhelmed by the success of his Columbus biography that later he embarked on an adaptation of Antonio Agapida's the *Conquest of Granada* (1829) and in 1831 he published *Voyages and Discoveries of the Companions of Columbus*. He was infatuated by Spain and its past.

The five-volume *Life and Voyages of Christopher Columbus* (later Irving published an abridged version) is a paragon of meticulousness and careful scholarship that has been praised by many for different reasons, among them Morison, the Spanish linguist Marcelino Menéndez y Pelayo, Alejo Carpentier, and Kirkpatrick Sale.[17] Colorful in its prose, it resembles a novelistic adventure more than an academic treatise. Irving portrays the mariner as honest, ardent, unstudied, impulsive, philosophical, kind to the Indians, saddened and overwhelmed by the ingratitude and violence of those he knew, devoted to his vision, never selfish, and never avaricious or blindly ambitious. In Irving's eyes, Columbus was a man of genius, with only a few defects, whose efforts were blocked by the obstacles set in his path by the Spanish court and the mediocrity around him. He let his life be ruled by superstition and foolishness, though he believed that Christianity was the only legitimate faith and that the natives were idol worshipers who needed to be baptized. He stumbled, committed mistakes, lost his temper, at times was insensitive. Notwithstanding, Irving portrays him as truly outstanding.

> Great men are compounds of great and little qualities. Indeed much of their greatness arises from their mastery over the imperfections of their nature, and their noblest actions are sometimes struck forth by the collision of their merits and their defects. . . . In Columbus were

singularly combined the practical and the poetical. His mind had grasped all kinds of knowledge, whether procured by study or observation, which bore upon his theories. . . . In the discharge of his office he maintained the state and ceremonial of a viceroy, and was tenacious of his rank and privileges; not from a mere vulgar love for titles, but because he prized them as testimonials and trophies of his achievements. . . . His conduct as a discoverer was characterized by the grandeur of his views, and the magnanimity of his spirit. . . . He was desirous of colonizing and cultivating [the newfound lands], of conciliating and civilizing the natives, of building cities, introducing the useful arts, subjecting every single thing to the control of law, order and religion, and thus of funding regular and prosperous empires. (563–65)

A follower of Las Casas in his heartfelt condemnation of the Spaniards but not the mariner, Irving claims that, had Columbus's successors understood his true personality, sound policy, and liberal views, "what dark pages would have been spared in the colonial history" (566). Life in the new continent would have been peaceful, civilized, full of enlightened legislators, and populated by humble people.

Irving divided his biography into 18 books: book 1 covers the period from Columbus's birth up until his departure from Portugal; book 2 describes the characters of the Catholic kings, the admiral's dealings with the court, and the events in the Franciscan convent of La Rábida and follows the admiral up until his departure from Palos; book 3 deals with the first voyage; book 4 describes his arrival in the Caribbean islands, his transactions with the natives, and his return to Spain; book 5 covers his reception in Spain and the preparations for the second voyage; books 6, 7, and 8 deal with his cruise among the Caribbean islands and his explorations of various territories; book 9 brings him back to Spain to prepare for the third voyage; books 10, 11, and 12 cover the establishment of military posts and communities in Hispaniola, Ciguay, and Xaragua; book 13 details the mariner's problems in the Spanish court and his dealings with the envoy, Francisco de Bobadilla; book 14 covers his imprisonment and return, for the third time, to Spain in order to appear in court; book 15 is concerned with the fourth voyage to Honduras, the Mosquito Coast, Costa Rica, and elsewhere; book 16 describes his troubles in various mutinies; and books 17 and 18 deal with the war with the natives in Higuay, his final return to Spain, and his death and include some observations on his character. Nothing is left out—Irving's is a *total* biography that includes every minutia, every step, every thought, every dream.

Certain facets of Columbus's life clearly fascinated Irving, including the rumor of the unknown pilot and Vinland. His Columbus is all-hearing, all-seeing, and capable of distinguishing between truth and falsehood. In Book 5, for instance, trusting Ferdinand's opinions in *Histoire*, he explains how the Genoese came to be certain that the earth is round. Basing his hypothesis on Ptolemy and Marinus of Tyre, Columbus observed that, out of the 24 hours in a day, during the 12 daylight hours the sun travels from east to west; during the remaining 12 nightime hours, perhaps the sun follows a similar pattern beyond human eyes. Therefore, he could travel to the Indies westward from the Strait of Gibraltar. His opinions, according to Irving, were confirmed when he heard that a Portuguese pilot had sailed 450 leagues to the west of Cape St. Vincent and found a piece of carved wood not worked with an iron instrument. Afterwards, he heard the report of a mariner from Santa María de la Concepcion Island who, on his trip to Iceland, saw land the rest of the crew thought to be Tartary. "Other stories of a similar kind are noted, as well as rumors concerning the fancied islands of St. Brandan, and of the Seven Cities, to which, as has already been observed, Columbus gave but little faith" (Irving, 28–29).

Always in control of his technique, Irving often takes advantage of an intriguing scene to invent, to improve the ambiance, to add suspense. Morison singles out one scene in which the mariner defends the roundness of the earth in front of a skeptical group of mathematicians, astronomers, and geographers at the University of Salamanca. The description runs for several pages, but the whole encounter is without basis: to begin with, the institution is nowhere to be found. According to Morison:

> Washington Irving, scenting his opportunity for a picturesque and moving scene, took a fictitious account of this nonexistent university council published 130 years after the event, elaborated on it, and let his imagination go completely. The result is that wonderful chapter where "an obscure navigator, a member of no learned society, destitute of all the trappings and circumstances which sometimes give oracular authority to dullness, and depending on the mere force of natural genious," sustains his thesis of a spherical globe against "pedantic bigotry" of flat-earth churchmen, fortified by texts from the Bible, Lactantius and Saint Augustine, until he began to feel nervous about the Inquisition. . . . A gripping drama as Irving tells it, this has become one of the most popular Columbian myths; for we all love to hear of professors and experts being confounded by simple common sense. (89)

The secret agenda of *The Life and Voyages of Christopher Columbus*, no doubt, is to make Columbus a bridge between the early Republic and the old Europe. By identifying himself as a U.S. writer living in Great Britain and Spain, he gave his biography a symbolic status: he, Washington Irving, a lover of Germanic folk tales, a humorist in exile, a man of letters, a writer with no North American colleagues, wanted to be recognized as the facilitator of communication between one side of the Atlantic and the other. His image of the navigator was that of a visionary who made two worlds unite, two realities improve, by accepting their similarities and differences. "The writing of lives," says Leon Edel, "is a department of history and is closely related to the discoveries of history. . . . No biography is complete unless it reveals the individual within history, within an ethos and a social context" (4). Irving's task was to place Columbus in context—in a context very similar to his own.

= Goodbye, Columbus =

Washington Irving's eighteenth-century precursors in writing about Columbus include William Robertson. Among his successors are Alexander von Humboldt, Henry Harrisse, José M. Arsenio y Toledo, Justin Winsor, and Filson Young. Twentieth-century biographers include: John Boyd Thacher, who published his three-volume work between 1903 and 1904; Jacob Wassermann, a German intellectual who wrote *Columbus: Don Quixote of the Ocean* in 1929, a biography that is loosely based on facts suggesting the admiral's possible role as "a Jewish traitor" and that compares him to the novelistic *hidalgo* of Cervantes, a character full of chivalous dreams and confusion between reality and fiction; the Nordic scholar Björn Landström, who produced a profusely illustrated biography in 1966; Alfred Crosby; Felipe Fernández-Armesto; the Italian scholar and diplomat Paolo Emilio Taviani, who after careful research in Venice and Genoa produced a four-volume biography between 1974 and 1984; Gianni Granzotto; and Ilaria Luzzana Caraci. Other contemporary biographers and researchers include Salvador de Madariaga, G. R. Crone, Carl Sauer, Benjamin Keen, Cecil Jane, Jorge Campos, Otto Schoenrich, Troy Floyd, Gabriel Verd Martorell, and Fredi Chiappelli. The unifying theme in all their works is a dialectic between departure and arrival, between darkness and light, between modernity and the Renaissance mind.

Madariaga is an important case in point. An Iberian statesman and scholar born in 1886, he held several diplomatic posts in Europe and the United States, was a dissident who spoke out against the regime of Francisco Franco, taught at Oxford University, and published several biographies, among them one on Hernán Cortés, another on the nineteenth-century South American *libertador* Simón Bolívar, and a third on the Genoese. Although not quite documented, its main thesis is that Columbus, by birth a Genoese Roman Catholic, kept the traits and habits of his Jewish ancestors.

The suspicion, I should say, was not Madariaga's alone. Before him, D. Meyer Kayserling and Henry Vignaud pondered the idea,[18] but Madariaga's forceful, if ill-supported arguments, published in 1939, made him a champion of this cause célèbre. Also linking Columbus to Don Quixote, he seems to have been inspired by Jacob Wassermann. (To give credit to his views, he opposed Morison and the Spanish linguist Ramón Menéndez Pidal.) Since then other supporters have come along, including Cecil Roth and Simon Wiesenthal, who in *Sails of Hope* (1972) "unquestionably" linked the expulsion of the Jews from the Iberian peninsula to Columbus's first voyage.[19] His opinion was that in sailing westward, the navigator, a man deeply in touch with the Jewish community in Spain and perhaps a *converso*, was looking for the land inhabited by the lost tribes of Israel. Instead, he came up with the ultimate escape for crypto-Jews escaping the Spanish Inquisition.

= The Harvard Professor =

Yet without doubt the most valuable and authoritative contemporary biography is Morison's magnum opus, *Admiral of the Ocean Sea*. The style is meticulous, clear-cut, and always impartial. His personal passion for the sea informed his research and became the volume's leitmotiv. In the preface he explains: "This book arose out of the desire to know exactly where Columbus sailed on his Four Voyages, and what sort of seaman he was. No previous work on the Discoverer of America answers these questions in a manner to satisfy even an amateur seafarer. Most biographies of the Admiral might well be entitled 'Columbus to the Water's Edge' " (xv).

It would be a mistake, nevertheless, to think that only nautical matters concern Morison. The biography begins with a comprehensive description of Columbus's birth and early years in Genoa (1451–73), his travels to Portugal (1476–85) and Castile (1485–90), the enterprise of finding a new route to the Indies, and the mariner's technique in getting the queen's consent (1489–92). Morison examines the available facts about Columbus's obscure childhood and adolescence with a meticulous, scientific, nonpartisan eye, thereby putting to rest some false rumors about the mariner's connections with his colleagues and, according to some, his "treacherous personality" (the Jewish ancestry, the tale of the unknown pilot, and so forth). Morison's discussion of the mariner's fluency in the Spanish language, based on the studies of the Iberian philologist Ramón Menéndez Pidal, is fascinating, as is his analysis of the 45 or more apocryphal and authentic Columbus signatures preserved throughout the centuries. Most of them include an elusive pyramid arrangement of the letters *S, X, Y,* and *M.* In examining these graphic and syntactical elements, Morison acknowledges the literary dimensions of the unsolvable detective story unfolding around the mariner. Was he bookish? Did he learn to speak Spanish in Portugal or in Seville? Did his signature embody some sort of Hebraic code, a secret, cabalistic message available only to the initiated?

Divided into five major parts, each containing between 5 and 17 chapters, and including drawings of the three caravels and custom-made detailed charts of every voyage, the heart of *Admiral of the Ocean Sea* is an analysis of the oceanic routes of Columbus. The information is mostly based on the navigator's own reckonings, but also on a Harvard expedition made in 1939, just before World War II, in which Morison participated. He studies each of the trips: the first (1492–93), from San Sebastián and Palos to San Salvador, and from Roca de Sintra, near Lisbon, to Hispaniola; the second (1493), from Dominica to San Juan Bautista to Hispaniola, Juana, and Jamaica; the third

(1498), from Madeira and the Canary Islands to Dominica and Venezuela; and the fourth (1502–03), to Central American territories known today as Honduras, Nicaragua, and Costa Rica. Morison tracks the money and crew that accompanied the admiral and describes his perils in planning each trip. Important data about the size, model, speed, and architecture of the three caravels—the *Niña* and the *Pinta* were both small-scale vessels, and the *Santa María* was not exactly a caravel but a *nao*, a bigger ship—help to explain why the first and second could survive hurricanes while the last suffered a shipwreck (109–34). Using his marine knowledge, Morison sets out to describe Columbus's character and vulnerabilities, his courage and weaknesses, his Christian views, and his oral and written narrative style (through the glass darkly of Bartolomé de Las Casas). At the end, the historian allows his own personal feelings to surface. After such a tumultuous, agitated life, Morison wishes the mariner had departed from this world with a sense of satisfaction and fulfillment. He describes Columbus's last pious words as, "*In manus tuas, Domine, commendo spiritum meum* (In your hands, Lord, I commend my spirit [my translation])."

> So died the man who had done more to direct the course of history than any individual since Augustus Caesar. Yet the life of the admiral closed on a note of frustration. He had not found the Strait, or met the Grand Khan, or converted any great number of heathen, or regained Jerusalem. He had not even secured the fortune of his family. And the significance of what he had accomplished was only slightly less obscure to him than to the chroniclers who neglected to record his death, or to the courtiers who failed to attend his modest funeral in Valladolid. The vast extent and immense resources of the Americas were but dimly seen; the mighty ocean that laved their western shores had not yet yielded her secret. (669)

Morison's Columbus is a compassionate, sensitive genius who changed the course of history. He portrays the mariner as a stubborn man of convictions and the owner of an indefatigable sense of wonder unequaled since the Greeks. Neither a hero nor a saint, his protagonist is a capable sailsman, a daring man ready to embark on a larger-than-life adventure. As a historian, Morison focuses on the man, not on the implications of his behavior. He is unconcerned with Columbus's legacy or with insinuations that the admiral was an evil colonialist, an abuser of natives. Says John Noble Wilford,

> Morison wrote [*Admiral of the Ocean Sea*] in 1942. In the foreword to a new edition in 1983, David Beers Quinn, another distinguished historian of exploration, praised the book's dramatic sweep and literary style, but noted that "there are other perceptions of the Discoverer that must now be taken into account." Quinn feels that Morison ignored or dismissed Columbus's failings. Columbus, Quinn writes, "cannot be detached from the imperialist exploitation of his discover-

ies and he must be made to take some share of responsibility for the brutal exploitation of the islands and mainlands he found." Times and sensitivities change in less than half a century, and so can the telling of history. (xii–xiii)

= Militants and Journalists =

With the quincentennial, politicized biographies with clear ideological agendas proliferated; many pictured Columbus as a rascal, a dishonest male-factor. Even the supposedly unprejudiced and impartial biographers had to take a stand. The writers were either militants ready to embark on unforgiving diatribes or influential journalists writing about the animosity against the navigator. This opposition was best epitomized in Kirkpatrick Sale and John Noble Wilford.

A journalist and political activist born in Ithaca, New York, with a record of anti–Vietnam War protest and environmental activism, Sale is also the author of *Human Scale* (1980) and *Power Shift* (1975). After more than a decade of research, looking for every possible fingerprint left by the admiral in Europe and in the vast Americas, Sale published in 1990 his controversial, book-length essay, *The Conquest of Paradise*. The first part is devoted to historical and biographical descriptions of the admiral's nautical ignorance and miscalculations. The second deals with how the British colonies carried on his ecologically disastrous legacy. And the final part focuses on perceptions of Columbus in history and art. This is not an orthodox, straightforward biography; it is an examination of the mariner's legacy. Although useful, erudite information about his upbringing, nautical odyssey, and isolated de-cline is given, Sale's goal is to analyze the aftermath of 1492. Within each of the 13 chapters he introduces a contextual chronology that lists both the immediate and long-term consequences of Columbus's acts. And in the tradi-tion of Bartolomé de Las Casas and his "black legend," Sale unequivocally attacks the navigator for opening the door to a natural and human holocaust of unimaginable proportions.

More than anybody else, the objects of Sale's pity are the native North American Indians and their environment. He laments the disappearance of their mythology and their overall destruction. His method is to approach the conquest from the victim's viewpoint. In an inspired section, he claims:

> There exists [in North America] a nineteenth-century "bible" with the title *Oahspe*, said to have been influential among the Irokwa of the last century, which purports to be the words of "Jehovih" transmitted through a Dr. John Ballou Newbrough in 1881, in which Christopher "Columbo" is mentioned as playing a special part in the Design of God. In "one of the plans of God for redeeming the world"—a world

which He acknowledged had fallen upon sinful times—Columbo was visited by the heavenly hosts and inspired by them "to go with ships to the westward, across the ocean," there to find for Europe "a new mortal anchorage," "a new country, where only the Great Spirit, Jehovih, is worshiped." He makes the momentous voyage, but the news of it is discovered by the agents of Satan, "the false Kriste," and his angels "did set the rulers of Spain against Columbo, and had him cast in prison, thus breaking the chain of inspiration betwixt Columbo and the throne of God"—and it is these evil spirits that instead lead the people of Europe across the ocean "to the countries Columbo had discovered" and there, to the consternation of Heaven, did "evil take its course."

So it may have been. However one may cast it, an opportunity there certainly was once, a chance for the people of Europe to find a new anchorage in a new country, in what they dimly realized was the land of Paradise, and thus finally the way to redeem the world. But all they ever found was half a world of nature's treasures and nature's peoples that could be taken, and they took them, never knowing, never learning the true regenerative power there, and that opportunity was lost. . . . As is inevitable with any war against the word of nature, those who win will have lost. (369–70)[20]

Some, such as Karl Meyer, scorned *The Conquest of Paradise* as inaccurate and misguided, but others prized it as a warning to a planet on the brink of ecological disaster. After the book's publication, Sale often had to clarify and defend his position. He argued that he had actually dismissed Columbus as an incompetent and an impostor, a mariner who was careless about protecting his ships and cruel toward the natives, but that he had not made Columbus an easy target and did not write the book to indict him. Instead, Sale's animosity was directed against the thoroughgoing evils of the culture of Europe, not only the Spanish and the Roman Catholic nations but the whole continent. North America has inherited the worse of the Old World.[21]

If Kirkpatrick Sale takes the role of the partisan historian, John Noble Wilford, a Pulitzer Prize–winning science reporter for the *New York Times*, navigates with impartiality as his banner. Divided into two parts and a total of 17 chapters, his 1991 biography, *The Mysterious History of Columbus*, is openly revisionist. As he states in his preface, his book is not a history of a famous figure but a history of the history. "The purpose of this book," Wilford argues, "is not to present a full-scale biography of Columbus. It is to tell the story of the story of Columbus—that is, to describe what we do know about him and his achievements and how this knowledge has come down to us, and also to review and assess the numerous questions that persist and cause such heated dispute among historians" (xi).

From Peter Martyr, Oviedo, and Las Casas to Morison, Taviani, and Sale, Wilford's list of the various biographers details mistakes, rumors, and myths.[22] He uses his reportorial approach to dissect every detail, every echo in time.

The style is compact and straightforward but lacks the beauty of literary biographies; very matter-of-fact and newspaperish, the book is distant and unengaged in its conclusions. A typical section is "His Place in History": offering no personal opinions on Columbus, Wilford describes the admiral's stature as perceived during various periods of history, each as relative, as subjective as any other. He quotes a verse by James Russell Lowell ("The idol is the measure of the worshipper"[23]), uses a metaphor by Walt Whitman (history is made of "ever-shifting guesses"[24]), and then goes on to discuss a number of mostly U.S. poets and historians (Joel Barlow, Herbert Butterfield, among others) who have appreciated through art Columbus's stature. But Wilford never takes a risk, never assumes an individual position. His agenda is to show that the admiral's image has suffered an intriguing, complex metamorphosis through time. Ultimately, he argues, "Columbus's place in history can only be judged in relation to the place accorded [to] America in history over the last five centuries" (265).

<h2 style="text-align:center">= Encore =</h2>

John Updike once claimed that what we love about fiction writers is their willingness to dare to submerge themselves, to give up, in behalf of brutal reality, the voice of a wise and presentable man.[25] Biographers, on the other hand, appear to us in suit and tie: they are knowledgeable, courteous, often predictable. From Ferdinand Columbus and Bartolomé de Las Casas to Washington Irving, Samuel Eliot Morison, Kirkpatrick Sale, and John Noble Wilford, each of the Genoese's biographers, some more ambitious than others, some more politically oriented than others, has tried to capture the evanescent moments in the navigator's life from the perspective of his present reality. Careful readers quickly notice how often they repeat each other: the same handful of scenes, reworked time and again, reconstructed with not-too-different words in quasi-identical settings. Of course, considerable new data have been found since *Histoire* and *History of the Indies* were written: the mariner's birthdate, for instance, was believed for some time to have been 1436; then it was moved to 1452 before finally being set at 1451. But one cannot avoid a feeling of discomfort, an overwhelming sense of repetition. Borges's "book of books" is certainly not without flaws.

Enter the creative writer, a guy of talent, a craftsman ready to play with real facts and his imagination. As Updike said, an artist mediates between the word and the mind, a critic merely between minds.[26] After numerous biographies and innumerable academic studies and research papers, Columbus the man remains a mirage of memory.

3

Facts on File

WHO *WAS* CHRISTOPHER COLUMBUS?[1] THE ANSWER IS IN THE eye of the beholder. If biographers have described him according to their own bias ("the only good biography," said Elizabeth Hawthorne, the Salem novelist's sister, echoing Thomas Carlyle, "is one that ought not to have been written"[2]), novelists, poets, and playwrights are more likely to fabricate, to imagine, to innovate, to idealize. History has not, of course, granted us a photograph of the admiral, but portraits abound. Most of the approximately 70 surviving paintings, done from 1506 to the present, are based in the imaginations of the different artists: Ridolfo del Ghirlandaio (circa 1530), Tobias Stimmer (1575), Theodore de Bry (1595), Daniel Chodowiecki (1791), Karl von Piloty (circa 1850), Niccolo Barabino (1887), Eduardo Cano de la Peña (circa 1890), George Edmund Varian (circa 1900), Joaquín de Sorolla y Bastida (circa 1900), and Leonardo Lasansky (1984).[3] These approxima-tions of Columbus's countenance have been inspired by the many biographi-cal accounts describing him, such as his son Ferdinand's in *Histoire*:

The Admiral was a well-built man of more than average stature, the face long, cheeks somewhat high, his body neither fat not lean. He had an aquiline nose and light-colored eyes; his complexion too was light and tending to bright red. In youth his hair was blond, but when he reached the age of thirty, it all turned white. In eating and drinking, and the adornment of his person, he was very moderate and modest. He was affable in conversation with strangers and very pleasant to the members of his household, though with a certain gravity. He was so strict in manners of religion that for fasting and saying prayers he might have been taken for a member of a religious order. And he was so great an enemy of swearing and blasphemy that I give my word I never heard him utter any other oath than "by St. Ferdinand!" and when he grew very angry with someone, his rebuke was to say, "God take you" for doing or saying that. And when he had to write anything, he always began by writing these words: *IESUS cum MARIA sit nobis in via*. And so fine was his hand that he might have earned his bread by that skill alone. (9)

Oviedo, for his part, believed the navigator to be a man of good stature and appearance, muscular and taller than average; in his estimation, Columbus's eyes were very lively, his hair red, his face somewhat ruddy and freckled. In the same vein, Bartolomé de Las Casas describes him in *History of the Indies* as more than middling tall, with a long face, an air of authority, an aquiline nose, blue eyes, and a light complexion tending to bright red; Las Casas also depicts him as gentle, modest, cheerful, eloquent, and forceful in negotiation. And Washington Irving saw Columbus as a tall, well-formed, muscular man with an elevated and dignified demeanor. Morison uses these views to shape his own: "He was of a North Italian type frequently seen today in Genoa; tall and well-built, red-haired with a ruddy and freckled complexion, hawk-nosed and long in visage, blue-eyed and with high cheekbones" (47).

From what we know for certain, Christopher Columbus seems to have had a rather conventional life up until the crucial trip from Palos in 1492. He was born in 1451,[4] by most accounts in Genoa,[5] a port in northern Italy known for its shopkeepers. Little is known about his early childhood and adolescence. Some speculate that he often got into Turkish and Venetian ships anchored near the shore; others believe that he dreamed of becoming a poet. As far as historians can tell, his father Domenico was a master weaver and a proud Catholic—although Wassermann, Madariaga, and Posse argue that he had Jewish ancestors persecuted by the Spanish Inquisition and had become a *marrano*. His mother was Susanna Fontanarossa, the daughter of a weaver. Bartholomeo, his younger brother, later raised money in Britain for Christopher's cause. According to some chronicles of the time, the two teenage brothers rejected the family trade; they preferred being wool carders and even cheese makers. Domenico and Susanna had more children, some of whom died young. Little is known about the fate of these family members, with the exception of Giacomo, better known as Diego, a boy some seven years younger than Christopher for whom he cared very much, to the point of having Diego join the crew of the second voyage (Morison, II). Up until 1473, when he was 22, Columbus lived in his hometown and in Savona. What money he earned he contributed to the family finances.

= Polyglotism and Translation =

Names, William of Occam thought, embody the essence of their referents.[6] A word about the navigator's surname is thus required. In Italian, Colombo means dove.[7] The biblical symbolism is easily traceable: after the deluge, when Noah wanted to know if the world was safe to reinhabit, he sent a dove forth from the ark. Since then the mythical connotation of the bird is that of a link between the old and new, a creature of peace, a prophetic image of better times. Paul Claudel, Stephen Marlow, and Carlos Fuentes make use of this onomastic coincidence to underscore the admiral's quiescent personality and progressive enterprise. But more important than his surname is his first name: Cristóforo, Cristóbal, Christopher, the three variants all refer to Christ, the messiah, the redeemer, the subject of gospels. It was a custom of the late Middle Ages to name a child after the patron saint of his or her day of baptism; Morison links St. Christopher's legend to the fate of Columbus. Having been a pagan, St. Christopher decided to look for Christ. A hermit told him that the only way to find Him was through systematic fasting and prayers. But St. Christopher refused to follow that method and asked for another assignment. The hermit then suggested that he help people cross a dangerous river without a bridge. St. Christopher built a hamlet near the shore and began escorting passersby across the river. One night, a child asked him for help getting across the waters. St. Christopher put him on his shoulders. As he crossed the river, he noticed that the child's weight was increasing almost intolerably, as if he had on his back "the whole world." Later he was told by the hermit that, indeed, he had borne upon his back the whole universe. Says Morison, rather piously:

> This story would certainly have gone home to the boy Christopher who was father to Columbus the man we know. He conceived it his destiny to carry the divine word of that Holy Child across the mighty ocean to countries steeped in heathen darkness. Many years elapsed and countless discouragements were surmounted before anyone would afford him means to take up the burden. Once assumed, it often became intolerable, and often he staggered under it; but never did he set it down until his appointed work was done. We may fairly say that the first step toward the discovery was taken by the parents of Columbus when they caused him to be baptized Cristoforo in some ancient church of Genoa, one day in the late summer or early fall of 1451. (10–11)

A most debatable topic about Columbus's background is the tongue he spoke and frequently misused in writing, Castilian Spanish. Where did he learn it? When and among whom? His native idiom was Genoese. He also spoke Marinaresco, Italian, and probably Tuscan. In addition, vernacular Latin was available during his childhood. He learned Portuguese, the exciting language of trade, science, and navigation, along with the lingua franca of seamen, in 1476 or after. He may have used Portuguese as a mariner when traveling to Africa, Iceland, Ireland, and England. He visited Lisbon in May 1476 and worked there for intervals as a skilled cartographer between 1477 and 1485, by which time he had learned to write Portuguese as well.[8] Perhaps during that period he learned a Castilian full of *lusismos*—bits of Portuguese—although it is not totally clear. What is certain is that he was a true polyglot, a man of multiple tongues. Todorov's assertion that he lacked any notion of verbal plurality, that he was thus unlikely to have understood the essential linguistic difference between himself as a European and the Aztecs and other natives of the Americas, is simply untrue. With an enterprising, adventurous spirit, the mariner was a voracious speaker of foreign tongues, a capable handler of different locutions (Navarrese, Cantabric, Galician, and so on). Though he seldom learned to write them he picked up many of the languages he encountered in his travels.

When Columbus moved to Palos in Andalusia in 1485, by most accounts his partial knowledge of Spanish was already a true asset. Ramón Menéndez Pidal, a famous lexicographer who wrote masterful studies of Spanish golden-age (1450–1580) dramas and the prose of Cervantes, published in 1942 a small but influential booklet, *The Language of Christopher Columbus*.[9] Although the text is devoted to various linguistic topics (the poetics of Santa Teresa de Jesus, for instance), the section on the admiral is the main course. Menéndez Pidal's clear-cut thesis goes against the view that the mariner was of Jewish heritage, especially that idea as promoted by Madariaga.[10] Menéndez Pidal thinks that Columbus never learned to write Italian in his childhood, that he spoke only Genoese and perhaps some commercial Latin, and that his Spanish was made easier by his almost native Portuguese, which he acquired because of his family trade and business in his adolescence. The scholar proves that Columbus learned Spanish from his daily experiences in the western harbors of the coasts of Portugal. In the diary of the first voyage and in some of his letters, the navigator's spelling—such as *mondo* instead of *mundo, se intenta* instead of *se entienda*—can be traced to Portuguese influence.

Columbus as a writer with a rich vocabulary should be placed alongside authors such as Baruch Spinoza, Franz Kafka, and Joseph Conrad, all of whom left a mark in a tongue other than theirs. Gustavo Pérez-Firmat, a Cuban poet and another polyglot, once said that being often forced to communicate in English, not Spanish, ended up falsifying his message.[11] Reading the admiral, one hardly gets a sense of there having been a loss in translation.

Though not his *lingua naturalis*, Spanish became the idiom that, however erratic his syntax and grammar, he used resourcefully. Critics such as Robert Parks justifiably claim that his prose is highly interesting, full of vivid descriptions and zeal for the faith, although often a bit fanciful, excessively imaginative. (The Orinoco, for instance, was in his eyes the Garden of Eden's fourth river.)[12] A superficial look at his narratives, the authentic as well as those transcribed by Bartolomé de Las Casas, does show his prose style to be versatile, powerful, and engaging.

=   The Universe as Thesaurus   =

Between 1473 and 1476, from the age of 22 to 25, Columbus became a business agent of the Genoese entrepreneurs Paolo di Negro, Ludovico Centurione, and Nicoló Spínola. As their employee, he traveled extensively. He made trips throughout the Mediterranean and reached even Africa. The companies he worked for had subsidiaries in Seville, Flandes, and France. At some point, in 1476 or after a boat Columbus was on destined for England sank near Cape San Vicente and he ended up visiting Lisbon. He soon moved to Portugal, where sometime around 1480 his marriage to Dona Felipa Perestrello e Moniz took place.

The marriage is surrounded by mystery. His wife came from a distinguished noble family with origins in Piacenza, whereas Columbus had a humble Italian background. Why was he considered an attractive suitor? The answer is unknown. Spirited, full of oceanic dreams, a voracious reader (in Latin) of Marco Polo's *The Book of Marvels* (also known as *The Book of Marco Polo*)—he owned a 1485 edition of the the Venetian voyager's text, which he annotated and kept constantly at his side[13]—perhaps he wanted to improve his standing in society. By marrying into the upper class he gained prestige and an open door into monied Portuguese circles. But he must have been a promising prospect, otherwise no engagement would have taken place. According to Ferdinand's *Histoire*, he met Felipa during church services in Lisbon. The oldest of two daughters of Bartholomew Perestrello and Isabel Moniz, little is known about her physical appearance, her background, or her love for Columbus. Also unexplained is her early death. The only certainty is that in 1485, when the admiral left Portugal with his son Diego—born around 1482 (Menéndez Pidal, 16) and named after the admiral's brother—she lay buried in the church of Carmo.

Sometime in the next year he may have traveled to Guinea. He also proposed his idea of finding a new route to the Indies to King Juan II of Portugal. He had concluded that the earth is spherical and was sure he could reach the mythical Cipangu and Cathay—the lands explored by Marco Polo and rich in silk and spices—without having to cross the powerfully defended Turkish line in the Mediterranean. If correct, he could open a new commercial route. But he was ignored. Depressed and disappointed, at the end of 1485 Columbus traveled to Spain, hoping to talk to Queen Isabella about his plan in Córdoba on 20 January 1486; perhaps rich Spanish businessmen close to the kings would support him. Up until the climactic year of 1492, their troublesome six-year dialogue, with its thousand ups and downs, was marked by distress, sadness, immobility—a general sense of defeat.

The relationship between Columbus and the skeptical, stubborn monarch has been the subject of endless speculation. In *The Harp and the Shadow*, Alejo Carpentier suggests there was a sexual component to their relationship,[14] but Morison, more cautious and objective, believes such a passion to have been an unreliable rumor (96–103, 106–7). The sovereign was a mature beauty in her forties, a lady with a very strong personality.[15] Having had his project rejected by Juan II of Portugal, Columbus, according to the rumor, decided to use his masculinity to gain access to power. By some reports, the lovers met at night, a time when Isabella would pay attention to Columbus's pleas. But during the day she ignored him. Knowing how to play his cards, says the rumor, the mariner threatened at one point to blackmail the queen by taking his project to France. To keep him in Spain, the Catholic queen supposedly told him she would borrow money from Luis de Santángel, an *escribano de ración*, or chief accountant, who according to some accounts, was a *converso* and needed to satisfy his bosses, the monarchs, to retain his power and not be expelled from the Iberian peninsula like other Jews.

Whatever the truth is, up until 1492 Columbus's many pleas to Isabella for support were rejected. At times the reason given was Spain's political turmoil; at other times the monarch was simply in a bad mood. Around 1490 a committee headed by Hernando de Talavera, the queen's confessor, considered the whole enterprise and judged it to be unappealing to the kingdom. (According to Bartolomé de Las Casas in *History of the Indies*, they categorized the mariner's project as "impossible and vain and worthy of rejection" [vol. 1, 17].)

During this period another woman entered his life. Still in his thirties, a widower and a father, he met the lower-class Beatríz Enríquez de Arana. They became lovers, and in August 1488 she gave birth to a bastard son, Ferdinand, who would eventually make his claim as his father's heir and write one of the first biographies. The admiral's liaison with Beatríz became an issue almost four centuries later when, from 1857 to 1867, Pope Pius IX and his successor attempted to have Genoese canonized. Count Antoine François Félix Roselly de Lorges wrote his now-infamous biography, *Christopher Colombus: A History of His Life and His Voyages* (1856), in which he embellished some aspects of the mariner's life, including the fact that he had married twice, his second wife being a well-educated Spanish beauty. Supported by Léon Bloy and other, Roselly de Lorges led the movement to canonize Columbus, while Angelo Sanguineti, an Italian, counterattacked by demolishing his arguments and exposing his misrepresentations and misreadings.[16] As expected, in the end the admiral's candidacy was revoked by Pope Leo XIII.

= Syphilis, Ultima Thule, = and the Unknown Pilot

Several myths haunt the navigator's history. One is that he introduced syphilis to Europe in 1493, after his first voyage, not personally but through one of his crew members. Promoted by Ruy Díaz de Isla in his book of clinical observations, *Treatise on Venomous Sicknesses* (1539), the claim is that *pinta*, from which endemic syphilis, venereal syphilis, and yaws are derived, entered Spain and Portugal from the caravel with the same name when the navigator and his crew returned from the Caribbean. Francisco Guerra, in his careful examination, "The Problem of Syphilis" (1976), strongly disagrees. He objectively proves that pinta came from animals in Africa and moved from there to Siberia and America.[17] Yet the unfortunate rumor persists, tarnishing Columbus's reputation.

Another rumor, not quite as improbable, is the one about the admiral having traveled as an adolescent to Iceland. Supported by Las Casas, this story also appears in *Histoire*: Ferdinand Columbus says that in 1477 his father visited Iceland—referred to by Ptolemy centuries before as Tile or Ultima Thule (Morison, 61–63). The inhabitants knew that they did not live on the edge of the earth but that their land was a bridge to another. The admiral quickly gathered information about the lands across the Atlantic, especially about Leif Eriksson's Vinland[18] in a location the future would know as New England (Morison, 25–26).[19] In his typical journalistic style, John Noble Wilford has this to say about Vinland:

> In time the Norse proved Thule not to be the ultimate land, but only one destination in the northern ocean where no more than 500 miles separates landfalls. From Iceland these hardy seafarers, led by Erik the Red, an outlaw from both Norway and Iceland, found their way in the tenth century to the southern shore of a new land. With the instincts of a real-estate developer, Erik disregarded the frigid evidence around and, hoping to promote colonization, named the place Greenland. In 986, another Norseman, Bjarni Herjolfsson, became lost trying to reach Greenland and came upon the coast of what would prove to be North America. But he showed no interest. Without so much as going ashore, he returned and made it to Greenland. In subsequent decades, the Norse under Erik's son Leif Eriksson went looking for the coast Herjolfsson had glimpsed. They came first to the rocky littoral he called Helluland, probably present-day Baffin Island, and then to a wooded coast of a place he named Markland, probably Labrador. Finally, Leif reached a land to the south where

the wild "grape" (red currant?) grew. The Norse called it Vinland the
Good, a place now assumed to be Newfoundland. (5–6)

As we know today, Columbus was not the first foreigner to reach the
Americas—not even the second or third. Rumors have it that besides the
Vikings, many European sojourners "discovered," and some settled in, the
Americas—including the second-century Jewish members of the ten lost
tribes of Israel, a Chinese Buddhist who visited Mexico in the fifth century,
the Irish monk St. Brendan, and Prince Madoc of Wales.[20] But Eriksson's
Vinland acquired the magic of a myth—an occult place of the human imagination, a utopia. The legend insinuates that the Genoese had prior knowledge
of a reality beyond the Canary Islands, of a place that existed not only in his
dreams but also in the maps of Icelandic contemporaries.

An excellent scholarly book on the topic, not yet translated into English,
is *Ultima Tule* (1942) by Alfonso Reyes.[21] Born in 1889, Reyes, a Mexican,
was a member of an artistic group devoted in the 1920s and 1930s to the
renewal of national letters.[22] An ambitious and prolific writer whose complete
works total 22 volumes, his text on Iceland, Ultima Thule, and Vinland
discusses the hypothesis that the Americas, as reality and as utopia, existed
in the European mind long before Columbus. From a philosophical viewpoint,
he ponders the rumors about the early Jewish, Oriental, and Nordic travelers,
paying particular attention to the saga of Eric the Red (a topic that appears
in William Carlos Williams's book of essays *In the American Grain* [1925]),
to Plato's idea of Antarctica (*Timeo, Critias*), and to Seneca's view of a reality
beyond the ocean (*Venient annis secula seris, quibus oceanus vincula rerum
laxet, et ingens pateat tellus, typhisque novos detegat orbes; nec sit terris
Ultima Thule* [the years will come, in the succession of the ages, when the
Ocean will loose the bonds by which we have been confined, when an immense land shall lie revealed, and Tethys shall disclose New Worlds, and
Thule will no longer be the most remote of countries].) Reyes discusses the
rivalry between Columbus and Amerigo Vespucci, the naming of the new
continent, and his difficult standing as commander-in-chief of the caravels.
What is fascinating about Reyes's study is that he shows how historically
irrelevant the navigator is if the rumor about his Iceland connection is true.

One other legend surrounding Columbus is the one about the unknown
pilot. Fernández de Oviedo y Valdés, in 1535, first discussed this story in
writing. Later on Las Casas argued that in Santo Domingo people talked
about the story as if it had been true. And since his time other historians,
from the Inca Garcilaso de la Vega to Morison, have developed it. Here is a
summary: A ship sailing from Spain to England, full of merchandise, was
struck by a terrible storm and pushed westward to the Americas (Morison,
62).[23] The crew, after observing the naked natives practice their rituals and
customs, returned to Europe, but not before suffering another major natural
disaster in which many died. The only survivor was an anonymous pilot,
although some claim that he was Alonso Sánchez, a man from Palos or Huelva

or Portugal. He was very sick. Since he was a good friend of Columbus, the admiral took him into his home and nursed him. Just before he died in his sleep, the pilot told Columbus everything about what he had seen in the territories across the Atlantic. He even gave the admiral a detailed chart, though in great secrecy. Thus has the myth of Columbus's "personal secret" traveled through time.

One can easily see how this thesis fits with that of Vinland. In both, some crucial information is delivered to the 27-year-old mariner during his Portuguese period, hence making him an inside trader in some "hidden" intelligence of great value. As the reader will find out in Part 2, writers like Alejo Carpentier and Abel Posse think that Columbus was not a prophet but a charlatan, an impostor—a thief who stole from the unknown pilot and his Nordic precursors the truth that made him famous.

= La Rábida =

An all-time favorite scene of biographers, playwrights, and novelists is said to have taken place just a year or so before the first voyage. Promoted by García Fernández, a physician from Huelva, in testimony delivered in 1513, the legend may not be true, yet its powerful message is fixed in the memory of many, among them Paul Claudel and Nikos Kazantzakis. According to the doctor's account, the admiral, poor, hungry, and disappointed, appeared with his son Diego, already nine years of age, at the gates of La Rábida, a Franciscan monastery in Andalusia within a long walk's distance from Palos. He asked for help from the friars and requested food and water for his child (Morison, 80–81, 158–59). Fernández claims the event took place in 1491. If it did, it was preceded by a previous encounter sometime around 1484–85, when Columbus left Diego at the monastery as soon as he arrived in Spain. On that occasion he met Antonio de Marchena, an astrologer and a noted Franciscan who probably directed his attention to the Church's scholarly material that might validate his oceanographic claims. Sensing the potential in the mariner's project, Marchena became his advocate and began supporting his cause with the dukes and counts who could offer money. Columbus always kept his dedicated friend in very high esteem, yet after many ups and downs nothing substantial came of Marchena's efforts. Time passed. Columbus returned six years later to La Rábida to pick up Diego and ended up meeting a second friar, Juan Pérez, the guardian of the monastery and the queen's confessor, a man of wisdom who indirectly decided Columbus's future and that of humankind. Tired of courting Queen Isabella and noblemen without success, Columbus had already made up his mind to go to France to look for financial help. Before leaving Spain, he decided to deliver his child to his sister-in-law in Huelva. But Pérez heard of his nautical plans and asked him not to leave Spain. He summoned Dr. Fernández and the powerful ship owner and administrator Martín Alonso Pinzón for a private conference. After their discussion, Pérez decided to write a personal letter to Isabella asking her to support Columbus. And after a few more dealings, the admiral finally got his money—2,000,000 maravedis (around $14,000 dollars) (Morison, 98–99, 103). He also became close to Pinzón, who later took command of the *Pinta* and gathered some of his brothers and other family members (Diego Pinzón, Francisco Martín, and Vicente Yáñez Pinzón), as well as several Palos inhabitants, to be part of the crew.[24]

The La Rábida story certainly has religious connotations. The admiral is seen in the role of Jesus during his spiritual pilgrimage from misery and suffering to love and perfection, from blindness to enlightenment. Whatever Columbus's personal beliefs may have been, the fact that the Franciscan friars—who practiced poverty and modest means as a political stand within the institution of the Church—helped Columbus out adds an obvious Christian dimension to his glory. Kazantzakis even describes Columbus's stay at the monastery as a season of revelation—an occasion to witness an apparition of the Madonna and to battle the forces of evil. Pinzón is perceived as a hypocritical friend, a potentially dangerous enemy who accused the admiral of killing the unknown pilot who had crucial information about a land across the Atlantic.[25] Yet the Genoese, as a true messiah with divine power, overcomes every earthly obstacle he encounters and champions kindness and benevolence.

= The Ocean Blue =

Eight years of supplication elapsed. The financial support came through, as well as the backing of Queen Isabella. Columbus got ready for his voyage, the first of four. His sailing tools were the astrolabe, the marine quadrant, a handful of compass cards, and pure intuition.[26] He sailed from Palos, north of Cadiz and the Strait of Gibraltar, through Gomera in the Canary Islands, and from there to the Caribbean. The day of departure was 3 August 1492. The chief vessel was the *Santa María*, the property of Juan de Costa. It carried some 45 men. The *Pinta*, commanded by Martín Alonso Pinzón, its owner together with Cristóbal Quintero, carried 25. And the *Niña*, the property of Juan Niño, carried 20 men and was under the command of Vicente Yáñez, a brother of Pinzón. During the journey of more than 70 days, the crew on the ships lost faith in the enterprise and rebeled. Columbus maintained order by promising to reach land very soon and by suppressing the offenders. His rivalry with Pinzón, due to a clash of personalities and opposing drives for power, ended when Pinzón disagreed with Columbus's decisions and, on 6 October, insisted that the caravels had to travel southwest to the island of Cipangu. A day later the crew sensed a false landfall, and on 9 October the caravels sailed on good weather and a fresh ocean as clean as a river. Soon after they witnessed, in the magisterial open sky, migrating birds, a probable indication of nearby land. Still, a mutiny attempt took place on 11 October, and at 2:00 A.M. on the twelfth Columbus reached Guanahaní.

The exact site he reached has been the subject of much debate. In 1747 Mark Catesby identified Guanahaní as Cat Island. Some 80 years later, in 1825, Navarrete believed it was Grand Turk Island, as did Washington Irving. A. B. Becher, in 1856, thought the place to be Watlings Island. In 1882 G. V. Fox argued it was Semaná Cay, and in 1926 H. C. F. Cox identified Watlings Island as San Salvador, a view supported by Morison in *Admiral of the Ocean Sea*. In 1961 Robert Fuson argued in favor of Caicos, not Watlings, and Arne B. Molander in 1981 that Columbus must have landed at Egg Island, off the north coast of Eleuthera. Most recently, in a *National Geographic* essay published in November 1986, Luis Marden concludes that Semaná Cay is Guanahaní (Provost, 85–93).[27] Now the consensus is that, indeed, Guanahaní was Watlings Island.

= Ordeal and Decline =

The odyssey of the first voyage has attracted more attention than any of the admiral's subsequent trips, which took him to Puerto Rico, the Leeward Islands, Venezuela, even Central America. In 1494 Columbus's brother Bartholomeo explored Haiti while the crew made inland expeditions to Cibao. That is also the year of the landing in Cuba and Jamaica. Between 1496 and 1498, before even the third voyage had taken place, the admiral had reached Trinidad, and after expeditions to Venezuela he finally realized he had found a continent, although he still thought it was part of that fabulous land described by Marco Polo. In Hispaniola he founded a colony and became the sole governor, with legislative power bestowed by the Spanish monarchs.[28] He supported the slave trade and was vainglorious about his role as administrator and supreme ruler, creating a feeling of discomfort among his peers. In 1499 Alonso de Hojeda and Amerigo Vespucci, with a few pilots and mapmakers, reached the Gulf of Paria, Aruba, Curaçao, and Maracaibo. In the eyes of Europeans, Vespucci was the true hero of the whole enterprise of discovery, and his appelation was used to name the continent.[29]

During the next couple of years, difficult political and social circumstances—rebellions by the Tainos Indians in Jamaica, which Las Casas proudly described and used for his cause in *History of the Indies*, mutinies aboard the different caravels and rebellions on land, hurricanes, and other natural disasters—infuriated the Catholic monarchs and made Columbus's standing precarious. Judging by his character, he was unfit to rule. Understanding the gigantic size of his adventure, Ferdinand and Isabella decided to take fast action. They regained control of the new colonies, and in 1500 a legal order was sent from the court to replace the navigator as governor of Hispaniola and to quickly return him, together with his brother Diego, to

Spain in chains aboard the caravel *Gorda*. Columbus arrived in Cadiz in October, exactly eight years after his glorious 1492.

Nevertheless, a fourth and final voyage was still in Columbus's future. Feeling pity and remorse over their treatment of him, the kings set him free. He then moved to Seville and began to campaign heavily for new financial and political support. Among his many strategies to regain the favor and patronage of Spain's rulers was to write a letter to Pope Alexander VI, asking him to supply missionaries to convert the natives in the Americas to Christianity. Columbus also wrote directly to Isabella and Ferdinand trying to persuade them to authorize and finance another trip. They agreed on 4 March 1502. Just before his departure he completed and made copies of *The Book of Privileges*, a text he began compiling before the third voyage.[30] It was his account of his voyages and adventures in the New World. He sailed out again and reached Honduras, Nicaragua, and Costa Rica. But shipworms damaged one of his boats, the *Vizcaína*, which had to be abandoned. The situation got worse: two other vessels were in bad condition, and the unhappy crew was ready to return home, though they understood the present danger of never being able to reach Spain again. The result was a lack of esteem and trust for their admiral. The whole situation depressed Columbus. Anxious, distressed about the way kings and common men alike were abandoning him, and sure that his last chance was near its collapse, he wrote the moving *Lettera Rarissima* to the Catholic kings as a last attempt to rescue and restore his reputation.

> I came to serve [Your Highnesses] at the age of twenty-eight, and now I have no hair upon me that is not white, and my body is infirm and exhausted. All that was left to me and my brothers has been taken away and sold, even to the cloak that I wore, to my great dishonor. It is believed that this was not done by your royal command. The restitution of my honor and losses, and the punishment of those who have inflicted them, of those who plundered me of my pearls, and who have disparaged my admiral's privileges, will rebound to the honor of your royal dignity. The highest virtue, unexampled fame as grateful and just princes, will rebound to Your Highnesses if you do this; and the glorious memory will survive for Spain.[31]

Suffering from arthritis, Columbus lost control of his crew. He became the target of a conspiracy of hungry and disappointed crew members organized by Diego and Francisco de Porras, two brothers in command of the caravel *Bermuda*. Along with others, the Porrases robbed and incited the Indians to kill the admiral. An explosion of violence took place, and the Spaniards divided into two groups: those supporting Columbus, and those against him. On 12 September 1502, with 24 other people, the Genoese returned to Spain. The trip had not been triumphant. His reputation was in ruins, and as soon as he arrived in Spain he was ignored and ridiculed. His personal journey from obscurity to power and stardom, then to prison and recovery, had ended in victimization and silence—from darkness to light, then back to obscurity.

= The Invention of America =

The diary kept by Columbus during his first voyage, later transcribed by Bartolomé de Las Casas, reveals not only what he saw but how he understood the new reality his eyes were encountering. On 15 April 1493 the navigator wrote his famous "Letter to Luis de Santángel"—also known as "Letter to Sánchez"—another valuable document in which he confirms that, after days of sailing, he has finally arrived at a beautiful coast, part of a large archipelago he presumed to be part of the Indies.[32] Like Adam and Eve in the book of Genesis, he takes possession of the territory by naming the sights: San Salvador, Santa María de la Concepción, Fernandina, Isabella, and so on. He also describes the route of his voyage. Soon Columbus is compelled to describe what he sees: he tells Santángel that nature in this new land is colorful and beautiful, that palm trees almost reach the sky and never change leaves, as green as if they live in an eternal May that this new land contains unrecognizable, enchanting songbirds, marvelous fruits and herbs, vast, almost infinite landscapes, minerals and metals in unaccountable numbers, fecund soil, and rivers of gold.

His observations on the natives are fascinating. He refers to them as "inoffensive (without weapons)," "joyful," "running around naked," "good-natured," "fearful," and "handsome." If asked a favor, they readily comply without complaint. Easily pleased with "cheap, dangerous objects such as broken glass," they often confuse shining items with precious jewelry. (When Columbus saw the possibility of them getting injured with sharp crystal, he ordered his crew not to give them anymore.) Acknowledging them as religiously naive but not idolatrous, he encourages help from missionaries to convert whole tribes to Christianity. And how should their spiritual conversion take place? Since they are "ready and expecting change," they need only be shown the correct theological path, "a road to redemption" (Varela, 113). The navigator approached them, because of the language barrier, through captive interpreters.

Columbus claims to be shocked that, everywhere he goes, the Indians offer him goods and generous gifts. He sees them as confused. At first sight he believes they are not polygamists, although they offer women (at times, up to 20) to their landowners and kings. He also suspects they do not share the European idea of private property since, to his bewilderment, they share everything, especially food. Having been warned by *The Book of Marvels* of Marco Polo, he is amazed to not find any monstrosities, although he hears a rumor about an island inhabited by strong cannibals, and another populated only by women.

As a whole, the "Letter to Santángel" embellishes the reality of what

Columbus found in the Caribbean. The admiral should be congratulated for the persuasive power of his prose. His readers were a few influential people in Spain and, indirectly, the Catholic kings. Thus, his text is a tool to promote his talents, to enchant and captivate. He describes mines of gold and endless varieties of exotic species and bizarre fauna. By granting him power and support, he suggests, his adventure will bring power and profit to Spain.

His distortions and fantasies have, of course, infuriated many, especially South American and Caribbean intellectuals and artists. Their claim is that, by describing a fictional environment, Columbus enabled Europe to justify its imperialistic drive. Among the most articulate such critics is Pedro Henríquez Ureña, a twentieth-century Dominican Republic scholar who wrote engagingly and extensively about how the Americas perceive themselves and are seen by others. During the academic year 1940–41 he delivered the prestigious Charles Eliot Norton lectures at Harvard University, in which he offered a panoramic study of the plastic and narrative arts and aesthetic trends south of the Rio Grande.[33] He also made some observations on Columbus the writer, whom he portrays as a poor, unsophisticated, and syntactically deficient narrator with only two talents: a photographic memory and a need to exaggerate. He examined the navigator's use of adjectives and adverbs and his tendency to claim that everything is "unsurpassable" and "never before seen by human eyes" and concluded by suggesting that, as a master of imaginative distortion, the Genoese was a forefather of what would later be called magical realism. (This somewhat loose term refers to Hispanic America as a region where fiction and reality intertwine.)

The same idea is promoted by the Peruvian presidential candidate and *homme de lettres* Mario Vargas Llosa in his lecture "Novels Disguised as History: The Chronicles of the Birth of Peru," delivered at Syracuse University as a Jeannette K. Watson Distinguished Visiting Professor in 1988.[34] He suggests that the narrative accounts of the conquest and colonization of the Americas by soldiers and priests like Columbus, Cortés, Pizarro, Bernal Díaz del Castillo, and Bartolomé de Las Casas, because of the amount of fantasy in them, should be read as novels, as texts manipulating the truth—as compelling deception.

Along a similar line, Stephen Greenblatt, a professor at the University of California at Berkeley who is a leading figure in the "new historicism" and the author of essays on Prospero's language in Shakespeare's "colonial" drama *The Tempest*, focuses on the admiral's linguistic means of occupation. In *Marvelous Possessions: The Wonders of the New World* (1991), his 1988 Clarendon lectures at Oxford and Carpenter lectures at the University of Chicago, he tackled the concept of multiculturalism—a project of the 1980s to build up a "global culture" encompassing traditions and worldviews from South Africa to Hanoi, from Paris to Bogota—and studied its origin in Herodotus and Sir John Mandeville.[35] Greenblatt argued that Columbus was blind to the splendor of the Indians: to deal with anxiety-inducing wonder, he took possession of their foreign, exotic reality by means of language, by not only naming objects and customs but injecting into the Americas his communicational frame of mind. Greenblatt cites the example of the navigator colonizing an island in the Caribbean with no resistance from the natives. His thesis is that they could not contradict Columbus simply because they did not understand his language.

Carlos Fuentes, a Mexican novelist, essayist and diplomat, wrote and hosted a five-part BBC television series entitled *The Buried Mirror*, in which Columbus is portrayed as a mariner "driven by courage, the desire for fame, the thrill of discovery, lust for gold, and the duty to evangelize." And Fuentes continues: "How are we to understand the discovery of America? Aren't all discoveries basically mutual? The Europeans discovered the American continent, but the indigenous peoples of the Americas also discovered the Europeans, wondering whether these white and bearded men were gods or mortals. And whether they were as merciful as their crosses proclaimed or as merciless as their swords demonstrated."[36] The argument is clear: to understand the events of 1492 only from the European perspective is a mistake. Thus Columbus ought to be studied also as an invader, a colonialist.

From Henríquez Ureña to Greenblatt and Fuentes, especially after World War II, the feeling on both sides of the Rio Grande is that to keep using terms such as "conquest" and "discovery" in reference to the events of 1492 is a mistake. Earlier historians like William H. Prescott were not at all shy in using them to describe the clash between the Spaniards and the Aztecs or Incas, but the cultural climate in the late twentieth century has dramatically changed. The argument now is that in 1492 Columbus began a history of violence, repression, and abuse, and that his narrative descriptions of his newfound territories are falsifying, misrepresentative, and offensively sophistic.

= Life after Death =

The fourth voyage ended on 7 November 1504, in Sanlúcar de Barrameda. Queen Isabella died a few days later, and her daughter, the Infanta Juana, "La Loca," married to the Archduke Philip of Austria, acquired substantial power in Spain. No longer held in esteem at the court, Columbus thought, as a last recourse, to ask his son Ferdinand and his brother Bartholomeo to intercede in his behalf. They had done so in the past, but this time nothing came of it. (Although three years after his death, in 1509, Columbus's older son Diego was appointed governor of Hispaniola.) On 19 May 1506, Columbus ratified his last will in which he made Diego his sole heir, subordinating all other family members to him, including Beatríz Enríquez de Arana. The navigator was obsessed with regaining his "rights." Arthritis and depression, however, were his major obstacles during those last couple of years. He could hardly move, and changes of weather affected him constantly. Again he sought to reverse Ferdinand's decision to take away his power over the colonies—the only response was silence. The court moved to Salamanca and Valladolid. Columbus followed it with his plea, but his sickness had weakened him, and in the end his effort came to nothing.

He died on 20 May 1506, in neglect, almost forgotten.[36] His body was not to be buried in peace; instead, it continued in the mariner's globe-trotting path. At the request of Diego, his corpse was transferred from Valladolid to Las Cuevas in Seville. It was then transported to Cuba. From there it supposedly was to return to Seville, but in a bewildering reversal, it ended up in the Dominican Republic. Kirkpatrick Sale describes its later odyssey:

> When France took control of Española in 1795, Madrid ordered that [Columbus's] remains be sent to safety in Havana; these were moved again after Cuba became independent in 1898 and shipped to Seville to be interred finally in the cathedral there in a tomb thought to be appropriate for the Great Discoverer. . . . Two decades before that, however, in 1877, a small lead casket was discovered and removed during the enlargement of the Santo Domingo cathedral, and when examined it was found to have two inscriptions with the name Cristoval Colon; in 1879 it was returned to the cathedral, and it lies there today in a tomb thought to be appropriate for the Great Discoverer. It is perhaps fitting that the bones of the man honored as the European discoverer of the Americas should lie, in a sense, on both continents. Fitting, too, that even in death he finds no home. (216)

So who *was* Christopher Columbus? After 1506 people began offering answers. With many rumors continuing to diminish his reputation, the search for intelligent clues to the mystery of his identity also continues. An admirable hero and the representative of sixteenth-century imperialism, a role model and a treacherous villain—the staggering asymmetries created by the many conflicting views have been a literary inspiration.

PART II

Lives of a Literary Character

When a writer calls his work a Romance, it need hardly be observed that he wishes to claim a certain latitude, both as to its fashion and material, which he would not have felt himself entitled to assume, had he professed to be writing a Novel. The latter form of composition is presumed to aim at a very minute fidelity, not merely to the possible, but to the probable and ordinary course of man's experience. The former—while, as a work of art, it must rigidly subject itself to laws, and while it sins unpardonably, so far as it may swerve aside from the truth of the human heart—has fairly a right to present that truth under circumstances, to a great extent, of the writer's own choosing or creation.

> —Nathaniel Hawthorne,
> *The House of the Seven Gables* (1851)

4

Masquerade

IN *THE USES OF LITERATURE* (1980), ITALO CALVINO, THE Italian avant-garde writer who died in 1985, wrote: "Whom do we write a novel for? Whom do we write a poem for? For people who have read a number of other novels, a number of other poems. A book is written so that it can be put beside other books and take its place on a hypothetical bookshelf. Once it is there, in some way or other it alters the shelf, expelling certain other volumes from their places and forcing them back into the second row, while demanding that certain others should be brought up to the front." Besides commenting on the readership a writer targets, Calvino, like T. S. Eliot in his essay "Tradition and the Individual Talent" (*The Sacred Wood*, 1920), offers a compelling theory on how books make history. The present, he argues, is made of current volumes, only a handful of which will survive on the hypothetical bookshelf of the future. While the past in literature is represented by a glorious display of titles that have overcome the mercilessness of time, deleted from human memory are those that, fortunately or not, succumbed to oblivion.[1]

Many books dealing with Christopher Columbus that are known today are indeed survivors. They made it into their future—the bookshelf that is our present. Yet a great number, perhaps ten or fifteen times as many as are available to us today, have been forgotten, left unnoticed in dusty library stacks or storerooms, perhaps known for a time to specialists but later excluded forever from the annals of remembrance. This chapter and the three that follow are the very heart of *Imagining Columbus*: a critical and personal library of selected poems, plays, novels, and short stories about the Genoese navigator, a compendium of outstanding fiction that may well prove that his life after death has been more fascinating than his earthly adventures.

As John Noble Wilford and Kirkpatrick Sale forcefully argue, once Columbus passed away in Valladolid on 20 May 1506, a period of silence and anonymity followed.[2] It took about 150 years for that period to end, yet once it did, the flow of narratives and poetic hymns became simply overwhelming.

Three essential elements of these fictions are the tongue, time, and country in which they were written. The scope, ideology, and aesthetic components of each of these titles ultimately depend on these elements. Take as an example James Fenimore Cooper's *Mercedes of Castile*, first published in 1840 after the writer had been living in Europe for several years. Its subject is the sentimental liaison between one Don Luis de Bobadilla, an Iberian sailor in one of Columbus's three caravels, and Ozema, an arresting Indian beauty he meets on an island in the Caribbean. The portrait of Columbus, a peripheral character, is quite benign: as a U.S. writer in an age of national consolidation, Cooper sees the mariner as adventurous, gay, even glorious. Cooper's interest in history is limited; his characters need only to fall in love to create a link between the two continents and bring on a happy ending. No enmity, no bitterness. In 1979, on the other hand, almost 13 decades later, *The Harp and the Shadow* by Alejo Carpentier is an indictment of the admiral's excesses, his abuse of power and thirst for gold. As perceived by Carpentier, Columbus is dishonest, wicked, flagrant, even scandalous. One novelist's tongue is English, the other's Spanish; one is a North American realist enthusiastic about his country's economic expansion and supportive of Europe's colonialism; the other, a Hispanic in a time of cultural reassessment and reevaluation of marginal civilizations. Two views, one literary character.

In the Old World, the early seventeenth century witnessed the very first narrative attempts that refer in passing to the navigator. Lope de Vega, the celebrated and very prolific Spanish golden-age playwright who wrote more than 400 plays as well as a fascinatingly persuasive manual on how to write for the stage (*The New Art of Writing Plays* [1609]), is among the first to have paid a fair amount of attention to Columbus. Published in 1614, his play *The Discovery of the New World by Christopher Columbus* is a humorous piece, seldom performed, in which the larger-than-life admiral is a symbol of exploration—in the words of Wilford, "a dreamer up against the solid forces of entrenched tradition, a man of singular purpose who triumphed, the embodiment of that spirit driving humans to explore and discover" (245). According to David Castillejo and other scholars, the comedy was written sometime around 1599, when Lope de Vega traveled to Seville to visit his mistress Micaela Luján while her husband, Diego Díez, was on the other side of the Atlantic.[3]

In English, no marginal literary references to Columbus can be found in Shakespeare, who died in 1616, more than a century after the Genoese. They are present, however, in John Milton's *Paradise Lost* (1667), a poem that includes the following lines:

> . . . . such of late
> Columbus found th' American, so girt
> With feathered cincture, naked else and wilde—
> (bk. *9*, l. 1116)[4]

British poets such as Algernon Swinburne and Alfred Tennyson pursued the Columbian interest in their act. Across the Atlantic, texts by Baptist Goodall, Robert Seall, Stephen Parmenius, and other British pilgrims and seventeenth-century writers in North America commended the mariner's courage or praised his undefeatable will.[5] Yet they hardly built up a complex, sophisticated portrait of any literary merit. Something similar occurred in Hispanic America during the baroque colonial period; Columbus was the subject of passing allegorical citations in religious sonnets, epistles, and essays by mystical nuns and clergymen, but most are unremarkable and now forgotten. Some Mexican writers, such as the *creole* hunchback Juan Ruíz de Alarcón and the poet Bernardo de Balbuena, praised him as a discoverer but failed to perceive his historic contribution to collective identity in the Americas under Spanish rule. More attention was given to the mariner in the verses and plays of Sor Juana Inés de la Cruz, a Mexican nun of great literary talent who was born in Nepantla in 1648 as an illegitimate child. With her lucid pen she wrote *First Dream* (1692), a metaphysical, Neoplatonic poem about the nomenclature of things earthly that recalls the art of Luis de Góngora and the views of Hermes Trismegistus.[6] In a *seguidilla*, stanzas of four or seven lines, written in honor of the Señora Condesa de Galve and published for the first time in 1692, Sor Juana includes the following reference to the admiral:

> A Columbus in her open,
> brave forehead,
> because among those in her Empire
> she's the most advanced.[7]

In an anthem, part of an *auto sacramental*, an allegorical religious play written in 1692 and titled "The Sacramental Martyr, Saint Hermenegildo," one of her many characters is Columbus himself. Appearing in scene 5, he talks with some soldiers. Here is his eloquent monologue:

> Fruitful Spain! I already kiss
> your sunny sands.
> Your oceans have overcome
> the many dangers and risks!
> I thank you, oh my God,
> for having entrusted
> this defeated creature
> with such an enterprise
> of stubbornly crossing across
> the Eccinoccial line!
> Congratulations, Europe,
> congratulations!
> There are more Worlds, more Empires,
> for your weapons to possess
> and your breath to capture!
> Leave behind the mistaken past
> of your forefathers,
> claiming that the end of the world
> wasn't beyond the horizontal edge!
> Oh, Hercules! Erase from your Columns
> the presumptous claim
> of *Non plus ultra*, because
> the control of Abila and Calpe,
> kept close for so long, is already broken!
> And you, my happy,
> gay companions,
> discoverers with clarions and music boxes
> of open Worlds,
> make it public, with sweet echoes:
> There are more Worlds, there is *Plus ultra*.
> people should come to see it!
> In a military tone,
> let it be clear to everyone:
> The Tórrida is inhabitable
> thanks to Heaven!
> *Plus ultra!* There are more Worlds,
> and we are coming to see them![8]

Sor Juana sings to Columbus's brave spirit and to his discovery of a new universe. She invites others to see, to appreciate what he has found. The fact that she is a Hispanic American, a devout Christian in a Carmelite convent in Mixcoac, later part of Mexico City, an inhabitant of the colonies, does not interfere with her sympathies toward the navigator. She addresses her monologue to *criollos*, viceroys, and the Europeans who were blind to the beauties of the newly discovered reality.

During the colonial period most literary references to Columbus occurred in poetry, and not coincidentally. After 1492 and during the European Renaissance, poems, either sensuously bucolic or scholastic, and rhymed theatrical dramas were the two predominant artistic genres. At the time of the unification of Aragon and Granada by the Catholic kings, streets and public plazas, mainly in the Iberian peninsula but also in southern France, were visited by troubadours singing lyrical verses. The Franciscan poets Iñigo de Mendoza and Ambrosio Montesino acquired a large following, and their style was imitated by anonymous *romances* (Spanish ballads) and *villlancicos* (religious songs or Christmas carols) everywhere from Castile to Andalusia. By the time the erotic and mythological Juan Boscán and Garcilaso de la Vega, followed by the metaphysical Lope de Vega, Luis de Góngora, and Francisco de Quevedo, emerged, the legend of the by-then defunct Columbus was still embryonic and hardly anyone was remembering him in sonnets. Constructing linguistic intricacies, these poets articulated inspired, at times labyrinthine ideas with beautifully insightful metonymies, oxymorons, and synaesthesises in octasyllabic and shorter-line sonnets (France, 23–54). In post-Milton England, the heroic poetry of the Augustans, from the Restoration of Charles II to 1750, also dealt with religious exhaustion and domestic imbroglios. And in France the poets of the Pléiade dealt with hopefulness, the destruction of sentiment and beauty, and the passing of things human. In general, poetry all over Europe served as music to the soul. Not until around 1739, when Samuel Richardson and Henry Fielding—recapturing the narrative tradition that originated with the picaresque writers of Spain, Cervantes, Daniel Defoe, and Jonathan Swift—began writing psychological narratives that focus on the emotional life of people, was the ground under poetry shaken. A new, encyclopedic genre took hold, an ambitious one that, in the words of John Barth, excludes nothing and attempts to mirror reality in all its candor and complexity[9]—the novel.

Around 1776 it was fashionable among poets and artists in the British colonies to perceive the admiral as an inaugurator of the patriotic experience, an indirect founding father of the Republic. If he lacked a real following in the preceding years, he gained one during the attempt to shape an independent collective identity in the British colonies; as an attractive historical figure, he became instrumental in the shaping of the national past. Propagandists, pamphleteers, revolutionaries, diplomats, intellectuals, even traders and businessmen found in his nautical odyssey support for their ideological breakup with England. They also saw him as a bridge, a link with the civilization of the Old World. North of the Rio Grande, among the first to celebrate him and transform his features into literary qualities was Joel Barlow, who wrote an epic entitled *The Columbiad* (1807) in his honor. Around the same time a minister named Jeremy Belknap wrote an essay entitled "A Discourse Intended to Commemorate the Discovery of America by Christopher Columbus," which he read in the tricentennial and included in his *Biographies of the Early Discoverers* (1792). Praising the admiral as a prophet, a messiah of sorts, Belknap glorified him as an originator of the United States:

About the middle of the fifteenth century . . . a genius arose, whose memory has been preserved with veneration in the pages of history, as the instrument of enlarging the region of science and commerce beyond any of his predecessors. . . . He had a genius of that kind, which makes use of speculation and reasoning only as excitements to action. He was not a closet projector, but an enterprising adventurer. . . . In the pages of impartial history, he will always be remembered as . . . a prudent, skillful, intrepid navigator. (Sale, 337–38)

In his essay, Belknap has God referring to the United States as a "sweet," "peaceful," "heavenly *Columbia*." This positive view of the mariner would prevail in North America. During the nineteenth century, in New York, Boston, and Chicago, Columbus was perceived by poets and writers as a precursor of modernity, a prophet, a man of invaluable talents. And after 1892, the consolidation of the nation as an international power, and the fact that only 100 years after gaining independence it had become a triumphant socioeconomic experiment compared with the poor and troubled countries of the Southern Hemisphere, contributed to Columbus's good standing among Anglo-Saxon artists, among them, the poets Ralph Waldo Emerson, Lawrence Ferlinghetti, Philip Freneau, Allen Ginsberg, Edward Everett Hale, Sidney Lanier, James Russell Lowell, Joaquin Miller, Walt Whitman, and William Carlos Williams.

In eighteenth-and nineteenth-century Europe a similarly patriotic, chauvinistic perception was promoted. The poet Madame Duboccage, in her thoroughly researched 1758 epic *The Columbiad: or, Faith Transported to the New World* portrayed the discoverer as a genius, a unifier of Europe and the Americas—or, in the words of the critic Moses Nagy, "an instrument of God's providential plans."[10] Ramón de Campoamor, an Iberian romantic, sang in *Colón* (1854) to his qualities as a Spaniard, disregarding his cruelty toward natives and his cultural nearsightedness. By the same token, Friedrich Nietzsche commented in poetic terms on Columbus's Genoese background.[11] But among Hispanics in Buenos Aires, Havana, Santo Domingo, and other cities of the region, perceptions were altogether different during the same period, even into this century. Those who make passing or full-length poetic references to him include Rafael María Baralt, Andrés Bello, Jorge Luis Borges, Rubén Darío, Narciso Foxá y Lecanda, Pedro Henríquez Ureña,[12] José María de Heredia, Leopoldo Lugones, José Martí, Pablo Neruda, Octavio Paz, José Joaquín Pérez, Father Fernando Portillo y Torres, Alfonso Reyes, and Ramón López Velarde. Ever since independence was won in Argentina and Mexico around the early decade of the nineteenthth-century America, the tone in South has been critical, antagonistic, and unforgiving. The candor and the fury can best be appreciated in "To Columbus," a poem written by Darío in 1892 (see chapter 6). The Nicaraguan *modernista* attacks the navigator for promoting a huge holocaust, for perpetrating chaos in an orderly land. If the idiosyncratic nature of North America enables its inhabitants to see

Columbus as a hero with an exceptional character, in places like Cuba, Puerto Rico, the Dominican Republic, Chile, and Venezuela, where history has been made up of multiple tragic encounters with foreign cultures and depression marks the collective identity, the Genoese is inevitably approached as a treacherous offender.

What about theater? During the Spanish golden Age of the fifteenth and sixteenth centuries, in the works of Tirso de Molina and Calderón de la Barca, among others, many characters traveled to the Americas and returned to the Iberian peninsula to tell stories of adventure, financial disaster, diplomacy, and violence. But with the already mentioned exception of Lope de Vega, none of these playwrights turned the navigator into a distinguished character. In France the encyclopedist Jean-Jacques Rousseau, inspired by Voltaire's *Alzire* (1736), which takes place in Peru and deals with the innocence of the savage, published *The Discovery of the New World* in 1740. Both Voltaire and Rousseau see Columbus as a symbol of resistance to mortality and human mediocrity. In England, Thomas Morton produced *Columbus: A World Discovered*, a play premiered in 1792 during the tricentennial celebration in Covent Garden in London. Rousseau uses the admiral as an excuse to discuss the difference between Europeans and savages in the Americas; he examines, within eighteenth-century parameters, the forces of civilization against barbarism and the attitude of the enlightened free-thinkers in metropolises like Paris toward the so-called inferior races. Morton, on the other hand, *Columbus* as a spiritualist. *Christophe Colomb* by Népomucène Lemercier premiered in 1809, and six years later a melodrama by Gilbert de Pixerécourt, *Christopher Columbus: or, The Discovery of the New World*,[13] was staged in the Théâtre de la Gaité. A century later operas by Félicien David and S. G. Pratt, an "ode-symphony" by Joseph Mery Chabet and Sylvain St. Etienne, an overture by Richard Wagner, and a chorale by Antonín Dvořák perpetuated this theatrical tradition. In the twentieth century Columbus has been the protagonist in plays by Fernándo Benítez, Paul Claudel, Nikos Kazantzakis, George Lansing Raymond, Guillermo Schmidhuber, and Alice Johnston Walker. Compared with the voluminous poetic and novelistic creativity on the subject, however, a fair conclusion is that the theater has generated considerably fewer works on Columbus. Even if the immediacy of the stage experience, as Peter Brooks puts it, transforms the myth into reality,[14] any cautious playwright knows that the larger-than-life scale of the Genoese and the need for a sophisticated setting can be obstacles in the staging process.

An altogether different situation obtains with the novel, which attempts to encapsulate the entire universe in words and paragraphs. If John Milton, Sor Juana Inés de la Cruz, and Jeremy Belknap saw Columbus as an allegory, in the novels of James Fenimore Cooper (*Mercedes of Castile* [1840]), Blasco Ibáñez (*In Search of the Grand Khan* [1978]), Abel Posse (*The Dogs of Paradise* [1985]), Alejo Carpentier (*The Harp and the Shadow* [1979]), Carlos Fuentes (*Christopher Unborn* [1987]), Michael Dorris and Louise Erdrich (*The Crown of Columbus* [1991]), Stephen Marlowe (*The Memoirs of Christo-*

pher Columbus [1987]), Ida Mills Wilhern (*The Son of Dolores* [1945]), Newton Frohlich (*1492: A Novel of Christopher Columbus and His World* [1990]),
and Rafael Sabatini (*Columbus* [1942]), he is a complex, multifaceted, vulner-
able individual—hero and martyr, villain and redeemer, discoverer and traitor.

Every novel on Columbus, even if it is experimental, is inherently historical. Some narrators, such as James Fenimore Cooper, are realists to the point
of chicanery. Others, such as Carlos Fuentes and Stephen Marlowe, have
inherited the ludicrous gimmicks of Laurence Sterne's *Tristram Shandy*:
their texts are not only unconventional but irreverent and anachronistic, their
goal, it seems, being to push literature to its limits. As Nathaniel Hawthorne
explains in the preface to *The House of the Seven Gables*, writers of prose
fiction are divided into two categories: the creators of novels, who aim to
depict, with "very minute fidelity, not merely . . . the possible, but . . . the
probable and ordinary course of man's experience"; and the generators of
romances, a product very much of the artist's own imagination.[15] The titles
studied here clearly are novels in the strict sense of the term—*ficciones*, in
Borges's terminology, fantastic pieces with a foot in history.

And the short story? Although they use historical material, the three to
be discussed in these pages are a bit rigid, zealous, more like essays. The first
("The Discovery of America") is by Umberto Eco, the Italian semiotician and
author of the thriller *The Name of the Rose*; the second is by the U.S. poet
William Carlos Williams ("The Discovery of the Indies"); and the third
("Christopher Columbus and Queen Isabella of Spain Consummate Their
Relationship, Santa Fé, January, 1492") is by Salman Rushdie, the controversial Muslim author of *The Satanic Verses* (1989) who was condemned to
death for blasphemy against Islam by Iran's top religious leader, Ayatollah
Khomeini. Oscillating between the quotidian and the exceptional, they play
with suspense yet remain flat, inert, dissonant.

Identity—the unequivocal nucleus of literature. Everywhere one finds
its manifestations: a character's desire to understand his place in time and
space, his sense of disorientation, his confusing inner motivations, his doubts
about God and his fellowmen. In the work of modernists like Luigi Pirandello,
Vladimir Nabokov, Jorge Luis Borges, and Samuel Beckett, the task of searching for one's identity is always difficult often a character, shouldering a bag
of unanswered philosophical questions is lost in a labyrinth of symbols and
anxieties; he looks at himself in the mirror only to find a mask, another self,
and not his authentic one. Masks, an ancient ritualistic and theatrical artifact,
have become the message.

Throughout his multicultural literary voyage, Columbus is a man of a
thousand masks. Many of them are metaphorical: in "Prayer of Columbus"
(1874) by Walt Whitman, the mariner, old and tired, delivers his own sermon
in the face of God. The poet's voice is the admiral's as well—two people
behind one single verbal mask. In *Christopher Unborn* by Carlos Fuentes,
on the other hand, Columbus is an embryo in a futuristic 1992—that is, a
science fiction mask à la Aldous Huxley or George Orwell. Columbus's masks

highlight various features, big and small, tragic and comic—an *homme de guerre*, a saint, an adored lover, a valiant patriot, a foolish buffoon. For analytic purposes, I have reduced them to three categories: those allowing Columbus to remain a common, unexceptional man; those transforming him into a villain; and those exalting his symbolic stature. As the reader will soon find out, the admiral as a literary character has an identity problem.

5

The Man

A SEA CAPTAIN, TRADER, JOURNALIST, ANTIUTILITARIAN, and prosperous gentleman of the early Republic, Philip Morin Freneau, who was a close friend of President James Madison, lacks a high literary reputation in the United States and abroad. Of Huguenot descent (his grandfather immigrated to New York in 1707), his style, oscillating between the satirical and the epic, did not gain him many enthusiasts and left no immediate successors. In fact, many of his contemporaries held Freneau in low esteem, among them George Washington, a political enemy who called him "a rascal."[1] Mary Weatherspoon Bowden, his biographer, sums up his precarious fame: "Any judgment of [his] worth as a littérateur is difficult. He set in train no literary school; if his work influenced any later artists, they did not credit it. . . . Today we can criticize most of his works as imperfect, as somehow defective. We can see where, in this essay or that poem, he excelled himself and achieved art. But other artists have achieved art more constantly."[2]

By today's values, perhaps Freneau's most outstanding contribution to the tradition of North American letters was his fascination with the native

Americans. Although he never really explored their customs and civilizations with the meticulous eye for detail of an ethnographic scientist, nor did he champion their civil rights (he was rebellious in character, but not a man ahead of his time), in his poems he focused on their plight. That alone makes him relevant. Yet like James Fenimore Cooper and Charles Brockden Brown, he approached them from a romantic, sentimental, even bucolic angle: they were the undeniable root, the essence of the by-then emerging nation—the victimized witnesses of a past repressed. Their contact with nature, their unsophisticated intelligence, their noble spirit, made them admirable, although not equal to the British Pilgrims.

In 1902 Fred Lewis Pattee, the editor of Freneau's complete works, proclaimed that the poet's interest was prophetic, that he predicted the role of the native Americans in the forthcoming art of the New World (*Freneau*, cx). And in *An Introduction to American Literature (1967)*, an overview of U.S. fiction since 1776, Jorge Luis Borges suggests that the theme is Freneau's legacy. Borges analyzes it in Freneau's most compelling piece, a poem entitled "The Indian Student: or, Force of Nature" (1788).

> Freneau tells the story of a young Indian who sells all his goods in order to acquire the mysterious learning of the white man. After painful wanderings he reaches the nearest university. He devotes himself first to the study of English and then to Latin; his professors foresee a brilliant future for him. Some maintain that he will be a theologian; others, a mathematician. Gradually the Indian, whose name is not revealed to us, begins to draw apart from his comrades and goes out walking in the woods. A squirrel, says the poet, distracts him from one of Horace's odes. Astronomy upsets him; the idea of the roundness of the earth and the infinity of space fills him with terror and uncertainty. One morning he goes away as silently as he came and returns to his tribe and his woods. The piece is at once a poem and a short story. Freneau tells it so well that no one can doubt that the facts were as described.[3]

After attending Princeton, Freneau became a mariner. He sailed several times to Bermuda and the Azores. An outspoken antislavery ideologue, he often criticized the English rule in the colonies. Columbus was a favorite historical figure of his; Freneau perceived him as a founding father of the Republic. The admiral's presence is felt in many corners of Freneau's oeuvre, beginning with "The Rising Glory of America," a vivid dialogue between three students on the greatness of the British colonies. Freneau cowrote the first version with a friend and fellow Princeton student, Hugh Henry Brackenridge. The text was read during the 1771 commencement and received applause. Published a year later in *The American Village*, it was reprinted in Freneau's 1809 collection. A decade and a half after, he revised and reprinted it under his sole name.

Although not strictly a revolutionary poem, "The Rising Glory" points

to the illustrious destiny of the United States and, indirectly, suggests its
autonomous future. What follows are the opening words by Acasto, one of
the three students:

> Now shall the adventurous muse attempt a theme
> More new, more noble and more flush of fame
> Than all that went before—
> Now through the veil of ancient days renew
> The period famed when first Columbus touched
> These shores so long unknown—through various toils,
> Famine, and death, the hero forced his way,
> Through oceans pregnant with perpetual storms,
> And climates hostile to adventurous man.
>
> (*Freneau*, 49)

Panoramic and ambitious, the dialogue between Acasto and his friends
Eugenio and Leander revisits the history, and travels through the vastness,
of the Americas but focuses on the present reality north of the Rio Grande.
Arguing on themes like progress and social improvement, Freneau and Brackenridge, through their protagonists, offer a vision of eminence and divine
grandeur as qualities found in the past in Memphis and Greece, in Rome and
Britain, and now inhabiting the Americas. True precursors of another New
Englander, the transcendentalist Ralph Waldo Emerson, the two poets encourage the emergence of new Homers, Miltons, and Popes to memorialize
the inception and continuity of the United States in this "messianic," "unsin-
ful" territory.

According to Freneau, in the second version of "The Rising Glory" (1786)
he retained only those verses originally written by him and added "a few
more." At 35, he had matured as a versifier and had a clear political agenda
directed against the British rulers. As Pattee and Bowden have noticed, every
favorable reference to England in the text was deleted in the revision; the
native Americans, referred to in the first version as "cruel," "wild as the
winds," "treacherous as hell," are now praised as advocates of autonomy and
change. And although Columbus is still referred to only marginally he clearly
has become a hero to Freneau.

In fact, by then he already had produced two full-length poems with the
Genoese as protagonist. Both belong to his first artistic period, from 1768 to
1781, when his views on the nation's heritage were shaped. Composed sometime between 1772 and 1774 (only two years before the Revolution), the texts
exemplify his obsession with the navigator: one is entitled "Columbus to
Ferdinand," and the other, "The Pictures of Columbus: The Genoese" (1788).
Although a 1786 edition of the poet's works states that the first was written
in 1770, Pattee found a June 1769 issue of *United States* magazine that
included it. Very brief in length (only 15 stanzas), its structure is that of an
address by the admiral to the Catholic king, in which he begs Ferdinand to

grant the financial support needed for him to travel across the Atlantic. Columbus's voice is premonitory and self-confident:

> Illustrious monarch of Iberia's soil,
> Too long I wait permission to depart;
> Sick of delays, I beg thy list'ning ear—
> Shine forth the patron and the prince of art.
> (*Freneau*, 46)

As a narrator, Freneau assumes two vantage points simultaneously: he is Columbus, and also a distant observer digesting the navigator's adventures. The maneuver allows him to offer an insider's as well as an outsider's perspective.

More than a conventional story poem, "Columbus to Ferdinand" is one scene, a static image with no action. The Genoese explains his anxiety to depart, his views of nature, his certitude. He knows, by pure intuition, of another continent west of the Canary Islands. His task is not to discover a new route to the West Indies but to allow the United States to make its entrance onto historical stage. Like his successor Washington Irving, Freneau's Columbus is a link between the old and the new, a man of reason and integrity who becomes a bridge, a communicating vessel between Europe and the Americas.

> When southward we shall steer—O grant my wish,
> Supply the barque, and bid Columbus sail,
> He dreads no tempests on the untravell'd deep,
> Reason shall steer, and shall disarm the gale.
> (*Freneau*, 48)

Nowhere in "Columbus to Ferdinand" can one find supernatural, symbolic, or quasi-divine attributes in the mariner. Freneau portrays him as humble and courageous, a freedom-fighter. He contextualizes Columbus's personal struggle in the frame of the prophecies of Seneca, the so-called sage of Cordoba. Freneau even quotes from Seneca's *Medea* (act 3, verse 375): "The time shall come, when numerous years are past,/ The ocean shall dissolve the bands of things, And an extended region rise at last" (*Freneau*, 47).

This uncomplicated poetic portrait of the admiral was developed in "The Pictures of Columbus: The Genoese," which comprises 18 "images," each with a total of between 25 and 65 verses with titles such as "Columbus Making Maps" and "Columbus Visits the Court at Barcelona." By means of monologues and objective descriptions, Freneau focuses on the admiral's odyssey, with its many hopes and disappointments. Compared with his other works, claims Bowden, this is a fairly good poem. Each of the pictures "presents a different aspect of Columbus's trials and discovery. Some pictures are dramatic dialogues, but others, more static and descriptive, are like the speech of the enchantress whom Columbus sought for her prediction. . . . Because of the shifting pictures, Freneau can show his versatility in painting the varied aspects of the man Columbus" (37).

If in "The Rising Glory" Freneau offers only scattered comments on Columbus's personality, in "The Pictures" he studies the navigator's adolescent years as a dreamer and explores his tense, "hypocritical" relationship with the Catholic kings. Freneau offers an explanation of Columbus's humble, "enlightened" psychology. In the opening sketch, Columbus reduces the universe to a map while exploring his intuition that another reality exists beyond the horizon. His love of humankind is unquestionable. Freneau makes him a common man of intelligence, uninhibited and courageous.

> This world on paper idly drawn,
> O'er one small tract so often gone
> The pencil tires; in this void space
> Allow'd to find no resting place.
>
> But copying Nature's bold design,
> If true to her, no fault is mine;
> Perhaps in these most regions dwell
> Forms wrought like man, and lov'd as well.
> (*Freneau*, 89–90)

The next scenes place the Genoese in dialogues with sorceresses, mirrors, King Ferdinand, and Queen Isabella. Once more, Freneau cites his favorite passage from *Medea*. He then shows that the compass was invented so that men like Columbus could wander to distant, unexplored lands. His thesis is that the first voyage was a proof of the eternal laws of reason: a divine power set the elements in motion for the navigator to achieve his goals—in other words, 1492 was an act of God.

Freneau's biographical information on the Genoese is, of course, incomplete. In 1788 Freneau had only partial knowledge of his life. Oviedo and Martyr, the only two well-known biographers, were unavailable in English. Not surprisingly, "The Pictures" delivers a vague, romantic, imprecise portrait. Descriptions of natural sites and of feelings and emotions predominate, not careful analysis of the life. And Freneau's secondary themes—once again, the native Indians among them—further embellish his work.

These noble savages' lives of peace and harmony with the environment are suddenly interrupted by the arrival of the white European man (Freneau, 117). Nevertheless Columbus is eventually amazed by their freedom and joyful spirit. (The same bucolic view informs Cooper's *Mercedes of Castile*.) He admires their directness and understands their perils. Nonetheless, he remains the hero and the object of the poet's attention. When in chains, he says:

Are these the honours they reserve for me,
Chains for the man that gave New Worlds to Spain!
Rest here, my swelling heart!—O Kings, O Queens,
Patrons of monsters, and their progeny,
Authors of wrong, and slaves to fortune merely!

(*Freneau*, 120)

In spite of its benevolent message, the poem's ideological stand is confusing. At one point, Freneau has Columbus justifying his 1492 trip to Queen Isabella as a mission for the Church to save lost souls "forc'd from Eden's shade" (*Freneau*, 102). Although we see Columbus's kindly feelings toward the aboriginal people, we also see that his arrogance makes him feel superior to them. In "Discovery"—still another early poem by Freneau on the topic of Columbus, written in 1772, between "The Rising Glory" and "The Pictures" (included in the 1786 edition of his complete works)—his stand against imperialism is similar, although here pessimism prevails. Like Bartolomé de Las Casas with his "black legend," but much less belligerently, Freneau accuses the Spanish conquistadores of colonialism, cruelty, and unmercifulness. Although Freneau does not mention the Genoese by name, his enterprise is indirectly examined, as well as Pizarro's in Peru. The natives are once more depicted as suffering victims and relics of the past, and the environment as a target of destruction. Religion and monarchy, in the poet's opinion, are the source of Europe's flaws.

Seek some new world in some new climate plac'd,
Some gay Ta-ia on the watery waste,
Though Nature clothes in all her bright array,
Some proud tormentor steals her charms away:
Howe'er she smiles beneath those milder skies,
Though men decay the monarch never dies!
Howe'er the groves, howe'er the gardens bloom,
A monarch and a priest is still their doom!

(*Freneau*, 88)

As suggested by these three poems, Freneau refused to equate Columbus with the enemy. The damage, for him, was perpetuated by others, not by Columbus. In the poet's eyes, the admiral was almost a saintly creature, one free of aggression: his lifelong battle was against the mediocrity and nearsightedness of his contemporaries.

= Prayer of Walt Whitman =

More than 100 years after Philip Freneau's idealized portraits, a more human and satisfying description of Columbus was delivered by Walt Whitman, whom Emerson called "North America's greatest poet." Born in 1819 on Long

Island, he began his literary career late, at the age of 36, after sojourns in printing and journalism that had taken him across the country and made him a powerful editor of a New York City daily. Before devoting himself to poetry, Whitman tried his luck on a temperance novel, *Franklin Evans: or, The Inebriate: A Tale of the Times* (1842), which was serialized in his own newspaper and elsewhere.[4] Later he devoted himself to the composition of *Leaves of Grass*. First published in 1855, that text underwent eight revisions, and numerous expansions over the next four decades, as if the writer dreamed of creating a perfect, unsurpassable, "organic" book with a life very much of its own. In his words, it was the attempt "of a naïve, masculine, affectionate, contemplative, sensual, imperious person to cast into literature not only his own grit and arrogance, but his own flesh and form, undraped, regardless of all models, regardless of modesty, or law; and ignorant, as at first it appears, of . . . all outside of the fiercely loved land of his birth."[5]

Embodying the risk-taking romantic mood, Whitman achieved something few poets ever do: he managed to become a creation of himself—"an American, one of the roughs, a kosmos" (*Leaves* [1855], 48). In the preface to the first edition of *Leaves of Grass*, he claims that "the United States themselves are essentially the greatest poem" ([1855], 6). Like Brackenridge and Freneau in "The Rising Glory of America," but with considerably more stamina, Whitman calls for a new poet to emerge, one in touch with the people, one able to translate into words the poetry of the entire nation. His worldview, no doubt, has to be seen in the context of the philosophical movement transcendentalism, a metaphysical and literary current based in Concord, Massachusetts, that was shaking the intellectual ground in New York during the middle of the nineteenth century. Its two most famous representatives, Emerson and Henry David Thoreau (both of whom loved *Leaves of Grass* and made pilgrimages to Brooklyn in 1855 and after to meet Whitman), placed the individual at the center of the universe, asked where and how the poet is to live in society, and tried to understand earthly matters not by accepting a certain abstract doctrine of knowledge but by ecstatic, intuitive, mystical communion with their immediate surroundings.[6] Octavio Paz considers Whitman to be "the only great modern poet who does not seem to experience discord when he faces his world. Not even solitude; his monologue is a universal chorus."[7]

"Prayer of Columbus," the brief, lyrical text discussed here, was first published in 1874 in *Harper's Monthly*. In a headnote the magazine editors, or Whitman himself, explain: "It was near the close of his indomitable and pious life—on his last voyage, when nearly seventy—that Columbus, to save his two remaining ships from foundering in the Caribbean Sea in a terrible storm, had to run them ashore on the Island of Jamaica—where, laid up for a long and miserable year—1503—he was taken very sick, had several relapses, his men revolted, and death seemed daily imminent; though he was eventually rescued and sent home to Spain to die, unrecognized, neglected and in want."[8] Alfred Kazin, the American critic, argues that Whitman's genius in his "old age" was to describe a world in transition.[9] And "Prayer of Columbus" is an expression of such a transition. The poet offers an image of the admiral undergoing a profound change: a lost soul full of doubts and uncertainties and ready to depart from this earth, he is becoming a historical and spiritual conscience. Moreover, Whitman is portraying himself as Columbus: *he* is the old man (the poem was published when he was 57), the insecure lost soul.

> A batter'd, wreck'd old man,
> Thrown on this savage shore, far, far from home,
> Pent by the sea and dark rebellious brows, twelve dreary months,
> Sore, stiff with many toils, sicken'd and nigh to death,
> I take my way along the island's edge,
> Venting a heavy heart.
>
> I am too full of woe!
> Haply I may not live another day;
> I cannot rest O God, I cannot eat or drink or sleep,
> Till I put forth myself, my prayer, once more to Thee.
> Breathe, bathe myself once more in Thee, commune with Thee,
> Report myself once more to Thee.
>
> (*Leaves* [1891–92], 328)

According to Gay Wilson Allen, one of Whitman's many biographers, the poem was written during the autumn of 1873 or winter of 1874, some eight years before Whitman's death. It was included in the sixth edition of *Leaves of Grass* (1876), in a section entitled "Autumn Rivulets" (*Leaves*, [1891–92], v–xx). Allen suggests that Whitman identified himself with Columbus.[10] He notes that in "Prayer of Columbus" Whitman is speaking about his own literary legacy, about his artistic life that was never fully accepted by his fellow poets in the United States but enthusiastically applauded in France and elsewhere around the globe.[11]

The text is an entreaty, a supplication, an act of worship. Columbus-Whitman appeals to God for an explanation, an insight into his own destiny. The divinity is the sole controller of his behavior, the depository of his knowledge, and the recipient of his feelings. That an almighty power appears as an indirect, silent respondent to the mariner's angst is fascinating: after his impious, sinful existence, he returns to truth and asks for forgiveness. In "Prayer of Columbus" he confesses his long-standing impatience and premonition of a future of glory.

> Thou knowest my years entire, my life,
> My long and crowded life of active work, not adoration merely;
> Thou knowest the prayers and vigils of my youth,
> Thou knowest my manhood's solemn and visionary meditations,
> Thou knowest how before I commenced I devoted all to come to Thee,
> Thou knowest I have in age ratified all those vows and strictly kept them,

Thou knowest I have not once lost nor faith nor ecstasy in Thee,
In shackles, prison'd, in disgrace, repining not,
Accepting all from Thee, as duly come from Thee.

                             (*Leaves* [1891–92], 328–329)

Unlike the 52 quasi-independent lyrics with a limitless protean narrator, "Song of Myself," which stands as an epic of American individualism and Emersonian self-reliance, this poem investigates the inner life of the protagonist in his last moments, his sense of loneliness and fragility.

Compared with "Columbus," a more conventional poem by Rubén Darío discussed in chapter 6, "Prayer of Columbus" reveals an insight about its author: Whitman personifies the individualist, the Protestant worshiper of unity. He does not scorn the Genoese for crimes committed against humanity, nor does he portray him as disoriented, violent, greedy, or manipulative.[12] History seems to be absent from the poem, or at best, a mere footnote. The North American's admiral is a man opening up his mind, a monologuist ready to account to God for all his mistakes and successes:

Is it the prophet's thought I speak, or am I raving?
What do I know of life? what of myself?
I know not even my own work past or present,
Dim ever-shifting guesses of it spread before me,
Of newer better worlds, their mighty parturition,
Mocking, perplexing me.

And these things I see suddenly, what mean they?
As if some miracle, some hand divine unseal'd my eyes,
Shadowy vast shapes smile through the air and sky,
And on the distant waves sail countless ships,
And anthems in new tongues I hear saluting me.

                             (*Leaves*, [1891–92], 330)

Whitman abandons the traditional meters of English verse and allows the sentences to flow, favoring a kind of "cadenced verse"—what the surrealists would refer to decades later as *la écriture automatique* (automatic writing)—in which the rhetorical phrase rather than the foot becomes the basic unit. As in other sections of *Leaves of Grass*, both the content and form of "Prayer of Columbus" express the poet's drive to take risks. The poem does not focus on Columbus's personal biography: nothing is said about his Italian upbringing, his four voyages, his writings. Instead, his sensibility and his inner struggle are at center stage: he is blind to his fortune, yet he foresees a symphony of voices and sounds in other tongues saluting his enterprise; his glory is uncertain, but the gamble was worth taking. In this sense the text can be seen as an expression of the egocentrism, the diversity, the disdain for history, and the desire for personal encounters with the divinity, of the Concord transcendentalists.

There is yet another reference to the Genoese in Whitman that needs mentioning. It is found in "Passage to India," inserted in *Leaves of Grass* in the fifth edition of 1872 and included in "Autumn Rivulets" just before "Prayer of Columbus":

> As the chief histrion,
> Down to the footlights walks in some great scena,
> Dominating the rest I see the Admiral myself,
> (History's type of courage, action, faith,)
> Behold him sail from Palos leading his little fleet,
> His voyage behold, his return, his great fame,
> His misfortunes, calumniators, behold him a prisoner, chain'd.
> Behold his dejection, poverty, death.
>
> (*Leaves* [1891–92], 329)

The fourth line, according to some, is one of Whitman's major Columbus images: the admiral is pure valor, impulse, and vision. It has been argued[13] that in this poem, the concept of westering as a passage to India, exemplified by the Genoese, is understood as the closing of the cycle of history and the restoration of man's lost harmony with nature. Thus, the mariner is not only a voyager but a visionary capable of making the globe a smaller, more hospitable place for humans. If, as D. H. Lawrence once said, Whitman "leaks out into the universe," his portrait of the admiral is that of a man without a milieu—a man who became his own universe.

= The Noble Savage =

Some 25 years before Whitman wrote his "Prayer," a romance, *Mercedes of Castille: or, The Voyage to Cathay* (1840) was written by a fellow North American, another romantic, one with a taste for adventure and for exploiting history to offer a suspenseful setting: the novelist James Fenimore Cooper, born in New Jersey in 1789 and considered by some critics to be the Sir Walter Scott of the United States. *Mercedes*, one of the writer's 50-odd volumes in which the literary craftsmanship can rarely be admired, belongs to his prolific second artistic period, 1839–43.

A deeply conservative man, Cooper was a defender of republican values at home and abroad. After settling in London, he returned to the United States in 1833, when Andrew Jackson was president and the spoils system—appointing loyal members of the ruling party to government posts—prevailed. Witnessing those who espoused his own democratic views slowly turn into a full-scale "mobocracy," Cooper combated public figures and got in trouble with the press. He had publicly retired as a novelist years before, having decided to devote his energy to other matters, but during that time he did not stop writing. Just the opposite—he produced a massive amount of work, most of which was social satire, such as *The Monikins* (1835), a depiction of social manners in the United States. But the result was unsatisfying to many, including Cooper himself. The nation at that time, in his own words, was "characterized by a respectable mediocrity" and did not offer enough inspiration.[14] Attacked by critics and rejected by readers who had applauded his earlier books, he returned in 1840 to the past, which had been the scene of his early success with the Leatherstocking tales, a saga beginning with the youth of Natty Bumppo, also called Hawk-eye, "the trapper," and Pathfinder, and concluding with his death. During that same year Cooper finished three tales, one of which was *Mercedes of Castile*.[15]

The principal setting, besides Spain and the Caribbean islands, is the ocean, as perceived by Columbus's crew. The sea waters are seen as an overwhelming natural entity—a dangerous, mysterious Leviathan, a stage on which civilization battles barbarism. This theme appears in several of Cooper's previous novels, including his third, *The Pilot*, published in 1824 and considered by many the first North American novel to deal with such a topic.

Published in Philadelphia by Lea & Blanchard after *The Pathfinder* (1840) and before *The Deerslayer* (1841), the general opinion of *Mercedes of Castile* was quite negative. Donald A. Ringe, a Cooper scholar, refers to *Mercedes* as a "wordy," "slow-paced" novel that can be "quickly passed over as the worst mature [one] he wrote." His attack does not stop there: "Despite the inherent drama of Columbus' first voyage, the book is intolerably dull; the lifeless characters recite long set speeches to one another; and Columbus, like Washington in *The Spy*, is dignified to the point of woodenness and helps set the tone of pompous solemnity from which the book never really emerges. Cooper was not at his best when writing true historical novels."[16] The novel opens with a three-page preface in which Cooper demythifies history—or better, adapts its cast of characters to his own imaginative needs. Arguing that "too much" has already been written about the Genoese, Cooper says he had to spend a substantial amount of time and energy in historical research to get his information straight. Nothing he read was conclusive:

> Some may refer to history, with a view to prove that there never were such persons as our hero and heroine, and fancy that by establishing these facts they completely destroy the authenticity of the whole book. In answer to this anticipated objection, we will state, that after carefully perusing several of the Spanish writers from Cervantes to the translator of the journal of Columbus, the Alpha and Omega of peninsular literature . . . we do not find a syllable in either of them that we understand to be conclusive evidence, or indeed be any evidence at all, on the portions of our subject that are likely to be disputed.[17]

His point, he argues at the end of the preface, is to *revise* history. Since nothing is definitive, there is room to interpret events, "to render future investigations unnecessary" (*Mercedes*, 7). While claiming to have read Washington Irving and the historian William Hickling Prescott to support his view—Prescott presumably gave him the data, irrelevant to his topic, on the conquest of Mexico and Peru[18]—the reader soon discovers that whatever accurate historicity can be found in the works of these two writers was largely ignored by Cooper.

Cooper's defensive position has an explanation in his personal life. The press had sharply criticized his democratic and religious ideas in 1838, when he forcefully attacked "radical" Protestant churches in the country, arguing that ministers were manipulating Christian truth and stirring people up emotionally. As a result, the Whig newspapers portrayed him as a merciless reactionary. The experience was not new: Cooper had been the target of animosity before, mainly as a result of his satire of North American and British idiosyncrasies. And in 1837 there had been a controversy over his property at Cooperstown, New York: apparently the land was used by some neighbors for sufferance while Cooper's family was absent, and when he complained, Cooper discovered that the neighbors believed it was their property. The result was very bad press. These affairs made him sensitive not only to public reaction but to mishandlings of data. Yet that is what he did himself in *Mercedes of Castile*. Obstinate, clogged, and unpleasurable, it suffers from almost every defect possible. At times paying too much attention to detail, the writer seems to forget the plot, turning it into a cartoonish display of marionettes always at the mercy of a manipulative, uninspired will. Long, tiresome dialogues run for 15–20 pages, supplanting action, character development, or conflict.

Made up of 31 chapters, the novel starts in Zaragoza in 1469, when Queen Isabella and King Ferdinand "make it convenient for themselves and their future" to marry. That episode, however, is only marginally the introduction. In chapter 4 the adventure moves to January 1492 in Santa Fé, where Luis de Bobadilla,[19] a young, "elastic" man with a "vigorous form" and a "handsome face" (*Mercedes*, 56), discusses with Friar Pedro, a court priest, the triumph of Christianity over the Moors in the Iberian peninsula. Luis is the hero of *Mercedes of Castile*; the heroine is Mercedes de Valverde, a beautiful and intelligent young woman, the daughter of the Marchioness of Moya, a very loyal friend and adviser to the queen. Their emasculated. voyeuristic, and platonic love is the book's leitmotiv.

A marginal character, Columbus is portrayed as a superior navigator and a genial pilot well accustomed to the sea. Through the dialogue between Don Luis and Friar Pedro, we learn everything about his background. "In mind, he hath outdone many of our most learned churchmen; and it is due to his piety to say that a more devout Christian doth not exist in Spain" (*Mercedes*, 58). Cooper also sees the Genoese admiral as brave, humane, and vastly knowledgeable. Mercedes finds him courageous, an adventurer with an enviable future. It is she who persuades Queen Isabella to fund Columbus's 1492 trip, an insupportable, clearly fictional thesis.

The mariner's triumphant will and launching of the *Niña*, the *Pinta*, and the *Santa María* are then described. The connection between Columbus and Mercedes is Don Luis, who gets involved, thanks to his "lovely" bride, in the mariner's navigations. The next few scenes, at the core of the novel, take place at sea, where the Genoese and his crew struggle to reach the rich land of Cathay, a fabulous kingdom described by Marco Polo. Their journey over the terrifying, turbulent ocean waters is a symbol of the epic struggle between civilization and nature, between man and his instincts. Cooper is clearly unconcerned with the rumors about Columbus's previous knowledge of Vinland and his contact with the unknown pilot. He also ignores Columbus's period in Portugal, the story of La Rábida, his personal relationship with Queen Isabella, and his family matters. In Cooper's eyes, Columbus was a valiant fighter and nothing more.

A decisive and suspenseful narrative twist is introduced when the ships reach Hispaniola and some of the Spaniards encounter, and eventually befriend, a group of natives. Don Luis de Bobadilla finds himself isolated with one, Mattinao. He is taken to Mattinao's village and after a while falls in love with Ozema, an aboriginal beauty. Cooper describes her in a feverish, romantic fashion, extolling the wild child of "nature" with a benevolent heart over the beauty standard of European society:

> She had reached her eighteenth year, without having experienced any of those troubles and exposures which are more or less the inevitable companions of savage life. . . . Ozema, in her person, possessed just those advantages that freedom from restraint, native graces, and wild luxuriance, might be supposed to lend the female form, under the advantages of a mild climate, a healthful and simple diet, and perfect exemptions from exposure, care, or toil. It would not have been difficult to fancy Eve such a creature, when she first appeared to Adam, fresh from the hands of her divine Creator, modest, artless, timid, and perfect. (*Mercedes*, 391)

Don Luis, though in love with Ozema, keeps in the back of his mind his desire for Mercedes back in Zaragoza. An imaginary romantic triangle is shaped in his heart. After much fuss, Columbus includes Ozema in the group of natives he is taking back to Spain. Back home, things get complicated: Mercedes is jealous, Queen Isabella intercedes, and for a while it seems that Don Luis has committed bigamy, since he married Ozema under Hispaniola law. As expected, at the end the female Indian sacrifices herself to honor the "civilized," educated passion of Mercedes and Don Luis. *Mercedes of Castile* concludes with the hero having his own ship, the *Ozema*, named in honor of the aboriginal martyr. He finds fame and money in the Indies and lives happily ever after with his wife Mercedes in Valverde, the principal state owned by her relatives. The lovers' felicity "was as great as could be produced by the connection between manly tenderness on one side, and purity of feeling and disinterested womanly love on the other." This is the moralistic last paragraph:

> At a late day, there were other Luis de Bobadillas in Spain, among her gallant and noble, and other Mercedes' to cause the hearts of the gay and aspiring to ache; but there was only one Ozema. She appeared at court, in the succeeding reign, and, for a time, blazed like a star that had just risen in a pure atmosphere. Her career, however, was short, dying young and lamented; since which time, the name itself has perished. It is, in part, owing to these circumstances, that we have been obliged to drag so much of our legend from the lost records of that eventful period. (*Mercedes*, 538)

Echoes of *The Last of the Mohicans* (1826) and *The Prairie* (1827), other works by Cooper, are everywhere. *Mercedes of Castile* is also a frontier story about the encounter between two cultures—or rather, about the ultimate accommodation of one to the rule of the other. Wilderness and barbarism are opposed to Christianity and reason. The protagonists are not intellectually sophisticated: the native Americans, understood as those from the Bahamas and the continent at large, are virginal, gullible, ignorant, immature, even foolish, and Ozema's relationship with Don Luis symbolizes that unbalanced, painful encounter between civilization and barbarism. When her people are massacred, she is rescued by her lover, then redeemed and sequestered in Europe. There, her language is, of course, incomprehensible; Don Luis teaches her to speak Spanish, thus subjecting her to a radical identity transformation. Not only is their interracial affair condemned by fate and by the conventions of society, but Ozema becomes a saint, a sufferer for love, a victim of history. In this setting, the Genoese navigator is only a peripheral, silent, unimportant, and impartial orchestrator of the love affair between Don Luis and Ozema—an unintentional matchmaker. In Cooper's eyes, the native of the Caribbean is equivalent to the "Redskins" and Mohicans of North America: their males are dangerous and unpredictable, but their females are fragile, well-built, tender, even sweet (Ringe, 81–82). Very much a nineteenth-century work of fiction, *Mercedes of Castile* may be seen as an affirmation of the fundamental Christian virtues and an examination of the selfishness and forbearance of the Europeans and the ingenuity of the natives. Far from capturing the cruelty involved in the events of 1492 and after, the novel centers on the conflicts of love and morality.

= Eco's Pendulum =

As an identifiable, historic character, Columbus has appeared tangentially in a handful of twentieth-century novels and short stories. Away from the spotlight, he is a shadow, an insinuation. An example is *1492: The Life and Times*

of Juan Cabezón of Castile (1985), by the Mexican poet and environmentalist
Homero Aridjis. In this work, Columbus personifies the hope for a better
future. Set in Seville and elsewhere in the Iberian peninsula in 1491 and
after, the story is about Juan Cabezón, a descendant of Spanish *conversos*
who grew up in Madrid to become a *pícaro*, a rascal much like Lazarillo de
Tormes. He lives in the street, uses his wits to escape justice, befriends
prostitutes, beggars, and dwarfs, and works as the keeper of a blind old man.
His wanderings allow Aridjis to describe the relationship between the three
major religious groups active in Spain at the time: Christians, Jews, and
Muslims. The book also opens a window on the atrocities and persecutions
of the omniscient Catholic Inquisition of the Dominican Torquemada. In the
last paragraph, after hearing rumors about the ventures of one Christopher
Columbus to new lands, Cabezón arrives at Palos to enlist as a crew member.
He departs through the Canary Islands and toward the Saltés River on 3
August 1492. A hopeful ending. The Americas prefigure a new reality, a
better life for a homeless *converso*.

One more appearance by Columbus as a minor figure is in "The Discovery
of America" (1963), a brief and hilarious short story by Umberto Eco, the Italian
semiotician and author of two best-selling novels, *The Name of the Rose* (1981)
and *Foucault's Pendulum* (1988). The purpose of this speculative, intentionally
anachronistic narrative is to make fun of modern technology. It depicts the
navigator's overseas adventure as projected by a television screen to some
20,000,000 viewers. At 7 o'clock on 11 October 1492, to monitor the event,
six Italian broadcasters and anchormen, with their guests, Martin Luther and
Leonardo da Vinci, are located in various crucial locations—among them, on
board the *Santa María*, at a Canary Island station, at a TV studio in downtown
Milan, at the University of Salamanca, and at the University of Wittenberg. As
they describe the exact moment Columbus is about to set foot in the Americas,
on 12 October, the television men try to analyze the political, territorial, religious,
financial, and scientific implications of this event, a moment when "man is
stepping out of the middle ages and taking yet another step in his spiritual
evolution."[20] And when the Genoese and his sailors descend on Guanahaní in
the Caribbean archipelago, a broadcaster, trying to hear the first words spoken
by a European in the New World, puts the microphone to Columbus's mouth.
"*Belin*, admiral," he says, "but they're naked!" ("Discovery," 67).[21] Just as
the commentators are attempting to descipher his puzzling message, the
story ends. A final monologue by one of the anchormen is offered:

> The spectacle being transmitted to us via the television camera is
> truly grand! The sailors are hurling themselves toward the natives, in
> great leaps, leaps and bounds, man's first leaps in this New World. . . .
> They're taking the mineral specimens right off the natives' necks and
> dropping them in huge plastic bags. . . . Now the natives are leaping
> too, trying to escape; and given the lack of gravity, they might hurtle
> into space too if the sailors weren't securing them with heavy

chains. . . . But now the natives are lined up in a civilized and orderly fashion, their heavy sacks full of the local mineral. The sacks are terribly heavy; it seems they're struggling as hard to transport them as they did when they filled them. ("Discovery," 67–68)

Eco ridicules modernity not only by showing the conflicting scientific view of a decisive historical event, but by portraying the centrality of that event to subsequent cultural injustice and aggression. He sets the record straight according to *his* interpretation: the Spaniards, he suggests through wittily contrived anachronisms, were slave traders and gold rushers; they traveled to the Americas not only to expand their geographical horizons but to enlarge their pockets.[22] Historical circumstances forced all of them, including Columbus, to behave accordingly—implying they were marionettes on history's stage.

= Sense and Sensibility =

Salman Rushdie, the London-based Indian author of *Midnight's Children* (1981) who was sentenced to death in 1989 by the Ayatollah Ruhollah Khomeini, Iran's Muslim leader at the time, for publishing his "blasphemous" novel *The Satanic Verses*, wrote a short story in 1990 about the Genoese's love affair with Queen Isabella. Unlike Aridjis and Eco, Rushdie not only makes Columbus central to history but also subjects him to an extensive, if sentimental, psychological scrutiny. Its long title is self-explanatory: "Christopher Columbus and Queen Isabella of Spain Consummate Their Relationship, Santa Fé, January, 1492."

Assuming a seduction of the female ruler by the mariner—a possibility that some biographers, such as Samuel Eliot Morison and John Noble Wilford, have resisted—the postmodernist Rushdie builds a schematic, matter-of-fact narrative around jealousy and betrayal, desertion and deceit. The action takes place in the present. Structuring his story as an impersonal interview rehearsed in the mind of an omniscient, objective detective in search of accurate historical facts, Rushdie pays tribute to the techniques of the experimental and playful French *nouveau roman* of the 1960s. In the story, history is but an intellectual game, a lottery of liabilities. A typical passage reads:

> *Does she torment him merely for sport?*
> Or: because he is foreign and she is unused to his ways and meanings.
> Or: because her ring finger, still hot with the memory of his lips, his breath, has been—how-you-say?—touched. Tentacles of warmth spread backwards from her fingers toward her heart. A turbulence has been aroused.
> Or: because she is torn between the possibility of embracing his scheme with a lover's abandon, and the more conventional, and

differently (maliciously) pleasurable option of destroying him by laughing, finally, after much foreplay, in his foolish supplicant face.

Columbus consoles himself with possibilities. Not all possibilities are consoling.[23]

Queen Isabella is a tormented woman; finding Columbus not only handsome but desirable, she favors him but never quite manages to fully comply with his supplications. He, on the other side, is constantly on the lookout for a proper device to capture her attention and obtain her uncompromised love. Their two personalities clash: she is mischievous and devilish; he is a proud yet petitioning foreigner (with an accent), an insecure person whose feelings are based on self-interest. In fact, the admiral's portrait is quite human: never enlarged to mythical proportions, he is a fragile, money-driven person obsessed with death. His future depends on whatever favors he can receive from Queen Isabella. He pursues her esteem and support against all odds and beyond the limits of his own skepticism. At one point, hesitating, losing hope, Columbus begins to daydream. Rushdie's method of intertwining fantasy and reality, in the spirit of magical realism, pays off: we cannot decide whether the admiral's perceptions are real or imaginary—whether his two feet are on the ground or he is hallucinating. Through dreams Columbus communicates with the queen:

> Isabella, in Columbus's savage dream, tears her hair, runs from the Court of the Lions, screams for her heralds. "Find him," she commands. But Columbus in his dream refuses to be found. He wraps around himself the dusty patchwork cloak of his invisibility, and the heralds gallop higher and yon in vain. Isabella screeches, beseeches, implores.
>
> Bitch, bitch! How do you like it now? ("Columbus," 34)

Predictably, Columbus returns to his senses in the following scene. Queen Isabella's heralds surround him. " 'Good news!' they shout. "The Queen has summoned you. Your voyage is wonderful news. She saw a vision, and got scared" ("Columbus," 34). The message is unequivocal: through a metalinguistic, suprasensory bridge, the admiral has communicated his hopes to Isabella. Hence, Rushdie indirectly proclaims, a divine force is manipulating world events. In a subtle way, human behavior is predetermined by God. By controlling our fantasy life, this almighty power arranged Columbus's intentions to fit perfectly into place. As a result, the Americas were discovered in 1492.

═══ Mr. Columbus Goes to Brooklyn ═══

Stephen Marlowe, a contemporary American novelist with postmodern inclinations, has written a ludicrous, straightforward, and long narrative about the mariner: *The Memoirs of Christopher Columbus*. Published in 1987, it is full of gimmicks and oblique devices. A graduate of the College of William and Mary in Virginia, Marlowe has written at least ten other novels; this one shows his lifelong passion for Tristram Shandy, the playful, humorous character created by Laurence Sterne. Such an affinity is clear even from the title page: claiming not to be the author of the book but a ghostwriter of sorts, an *ecrivain*, Marlowe steps behind Columbus as the "creator" of this joyful, irreverent "adventure." And a *with* is used: the navigator is presented as the author of his memoirs with Marlowe at his side.[24] As a result, the volume, though written in what is at times a shallow and repetitive prose, ought to be seen as a full-length autobiography, complete with deliberate anachronisms.

Marlowe uses numeous other narrative pyrotechnics: graphic signs are peppered throughout the pages; the plot advances one step and regresses two; a ludicrous examination of the novel as literary genre is conveyed through Columbus talking about Homer, the Bible, *Moby-Dick*, Dante, More's *Utopia*; like John Barth, Luigi Pirandello, Milan Kundera, and Felipe Alfau, Marlowe reflects on his authorial role while the characters feel like marionettes. Moreover, Tristram himself—sometimes as Sterne's protagonist, at other times as Isolde's tragic lover—appears as a phantom friend of the Genoese admiral. He symbolically takes his journals—that is, Marlowe's book—away from his desk to deposit in the libraries of history. If *Mercedes of Castile* is an example of nineteenth-century epic romanticism, *The Memoirs of Christopher Columbus* is a rambunctious, 569-page travesty, an offering of metafictional eccentricities set in seventeenth-century Spain but with the admiral speaking in a contemporary Brooklyn accent.

Humor is Marlowe's main agenda.[25] He opens with two epigraphs, one by Morison and another by C. V. Wedgwood; the spirit of the latter pervades the text. "History," states the historian, "is lived forward but it is written in retrospect. We know the end before we consider the beginning and we can never wholly recapture what it was to know the beginning only."[26] A map of the four voyages follows; then the 21-chapter text begins its festive serendipity. Columbus is at once the protagonist and the narrator. He constantly refers to present, future, and past events. For instance, he mentions the Gutenberg-Schöffer printing press, which, although "unfortunately" absent in his time, is an invaluable tool to publicize the news of a historical event. The navigator wishes he had had one to proclaim the success of his voyages.[27]

The biographical details of Columbus's life undergo major revisions to fit the jokes. Instead of his birth being in Genoa, for instance, it takes place in Spain. Other distortions of the facts abound: his family has an undeniable *marrano* background; his boyhood marks him as an encyclopedically knowledgable Renaissance man with an abrasive, relentless intellect; Beatríz Enríquez de Arana, the mother of his second son Ferdinand, is an orphan; and so on. This revisionist approach, in the style of John Barth, prevails in almost every corner of the book. In another irreverent scene, the linguistic encounter between the Spaniards and the natives on 12 October 1492 is hilarious:

nobody understands a word of what the Indians are saying. The foreigners
try Latin, Hebrew, Greek, Spanish, Portuguese, Arabic, Aramaic—but to no
avail. In the end, because they need to name the Caribbean island, the
Spaniards use a random expression from an aborigine's mouth: Guanahaní.

To understand Marlowe's narrative fiesta, it should be remembered that
he is a New York City boy: everything Jewish in his background is inflated.
The novel starts with a Passover seder at the house of Santiago Santángel,
father of Luis, "a Jew from Calatayud, now a New Christian, born Noah
Chinillo" (*Memoirs*, 1). Dealing with the onomastics examined by Morison
(Cristoforo as messiah), Marlowe sets a parodic scene, in this crypto-Jewish
family milieu, during the time of the Inquisition. Domenico Colombo and
Susanna Fontanarossa, referred to simply as "Papa" and "Mama," discuss
the various possibilities in naming their forthcoming child:

> "We'll call him Jesús."
> "*What?*"
> Mama had red hair and a temper to go with it.
> "I said, we'll call him Jesús."
> "Who," said Mama in a soft and deadly voice, "will we call Jesús?"
> "The boy. When he's born. He'll be baptized Jesús."
> . . . Two could play at that game. "Moses," Mama countered.
> It was Papa's turn to say what.
> "What?" Papa said.
> "We'll call him Moses. Moses Maimonides Colón," Mama said in
> a rapturous voice, warming to the mellifluous syllables of the name I
> would never have.
> ". . . the wrap," said Papa patiently. "Moses. An Old Testament
> name. A sure sign that we're backsliders. . . . Joseph," Papa sug-
> gested. "We can call him Joseph."
> . . . "I don't like it," Mama said.
> . . . Papa said suddenly: "What if it's a girl?" (*Memoirs*, 3–6)

No legends of Columbus's life are overlooked: his courtship of Queen
Isabella; La Rábida; the unknown pilot; his prior knowledge of Vinland; his
surprise on seeing the Indians in the Caribbean; and his carrying syphilis
back to Europe. As an intellectual writer, Marlowe is not interested in either
promoting or poking fun at the admiral's legacy of destruction and slave
trading; nor is he analyzing Columbus's larger-than-life glory. Instead, the
intention of this U.S. writer is to use a historical figure to play with time,
space, and information in an experimental narrative fashion. *The Memoirs of
Christopher Columbus* simplifies the admiral's odyssey, turning it into an
accessible intellectual game.

Under Marlowe's pen, the navigator is a jester, an epigrammatist, a
lampooner, a jokesmith, a reincarnation of Tristram Shandy—a regular kind
of guy with the humor of an S. J. Perelman, the abrasive wit of a Groucho
Marx, and the introspection of a Woody Allen. Stephen Marlowe's simple

message is that history is boring when seen as a collection of past events. The proper approach, he suggests, is to perceive it first and foremost as a source of artistic inspiration, though one never to be taken too seriously. The writer can play with names, dates, and references because the past is nothing but an invention—one novelists should draw upon.

6

The Villain

AS RECORDED IN MATTHEW 27:3–10 AND IN ACTS 1:16–20, Judas Iscariot, one of the twelve disciples, betrayed Jesus Christ for 30 pieces of silver; he led Roman soldiers to the garden of Gethsemane and identified Jesus with a kiss. Although he later repented and committed suicide, Judas had earned the infamous stature of *the* most detested villain in human history. Antinomians, like the evangelist Nils Runeberg in Borges's "Three Version of Judas" (1944), believe his evil actions were as useful to the universe as those of the ill-served messiah. Evil, for them, is a hidden dimension of good, part of the same metaphysical unit. As portrayed in literature, sacred or secular (Dante, Léon Bloy, G. K. Chesterton, and so on), Judas is a complex figure: a treacherous, deceiving bandit, but also the person who forced Jesus to assert his divine powers and establish a new order on earth.

Like Judas Iscariot, villains in literature are often cartoonlike: their offensive qualities are taken to extremes, but they may also be ridiculed. Lieutenant Jàvert in Victor Hugo's *Les Misérables* (1862), Mr. Wackford Squeers, the schoolmaster at Dotheboys Hall in Charles Dickens's *Nicholas Nickleby*

(1838–39), even the mysterious "Mister" Kurtz in Joseph Conrad's *Heart of Darkness* (1902), are embodiments of perversion, outrageous conduct, and cruelty. In his many reincarnations, Columbus, a selfish antagonist, a stingy conqueror, and a deceiver, is also seen as a villain—an aggressor who invited disaster.

This particular mask has flourished especially, although not pervasively, in Hispanic America. Since the nineteenth century, and in conjunction with the wars of independence—which gave rise to a continentwide collective consciousness—artists and intellectuals, from Rubén Darío to Alejo Carpentier and Abel Posse, began to see in the Genoese a symbol of holocaust and doom. In their eyes, he is a destroyer, a treacherous liar, an ignorant mariner. Because the lands south of the Rio Grande have suffered as a result of the so-called discovery of 1492 and its subsequent conquest, Columbus is regarded there as the originator of all pains. Of course, dissenting, more indulgent voices have contradicted this ideologically oriented portrait throughout the decades—but to no avail. The sabotage of the festivities of the quincentennial was but the culmination of this professed hatred. And with the emergence of multiculturalism in the United States, similar voices are joining that country's national debate: the native North Americans, robbed of their lands and traditions, their ancestors massacred by the Pilgrims and other colonizers, are accusing the admiral of precipitating their ruin. In this chapter I analyze some poems and novels written by Nicaraguans, Cubans, Argentines, and North Americans in which that perception is promoted: Columbus as evildoer—as another Judas Iscariot.

= Target of Animosity =

Rubén Darío—in the words of José Enrique Rodó, the "poet of poets" of Hispanic America[1]—is considered the leader of what in Hispanic America is known as the *modernista* movement, which occurred roughly between 1885 and 1915 and attempted to revitalize and unify the literatures of the entire area. Although carrying the same name, it is a totally different literary tradition from the Anglo-Saxon modernism of T. S. Eliot, Ezra Pound, James Joyce, and Virginia Woolf. In fact, there have been at least five narrative trends in Europe, the United States, and the Southern Hemisphere called modernism.[2] Darío belongs to the movement, with strong roots in European symbolism, art nouveau, decadence, and impressionism and with an admiration for Walt Whitman. These writers had a passion for minute details and ironic metaphors, precise language, and a view of the poet as medium. Octavio Paz has claimed that in Buenos Aires, Havana, and Mexico the *modernistas* were newborn nineteenth-century romantics adapting the European (especially Parisian) mood to their own restricted, but at times volatile, reality.[3] Along with the Cuban poet and revolutionary José Martí (who saw Whitman in New York City in 1887, at a conference in Madison Square Theater), the

Mexican poet Manuel Gutiérrez Nájera, the writers Leopoldo Lugones and Delmira Agustini, and others, Rubén Darío managed to create a new poetic voice that was unique to Hispanic America. He was the first South American litterateur to be taken seriously in Spain (by Juan Ramón Jiménez and Juan Valera), and all subsequent Hispanic American poets, including Pablo Neruda, Borges, Gabriela Mistral, and Paz himself, owe a personal debt to him.

Born in Nicaragua in 1867, he wrote *Blue . . .* , a book of prose and poetry (1888), at the age of 21; its innovative style changed forever the face of Hispanic literature.[4] His poem devoted to the Genoese was written in Spain where, sponsored by the governments of Chile and Nicaragua, he was participating in 1892 in the fourth centennial of the mariner's first voyage. In 1907 "To Columbus" was included in the collection *The Wandering Song*. As some critics have noticed, the poem belongs to Darío's period of renovation and rediscovery.[5] He was already in his fourth decade of life and his poems memorializing Caupolicán and other idealized glories of the Hispanic American past had been left behind. He was by then a crude realist, and eager to target the aggressor. In 1905 he published *Songs of Life and Hope*, a personal volume that included intimate verses about the function of poetry, swans as a favorite symbol, and his immortal sonnet "Fatal," about man's loneliness in the universe and his desire to overcome death. But the book is not free of political messages, as evidenced by an ode to Theodore Roosevelt. "To Columbus," although written earlier, is part of a later volume: it signals the return of Darío's focus to the tragic fate of the Americas.

The title suggests that Columbus is the subject and protagonist of the poem, but it actually deals with the consequences of his voyages, not with his personal life or his writings. The navigator, in Darío's eyes, is a mythological figure and an offender—the villain of the Americas. Unlike Whitman, he leaves out Columbus's inner thoughts, his fears and expectations. His purpose is to discuss the sad and painful aftershocks of 1492. Here is my own rough translation, the first to appear in English:

> Misfortunate Admiral! Your poor America,
> your beautiful Indian virgin of hot blood,
> the pearl of your dreams, is a hysteric
> with convulsive nerves and pale brow.
>
> A disastrous spirit possesses your land:
> where the united tribes once brandished their war clubs
> today rages perpetual war among brothers,
> people of the same race wound and destroy each other.
>
> The stone idol has been replaced
> by an enthroned idol of flesh,
> and each day the white dawn illuminates
> on blood and ashes the fraternal battlefields.

Rejecting kings, we gave ourselves laws
to the music of cannons and trumpets,
and, receiving the sinister favor of petty princes,
the Judases and the Cains are friends.

Drinking the scattered essence of France
with our native, semi-Spanish mouth,
we daily sing the *Marseillaise*
only to end dancing the *Carmañola*.

Treacherous ambitions have no barrier,
and dreamed-of freedoms lie smashed.
That was never done by our Indian chiefs,
to whom the mountains gave their arrows!

They were high-spirited, loyal and honest,
their heads were bound with exotic plumes;
if only the white man had been
like the Atahualpas and the Moctezumas!

When in the wombs of America the seed was planted
of the iron race that came from Spain,
Castile mixed its heroic strength
with the strength of the Indian from the mountain.

Would to God that these once-untouched waters
never reflected white sails;
that the astonished stars never saw
your ships reach the shore!

The mountains saw the aborigines,
as free as eagles, course through the forest,
after pumas and bisons
with the deadly darts in their quiver.

How much worthier is the uncivilized and brave chief
than the soldier who sinks his glory in the mud,
who made the Zipa groan under his carts
and the frozen Inca mummies tremble.

The cross you brought to us decays:
and after debased revolutions,
debased writers sully the language
used by Cervantes and Calderón.

Christ, thin and weak, wanders the streets,
Barrabas has slaves and grand uniforms,
and the lands of Chibcha, Cuzco, and Palenque
have seen panthers decked with honors.

> Sorrows, horrors, wars, constant fever
> has misfortune placed in our path:
> Christopher Columbus, poor Admiral,
> pray to God for the world you discovered![6]

Darío uses Columbus to condemn the holocaust perpetrated by the Spaniards against the Aztecs and Indians. The poem is made up of fourteen
quartets, each with lines of five to seven feet, and the consonant rhyme
scheme *abab*. The first and last stanzas make it clear that the poet is ad-
dressing his words directly to the Genoese: he wants Columbus to realize the
tragic result of his "discovering"—that is, conquering—the Americas. He
describes the natives' past as peaceful and heavenly, a state interrupted by
the coming of the conquistadores. He also upends the view that barbarism
was a quality of the Indians. Atahualpa and Moctezuma, he argues, were
more civilized than the Spaniards: they did not kill other human beings as
mercilessly. Darío refers here and there to what has been nothing but a
sorrowful ethnic mix: the hybrid Indian-European *mestizo* culture. He lists
the outcome of Columbus's trips: the replacement of idols and idol worshiping
by the omniscient figure of *hacenderos*, or corrupt landowners; the self-
consuming civil wars; the debunking of aboriginal law; and the collapse of
revolutionary hopes. The overall tone is grandiloquent, even pompous, full of
sorrow and anger. Religion is the most powerful element: a critic of the
proselytism of the Church, the poet wants the admiral to notice Jesus, naked
and tired, wandering alone through the empty streets of Quito or Managua,
overtaken by famine and hunger. The legacy of Catholicism has been turned
upside down: in the Americas, Darío claims, the Redeemer is a homeless
man with nowhere to go. But even as this strong image is left reverberating
in the reader's mind, the poem asks the mariner to pray—to have faith that
things will not deteriorate even more!

Darío's message is quite different from Whitman's in "Prayer of Columbus."[7] The author of *Leaves of Grass*, a true son of the United States and a
searcher for the love and the orgiastic embrace of the masses, was an individualist interested only in the personal, unique achievement of the Genoese;
Darío, on the other hand, giving no clear sign of ever having read "Autumn
Rivulets," perceived the consequences of 1492 and believed that Columbus's
voyages only brought disgrace to the New World. Whitman looks at death
through the mariner's eyes; the Nicaraguan carries on his back the suffering
of his fellow South Americans. The U.S. poet's protagonist is moved not by
sadness but by intellectual curiosity. Darío's Columbus, by contrast, is a
propagandist.

= Confessions of an Actor =

A professional musicologist who wrote a history of Cuban music, Alejo Carpentier lived in Paris when the surrealists were seeking notoriety. It was this writer who coined the term *lo real maravilloso* (magical realism) after his 1943 trip to Haiti, where he discovered a reality far richer than any fantasy ever dreamed up by André Breton, Tristran Tzara, and the other surrealists.

Born in Havana in 1904, Carpentier lived for many years in France and Venezuela. Along with the Guatemalan Nobel Prize–winner Miguel Angel Asturias, he is now considered a leading precursor of the literary boom that emerged in Latin America during the 1960s and gave international recognition to the pens of Gabriel García Márquez, Carlos Fuentes, Mario Vargas Llosa, and Julio Cortázar. Quintessentially baroque in his prose style, nurtured by the poets of the Spanish golden age, he wrote *Ecué-Yamba-O* (1933), a novel about the African heritage in Cuba; a Descartian narrative about dictatorship titled *Reason of State* (1974); and the remarkable *Explosion in the Cathedral* (1962), which takes place during the French Revolution and features the first guillotine ever to travel to the Caribbean. Other books of his are narrative experiments that attempt to tell a story in reverse or ambitiously examine the musical, political, and literary life of the twentieth century. His last book, *The Harp and the Shadow*, revels in his encyclopedic vocabulary and explores his lifelong preoccupation: the troublesome interaction between Europe and the Americas.

Originally published in Havana by the state publishing house, Editorial Letras Cubanas, in 1979, one year before Carpentier's death,[8] *The Harp and the Shadow* is a sophisticated, ambitious, daring, and polemical inquiry into the myth surrounding Columbus. By 1979 Carpentier, an enlightened intellectual who had been jailed in his twenties (in 1927) for political activities against the dictatorship of Gerardo Machado, had reluctantly embraced the revolution of Fidel Castro. He had returned to the country's capital in 1959, but his relationship with the new regime, as the Yale critic Roberto González Echevarría states in his comprehensive 1977 biography, was to remain ambiguous. Although he had arrived with the manuscript of a new novel in his luggage (*Explosion in the Cathedral*), he delayed handing it over to the publisher because he wanted to make changes that were more responsive to the new revolution.[9] Later Carpentier would be named director of the state publishing house, but in 1968, because of his ideological ambivalence, he lost his post and became cultural attaché in Paris, a job that kept him (once again) away from Cuba. While in Europe, Columbus's home continent and his own spiritual nest, Carpentier wrote *The Harp and the Shadow*.

Divided into three parts ("The Harp," "The Hand," and "The Shadow"), each in a different place and time, this scholastic novel is built around the effort to canonize Columbus in 1856 and afterwards. If the suggestion that the Genoese had Jewish blood has been widespread, in some European nations— France, Italy, Greece—his Catholic background has stirred up just as much emotional controversy. It culminated in Pope Pius IX commissioning Count Roselly de Lorges to write his book *Christopher Columbus: A History of His Life and His Voyages* (1856) in which the admiral is declared a devoted Catholic and another Jesus Christ. But since Pius died before the usual ten-year period in which the Holy Congregation of Rites examines the documents, the final decision was left to Leo XIII. Theological and civic journals all over the globe, including Hispanic America, began to investigate the religious dimension of the mariner. Almost a decade later, in 1869, when the Holy Congregation was asked to beatify the Genoese admiral, the findings by the ecclesiastical researchers were definitely not encouraging: not only had Columbus had children out of wedlock, but he never married Beatríz Enríquez de Arana, his bones were lost or misplaced in Seville, Santo Domingo, Havana, or elsewhere, and he died heavily endebted to Martín Alonso Pinzón. In the end, the sanctification did not take place.[10] Carpentier created his baroque narrative tapestry against this background.

The first part of *The Harp and the Shadow* takes place in Europe in 1856, when Pope Pius IX is beginning the process of canonizing the Genoese for his courageous "discovery." There is a flashback to the pope's youth, in 1823, when he traveled from Genoa to Santiago, Chile, in the ship *Héloise* to see if an apostolic mission could be sent to that region, a request that had been made by Bernardo O'Higgins, then head of the Chilean government, to Pope Pius VII. While in Rome this inexperienced clergyman encounters a succession of spiritual leaders (Leo XII is elected) before his voyage to the New World. Carpentier describes his intellectual and physical journey.

The second part, set three centuries earlier, is the confessional testament of Christopher Columbus himself—an exploration of what he saw, or wanted to see, during his trips to the Caribbean islands across the Atlantic. While the first and third parts are third-person descriptions, the second part uses the mariner's own voice, thus creating a feeling of intimacy and closeness. His autobiographical account, not surprisingly, starts in medias res: like Walt Whitman in his prayer, Carpentier chooses as a viewpoint the admiral's old age in Valladolid, where he was to die. Columbus looks back, reflecting on his actions and legacy. "They've gone to get the confessor," he claims:

> But it will take him a long time to get here, because my mule refuses to hurry when the road is bad (mules are fit only for women and clerics anyway); and to get the estimable Franciscan, who has vanquished moral confusion, they have to travel four leagues to the home of one of his relatives who is in need of extreme unction. Since I already have one foot in the grave, I'll use the time to marshal my thoughts, because I'm going to have to talk for a long time to say what I have to say, and I'm more daunted, perhaps, by how much I have experienced than by my illness itself. (*Harp*, 35)

Columbus is perceived as a poor mariner, a pathological liar, a lust-driven, untrustworthy, and impatient person—an actor of many masks. He is also par excellence a villain—such an egomaniac that he constantly confuses his own personal goals with those of his contemporaries. This rather conventional autobiography[11] is quite resourceful in using the information made available by Las Casas, Oviedo, Ferdinand Columbus, Irving, Morison, Madariaga, Taviani, and other major biographers, although Carpentier manages to put in Columbus's mouth words that some historians would consider doubtful, even dangerous. For instance, in Carpentier's treatment of the controversial tale of the unknown pilot and Columbus's prior knowledge of Vinland, the navigator receives the information from a crucial character in *The Harp and the Shadow*, one Master Jacob, a fictitious Jew and a paternal figure who resides in Galloway with a beautiful Scottish woman. A source of inspiration for Columbus's voyages, Master Jacob tells the young mariner that the Inquisition will soon begin torturing the Jews and examining the records of new Christians; that is why Jewish financiers such as Luis de Santángel are worried, he claims—in a device recalling Madariaga and Jacob Wassermann—and are anxiously moving their money. He also tells Columbus about the Vikings, about a land across the Atlantic, and about the many books about the Icelandic colonies, some real and others not, that were circulating in fifteenth-century Europe.

> Master Jacob gives me a shrewd look and tells me that more than two hundred years ago there were already a hundred ninety farms in Green Land, two convents of nuns, and even a dozen churches—one of them almost as large as the grandest the Normans had built in their lands. And that was not all. Lost in the fog, sailing phantasmal ships through hyperborean nights without dawn, cutting through the clouds by candlelight, those men dressed in hides had traveled even further to the west, and then still further, discovering islands, unknown lands, which had been mentioned in the treatise entitled *Inventio fortunata*, which I didn't know, but which Master Jacob seemed to have studied closely. Sailing even westward, farther and farther westward, a son of the redheaded mariner, called "Lief the Lucky," reached an immense land that he named "Wood Land."
> (*Harp*, 48)

We then travel with Columbus to Santa Fé and witness his courting of Isabella ("the name *Ysabel* . . . becomes for me the almost present image of the person to whom I owe my election and investiture" [*Harp*, 79]). In a scene that has made historians and critics uncomfortable, Carpentier transforms the Genoese into the queen's lover and narrates their sexual encounter. The Mexican scholar Juan José Barrientos claims this is one of the novel's greatest coups—taking the myth of their erotic liaison to an extreme. The mariner is the personification of the brave adventurer, and Isabella, a 40-year-old beauty abandoned by her husband, is the ideal lover (Barrientos, 52–53).

With amazing scholarship, Carpentier also comments—passionately, if not always accurately—on the mariner's knowledge of Marco Polo and the

Grand Khan, the constant struggles with his crew (for which he is never guilty), his ruling of San Salvador, and his escapist dreams and personal obsessions. Conscious of his historic mission, wanting everything for himself, he is anxious to be the sole person to shout "Earth!"—to take full, irrevocable control of the newly discovered territories.

Columbus's descriptions of the flora and fauna of the Americas, and especially of the aborigines, is patronizing; from the very beginning, the Genoese portrays himself as superior. He feels pity for the uncivilized people he encounters and wants them baptized immediately. They have "no arms except spears," he says, "no churches," "no dignity." To see them walk around shamelessly, "almost naked" puzzles and even infuriates him (*Harp*, 99). Carpentier's agenda in *The Harp and the Shadow* is to indict the Spaniards for their blindness and violence, both psychological and physical. The admiral's attitude toward the continent is best reflected in his answer to Martin Alonso's question, "Where have we arrived?" Columbus responds, "The main thing is, we have arrived" (*Harp*, 83). Uninterested in the new territory, his only care is for gaining fame and riches. The land in the Americas seems to him fertile, beautiful, substantial, good for producing species transferable to the peninsula (*Harp*, 101). Although Columbus is honest when describing the enchanting power of the New World, Carpentier makes the reader constantly aware of his true intentions: the Genoese is gold-thirsty, and he needs to impress his financial backers. In his letters and reports to the Catholic kings and the court, he assures them he will soon find the Grand Khan. ("The name of the *Grand Khan* resonates of gold, gold dust, gold bars, gold treasure chests, gold cask: the sweet music of gold coins clattering, spilling onto the banker's table: celestial music" [*Harp*, 88]). The Americas are just a gold mine.

Part 2 also includes Columbus's triumphant return to Seville, his discussions with Queen Isabella—who is also blinded by greed—his begging letter to the Pope, his reencounter with Master Jacob (who says, "I heard you've been to Vinland" [*Harp*, 115]), and the mariner's tragic end. *The Harp and the Shadow* returns full circle: the navigator is awaiting death in Valladolid. He thinks of himself as a new Moses on Mount Sinai, directing the people of Israel to Canaan. The typically Latin American symbol of the labyrinth recurs: Columbus accepts being lost in his own maze. His last words are:

> And yet, placed in the inevitable position of having to speak, the moment of truth having arrived, I put on the mask of the one I wish to be but was not: the mask that will become my death mask—the last of the countless masks that I have worn through my existence since its uncertain beginning. . . . And so it was that I took for my own—I who from ambition disregarded the laws of my people—those strictures dictated, on the eve of his death, to Moses, who like me was of uncertain birth, and like me, was an announcer of Promised Lands. . . . Now I see myself extricated from the labyrinth in which

> I was lost. I wanted to gird the earth, but the earth was too large for me. (*Harp*, 128)

The third part of Carpentier's novel, set in the early twentieth century, is an allegorical—that is, abstract—debate involving numerous intellectuals and artists, among them, Jules Verne, Léon Bloy, Karl Marx, Washington Irving, Bartolomé de Las Casas, the French poet and statesman Alphonse Marie Louis de Lamartine, and the German poet and dramatist Friedrich Schiller. As if history were judging their decision, the subject of their collective argument is the character and true intentions of the ambitious mariner. It concludes with the evidence against Columbus's saintliness, as perceived by Leo XIII, the successor of Pius IX.

The middle part of *The Harp and the Shadow* is fascinating, but the two parts framing it are self-indulgent, even complacent, not nearly as engaging. Yet as a whole the novel is an extraordinary display of historiographical inquisitiveness and stylistic maturity. Carpentier dares to awaken Columbus from his glorious eternal rest to denounce his foolishness, his mendacity, and his insatiable greed for gold.

= Lost in Hell =

Although comically irreverent in style and unconventional in historical approach, Abel Posse's *The Dogs of Paradise*, like *The Harp and the Shadow*, condemns Columbus as a villain. First published in Buenos Aires in 1987, the novel won the prestigious Rómulo Gallegos literary prize. An Argentine born in 1921, Posse is a journalist and diplomat and has written numerous articles for newspapers and magazines. Fame eluded him for years until the critical and commercial success of *The Dogs of Paradise*.

A postmodern narrative with anachronistic comments, it begins in 1461, when Columbus is ten years old, and ends in 1500 after the third voyage, when King Ferdinand signs an order to arrest the Genoese. In the same vein as Joel Barlow's *The Columbiad*, Posse does not restrict his cast of characters to the admiral's family and contemporaries (the King of Aragon, Juana "La Loca," Tomás de Torquemada, Pope Alexander VI, and so on), but also introduces Emanuel Swedenborg, Jean-Paul Sartre, Tzvetan Todorov, the New England Pilgrims, and other atemporally presented characters, as if Columbus's odyssey was a premonition of things to come. Told in a third-person voice, the novel intertwines, almost cinematographically, scenes in Tenochtitlán, in brothels and the Catholic University of Brussels, at the court of the Catholic kings, and events in Columbus's life. Divided into four parts— astrologically entitled "Air," "Fire," "Water," and "Earth"—Posse's technique is to intertwine occult knowledge with famous historical ideas: Bartolomé de Las Casas submerges himself in what looks to be Spinoza's philosophy of an absent God; Nietzsche's superman theory floats about; the concubinage of

Isabella and Ferdinand recalls Nazi Germany. The drama is perceived cosmically through obscene abstract forces fornicating, orgiastically chanting about the discovery of a paradise. And the Columbus who emerges in *The Dogs of Paradise* is, like Michelangelo or Botticelli, a passionate creator overwhelmed by his talent—a superman. As "a direct descendant of the prophet Isaiah," his only ambition is to find the earthly paradise.[12]

In fact, ambition is his trademark. Recalling Nikos Kazantzakis's dramatic portrait (see chapter 7), Posse's Columbus will do anything, including killing and lying, to achieve his goals and overcome any obstacles in his path. Speculation and intellectual fabulism are Posse's techniques for dealing with the unresolved mysteries surrounding the Genoese. After the birth of his child Diego, for instance, Posse suggests that Columbus either killed Felipa Perestrello e Moniz, his first wife, hiding her corpse without a trace, or sold her to Moorish white-slavers. "The fact is," says Posse, "that no one ever found the tomb of this person who from birth had been reserved a vault in the most fashionable cemetery of Lisbon" (*Dogs*, 90).

Never timid in his invention of bizarre possibilities, Posse deals with the unknown pilot by having Columbus say to the dying shipwrecked sailor: "Come on, don't die on me now. Talk!" (*Dogs*, 79). In Greenland, where Nordic missionaries settled and their community flourished, Posse claims: "In Rok, a city in Ultima Thule (Iceland), [Columbus] had tortured a Viking, and made him describe with his handful of Latin words the cost of Vinland where Bishop Gnuppon had landed during a pastoral mission" (*Dogs*, 80). The novel also revises segments of Columbus's journals and correspondence with Queen Isabella, King Ferdinand, and Luis de Santángel. His broken Spanish becomes the subject of a reflection on Argentina's idiosyncracies and slangs: "Colón, like many Argentines, was an Italian who had learned Spanish. His language was necessarily bastardized, macerated, dulcified, and explicatory—like the language common to the literature of the Río de la Plata. Colón said *piba* instead of *niño*, *bacán* for *bon vivant, mishiadura* instead of *miseria*, and *susheta* instead of *mujer*, words heard today only in tangos and the slang of the *lunfardo* poetry. During his relationship with Beatriz de Arana, in Córdoba, he had picked up the infamous all-purpose *ché*" (*Dogs*, 71).

The Aztecs and other native Americans had an ancient legend of the return of Quetzalcoatl as a bearded white man, and they therefore believed the discoverers to be divine. The novel describes the foreign visitors voraciously taking advantage of their empowered position to rape, assassinate, and rob. The natives are amused by the white men's aggressive sexuality. Posse wonders who is more barbarous, the aborigines or the Iberians.

> "We are not fucking savages!"
> All this frenzy amazed the natives. They could not understand the sudden eccentricities of the gods. They yielded courteously to their needs. They were puzzled by the bearded ones' curiosity about

ordinary parts of the body. And their panting effusiveness as they
undertook the most natural relations.

They found it comic that in the enthusiasm of their pairings the
gods imitated the exotic animals they had brought with them: they
grunted like the hogs, they brayed pathetically at the moment of
climax, and they trembled like jennies with the ague. (*Dogs*, 255)

Similar passages abound. Like Rubén Darío, Posse implies that excess
in the Americas was imported from Europe—with Columbus! This burlesque
description of the corruption, violence, and prostitution brought from abroad
reaches its climax in the novel's last part, "Earth": Posse suggests that Columbus enters paradise (*"Purtroppo c'era il Paradiso"*) while his ferocious companions become savage dogs who fight, metaphorically and concretely, to
take control of his newfound kingdom. Posse's message is that 1492 was a
carnage, an invitation to Satan to dance free in Spain as well as in its colonies.

=== The Dartmouth Secret ===

Novels about academics and whodunits that take place in university settings
were in vogue in the 1980s. With the success of *The Name of the Rose*,
Umberto Eco, inspired by Jorge Luis Borges, may be congratulated, or perhaps blamed, for making this type of novel popular. (To my mind, the best
example of it is *Possession: A Romance* [1991] by the British scholar and
sometime novelist A. S. Byatt.) Michael Dorris and his wife Louise Erdrich,
both successful U.S. writers, have not only villified the Genoese but done so
in an academic milieu.

Each of them is a prestigious novelist who has won the National Book
Critics' Circle Award—he in 1989 for *The Broken Cord*, she in 1984 for *Love
Medicine*. They joined forces in *The Crown of Columbus* (1991), which takes
place between Christmas 1991 and November 1992, that is, after the quincentennial. Divided into two major parts—"Four Discoveries," comprising about
nine-tenths of the text, and the 20-page "Four Returns"—the book has as its
protagonist a 40-year-old, nontenured Dartmouth professor named Vivian
Twostar. She has discovered in the college library a lost clue to one of "the
greatest treasures of Europe," to be found, she believes, on the Caribbean
island of Eleuthera, in the Bahamas.[13] She is a descendant of the native
Americans who preceded Columbus's arrival and thus has a consciousness
of the atrocities perpetrated by his followers. Like Joel Barlow's *The Columbiad*, *The Crown of Columbus* is concerned with the United States: Columbus,
a secondary figure in the novel, is seen as a conqueror of North America, the
one who opened the door to massacres of aborigines on the West Coast of the
United States. Little is said about South America and its plight. Less is said
about Columbus's origins and adventures, his voyages on the *Niña*, *Pinta*,
and *Santa María*, his passion for Marco Polo, or his dream of finding a new

route to Cathay. Only his landing in the Bahamas and a few passages from his journals, as well as a letter he wrote to Prince John dated in 1500, are treated.[14]

When Vivian is asked to write a historical paper on the admiral for the college's scholarly journal, she unexpectedly feels thrown into an existential abyss: here is her opportunity to aim all her anger at the figure of the "discoverer" and to give voice to the silent minority she represents. Her unlikely lover is Roger Williams, a poet and English Department superstar who is also looking into every book related to 1492 for an epic he is writing. Passion emerges between Vivian and the pedantic Anglo-Saxon academic; the result is an unexpected pregnancy that she wants to continue (although she is already the mother of a fatherless son) but Roger does not. The romantic scenes between them delay the plot; early on suspense is built up around "the secret" in the Dartmouth library pertaining to the circumstances of Columbus's first voyage. Dispelling the mystery will supposedly change our perception of history.

A miraculous invitation to Vivian and Roger from a Dartmouth alumnus to travel with him to Eleuthera opens up the plot. Readers are asked to believe that the Genoese brought with him a crown, a present from Queen Isabella, who after supporting the Genoese's 1492 ocean enterprise was persuaded to make him future emperor of all the prospective new territories.[15] But the invaluable object was lost. Vivian, Roger, and the Dartmouth alumnus, who after a short while in the Caribbean becomes their enemy, think they can find it in an obscure cave—that is, if the information in a handful of missing pages deliberately left out of the mariner's first-voyage journal, as transcribed by Fray Bartolomé de Las Casas and recovered by Vivian in the library, is correct. That's the secret. The current editions of the Mariner's diary have simply been censored—some deletions have been made. Crucial information is missing, and the protagonists of *The Crown of Columbus* set out to discover it without delay. In the climactic scenes, Vivian defends her life with karate kicks, and Roger recites memorized parts of his epic poem-in-process in the privacy of a secret and dangerous tropical catacomb. After they find the box containing the crown, Vivian's mother—also a native Indian, of course—tells her daughter:

> "What we have here is Europe's gift to America." Her words were paced, calm. . . . "What we have here is the promise, the pledge, the undiluted intent, the preconceived idea before any fact was known. This little nothing, this box anyone can lift, was the bond, was supposed to be a fair trade. And Columbus left it unopened. Never given. Never accepted. . . . Europe got America, everything and everybody in it and on it, and in exchange we were supposed to take . . . this."
> (*Crown*, 359–60)

In other climactic scenes, Vivian gives birth to her child and is recognized as a promising, bright female scholar, and Roger publishes part of his epic,

"Diary of a Lost Man" (*Crown*, 303–18), an expression of his inner doubts and a retracing of the Genoese's nautical trips. Roger's tranquillity derives from a daily reading of John Donne's religious sonnet "La Corona," a poem in praise of freedom and autonomy that he is trying to understand. The poem also informs the novel's message: that a collective consciousness should be raised among native Indians to counter the abuse with which history has plagued them. Thus, the crown of Columbus, once a symbol of colonialism and violence, is transformed into a divine gift—an illumination!

The Crown of Columbus attempts to reconstruct the past by adding a fictitious item that could eventually transform our established views of history. But the novel gets lost in another agenda: calling attention to how native Americans have been forgotten in the festivities surrounding the quincentennial of 1492. The North American Indians have been the preoccupation of many writers, especially Dorris, who has produced two important books: *Native Americas: 500 Years After* (1975) and, with Arlene Hirschfelder and Mary Lou Byler, *A Guide to Research on North American Indians* (1983). But the fact that Vivian is a descendant of this ethnic minority and is actively conscious of her heritage turns out to be of little consequence. Like some other literary works about the Genoese, such as Cooper's *Mercedes of Castile*, *The Crown of Columbus*'s premises are implausible: the only image of Columbus Dorris and Erdrich want to project is that of the originator of a sequence of tragic ecological and human holocausts.

7

The Symbol

A symbolic man is a man's name without a self.
—Zdenek Saul Wohryzeky,
An Improbable Life (1986)

IN 1851 POPE PIUS IX, AS PART OF THE PROJECT OF CANONIZ-
ing Columbus, asked the official historian of the Vatican, Court Roselly de
Lorges, to write a "pious" history of the admiral. He did so with such pompous
style, with such grandiose spirit, that the hero ended up in his 1856 work
larger than life, a reincarnation of Jesus Christ. Although de Lorges was
successful in literarily transforming the admiral into a redeemer, in the end
Columbus's sainthood was not granted by the Church.

The same unquestioningly Catholic tone was used by de Lorges's coun-
tryman and a favorite of Borges: Léon Bloy. Born in Périgueux, France, in
1846, Bloy, who loved to say that "no one knows who he is," perceived the
universe as full of mysticism and was drawn to redemptive ideologies. A
follower of the esoteric secrets of Cabala, he was certain that our reality is

nothing but a language we dream of deciphering but cannot since we lack the proper tools. His stoutly Roman Catholic novels, essays, and religious studies lacked any objectivity; his writing was unabashedly biased, intended to proselytize. In his *Revealer of the Globe*, published in three volumes in 1889, Bloy celebrated Roselly de Lorges, arguing that Columbus was to Europe what Moses had been to the people of Israel. Perfectly illustrating the allegorization of the mariner, he promoted Columbus as the carrier of a message and compared him to Jesus Christ, John the Baptist, Moses, St. Peter, and Abraham. "Columbus reveals all Creation," he said. "He divides the world among the kings of earth, talks to God in the Tempest, and the result of his plea is the patrimony of all mankind."[1] Once again the admiral had become a symbol—this time, transformed into a semi-god, a sign of divine intention.[2]

== The Cause of Patriotism ==

Roselly de Lorges and Léon Bloy are not alone: Joel Barlow, a North American, transformed Columbus into a time-traveler. A poet and politician born in 1754 in Redding, Connecticut, Barlow is perhaps the most important North American writer of the late eighteenth century who, along with Philip Freneau, was interested in the mariner.[3] The publication in 1787 of *The Vision of Columbus*, the first best-seller after the Revolution, sold to a limited list of subscribers, brought Barlow fame and placed him among "the most important United States poets of his time."[4] Among his readers were Benjamin Franklin, Lafayette, Alexander Hamilton, and George Washington. After almost two decades traveling abroad and writing humorous texts—including his mock-heroic poem *The Hasty Pudding* (1796), about the habits of the celebrated New England mush—Barlow decided in 1804 that it was time for a complete revision of *The Vision of Columbus;* he turned it into a magisterial epic entitled *The Columbiad*. Again it became a huge success. New additions and changes were made around 1807. Thus, two titles, two editions: one published in 1787 (though written four years earlier), the other in 1796 (but published eleven years later); the first a lyrical poem, the second an epic.

Barlow was originally considering a poem about Cyrus the Great, Daniel, Cain and Abel, and Joseph; only later did he decide to make the United States the sole protagonist of *The Vision of Columbus*. His purpose was to describe the founding years of the early Republic, to demonstrate the importance of the young nation from every possible angle. He explains his objective in the introduction: "The author, at first, formed an idea of attempting a regular Epic Poem on the discovery of America. But on examining the nature of that event, he found that the most brilliant subjects incident to such a plan would arise from the consequences of the discovery, and must be represented in a vision."[5] Thus, it is not Columbus who interests him, but Columbus's discovery.

In the 1787 edition the reader first sees a tired, old Columbus in jail. Although obviously a precursor, Barlow's admiral recalls Walt Whitman and some of the features Whitman gives him in *Leaves of Grass*: he is alone, his voice is honest, his tone is that of a sinner coming before God. His monologue refers to the discovery of the Americas and discusses his suffering. His visions are prophetic and philosophical: he sees the earth *sub specie aeternitatis* and comprehends his human endeavor from the viewpoint of divine judgment.

> I traced new regions o'er the pathless main,
>   Dared all dangers of the dreary wave.
> Hung o'er its clefs and topp'd the surging grave,
>   Saw billowy seas, in swelling mountains roll,
> And bursting thunders rock the reddening pole,
>   Death rear his front in every dreadful form,
> Till, tost far onward to the skirts of day,
>   Where milder suns dispens'd a smiling ray,
> Through brighter skies my happier sails descry'd
>   The golden banks that bound the western tide.
> And gave the admiring world that bounteous shore
>   Their wealth to nations and to kings their power.
>   (*Vision*, 126)

Divided into nine chapters, *The Vision of Columbus* has the navigator visited by an anonymous angel, a Virgil ready to accompany him on his journey and answer his innermost questions. Like in Cicero's *De Republica* and Athanasius Kircher's *Iter exstaticum*, Barlow's mariner embarks on an epistenological odyssey. In his first visions, Barlow describes the rivers and lands of North and South America. He then moves on to the inhabitants, arguing that those in the Southern Hemisphere are descended from Mediterranean peoples, and those in the North come from Siberia—that is, Asia. In a section important to the present controversy surrounding the quincentennial, Columbus asks the angel why the discovery resulted in so much destruction. The answer is a tale about Manco Capac, a governor of Cuzco, part of the Inca Empire before 1492. Barlow describes the political, military, and social order of these aborigines and compares Capac to Moses, Lycurgus, Muhammad, and Peter of Russia. He celebrates the Incas' intelligence and bravery and expresses his appreciation for the civilization south of the Rio Grande. He then gives the reader a view of the sorrowful destruction and violence perpetrated by Pizarro against the Incas.

From here on, the inhabitants of the Caribbean and of Central and South America are pushed to the margin. Barlow switches his focus to the United States. Portraying George Washington as a major hero, he describes the first Pilgrim settlers and the colonists' battles against Great Britain. This vision culminates in the spiritual triumph of the nation as a whole. In a couple of subsequent chapters, Barlow offers a metaphysical inquiry into the perfect system of government and the happiest state for mankind; his viewpoint was influenced by William Godwin, the English philosopher who was also the father of Mary Shelley. Columbus asks the angel, How can the perfection of earthly human life be achieved? The answer pushes *The Vision of Columbus* into utopian science fiction: Barlow portrays a futuristic society without frontiers, a global country with one unifying government ruling its citizens everywhere. Life, in such a reality, is harmonious, happy, and complete.[6]

By the time Barlow revised the first edition almost two decades later, his interests had changed; thus both the generic form and the content of the work changed drastically. Between 1786 and 1787, together with some members of the Hartford Wits (David Humphries, Lemuel Hopkins, and John Trumbull), he had produced the satiric epic *The Anarchiad*, which was first published anonymously in the *New Haven Gazette*. He subsequently reshaped the text of *The Vision of Columbus* as an epic because the genre "is particularly well suited to the portrayal of the [discovery] and civilization [of the New World]. . . . In writing his epical account . . . Barlow was unquestionably influenced not only by Voltaire's *Essay on Epic Poetry*, which would have lent credibility to his own belief that a modern epic need not adhere strictly to neoclassical rules, but by [the Inca] Garcilaso de la Vega's *Royal Commentaries of Peru*, Juan Francisco Marmontel's *Incas*, and [Alonso de] Ercilla's *Araucaniad*" (Fitz, 49, 52).

In the preface Barlow claims that his objective is "altogether of a moral and political nature."[7] He wishes to strengthen republican institutions and glorify the foundations of his country. The structure of *The Columbiad* is simple and straightforward: the angel, now called Hesper, is the spirit of the Western world that will take Columbus to the Mount of Vision to foresee the future of the North American continent. In two volumes and ten books (with substantial footnotes in the 1807 edition), Barlow describes the settling of the New World, especially the United States, and the rise of what he believes to be a glorious nation destined to lead all others. The biblical and puritanical influences are quite obvious: like the Israelites, the citizens of the United States have been chosen by God and are therefore unique and have a mission to accomplish.

Book 1 is an invocation of freedom. Columbus is seen in a Spanish prison, alone and forgotten. He ponders the great adventures of his life, from his birth to his imprisonment, and talks to Hesper. They quit the dungeon and ascend the Mount of Vision, which rises over the western coast of Spain. The Americas come into view across the Atlantic—mountains, rivers, lakes, and soil. Book 2 is a discussion of the manners and character of native Americans. Columbus wonders why the vast territory of the new continent is so ethnically diverse; among other reasons, Hesper offers the idea that the human body is composed of "due proportion of elements suited to the place of its first formation" (*Columbiad*, 60). A view of Mexico and Peru, of Cortés and the Incas, is given. The admiral questions the historical development of the civilizations in the Southern Hemisphere. Book 3 is about the Inca leader Manco Capac, in action in the Andes. Book 4 tells the story of the destruction of Peru, an event that makes Columbus grieve and encourages Hesper to comfort the mariner by promising a vision of future ages. Book 5 is confined to North America. It begins with the progress of the colonies and their troubles with the natives; a description of France and England's hostilities, which extended to America, follows. Then Gen. Edward Braddock's defeat and George Washington's heroism in saving "the relics" of the British army during the French and Indian War are followed by the actions of Gen. James Abercrombie, Baron Jeffrey Amherst, and Gen. James Wolfe in that conflict. Then comes the battle of Bunker Hill and the deaths of Gen. Joseph Warren and Gen. Richard Montgomery. Book 6 describes British cruelty to American prisoners, Washington crossing the Delaware River, and the battle of Saratoga. Barlow takes the opportunity to compare the United States and Greece. Book 7 evokes the coast of France and describes the struggle for independence by the British colonies while Europe undergoes a war between Spain, Holland, and France. Book 8 is a eulogy for the heroes slain on this side of the Atlantic and a hymn to peace. Hesper talks about progress and art in North America, sermonizing that, since the discovery of Columbus, the settlers of the new continent have been destined to subdue the formerly savage state of affairs. In book 9 Columbus's vision is temporarily suspended while he inquires into the slow development of science. Hesper answers by charting the progress in this area from the creation of the earth to the present; to explain the advancement of the human intellect, and he talks about the Crusades, Copernicus, Kepler, Newton, Galileo, Descartes, and Bacon. Finally, book 10 resumes Columbus's vision: he sees the present character of the different nations in the Americas and the future progress of (North American) society in commerce and inland navigation and in the acquisition of philosophical, medical, and political knowledge. An optimistic view of a generally harmonious future for humankind concludes *The Columbiad*.

Acknowledging his distortion of the chronological order of battles and other historical events, Barlow, in his preface, justifies doing so by arguing that in order to punctuate what's notable and motivating in the past to solidify the present, he had to accommodate his own poetic goals. And why use the image of Columbus as the leading narrative figure? In his correspondence and private papers, Barlow referred to the Genoese as the greatest man on earth (Ford, 63). Using him, as Washington Irving did, as a link between the past and the future, between West and East, Europe and the Americas, allowed Barlow to make his native country, the United States, the real protagonist of his ode. As Ford puts it, *The Columbiad* is unquestionably a nationalistic anthem—a patriotic celebration of the inevitable progress of democracy in the United States (83–4). Barlow also discusses the principles of good government and how to achieve the happiness of humankind; in fact, the preface to *The Columbiad* opens with a discussion of Homer and Virgil. Barlow then states his true intentions:

In the poem here presented to the public the objects, as in other works of the kind, are two: the fictitious object of the action and the real object of the poem. The first of these is to sooth and satisfy the desponding mind of Columbus; to show him that his labors, tho ill rewarded by his contemporaries, had not been performed in vain; that he had opened the way to the most extensive career of civilization and public happiness; and that he would one day be recognized as the author of the greatest benefits to the human race. This object is steadily kept in view; and the actions, images and sentiments are so disposed as probably to attain the end. But the real object of the poem embraces a larger scope: it is to inculcate the love of rational liberty, and to discountenance the deleterious passion for violence and war; to show that on the basis of the republican principle all good morals, as well as good government and hopes of permanent peace, must be founded. (*Columbiad*, vii–viii)

The poet makes numerous mistakes when introducing Columbus, most resulting from the lack of historical information at the time. Barlow claims, for instance, that the Genoese was born in 1447 (*Columbiad*, 1),[8] which generates an inconsistent chronology of events. He also mistakenly claims that Columbus looked first for financial support not from the courts of Portugal and Spain but from the senate of Genoa, supposedly because he felt he owed something "to the country that gave him birth" (*Columbiad*, 6); that he "married a Portuguese lady, with whom he had two sons, Diego and Ferdinand" (*Columbiad*, 3); that he spelled his name in Spanish Cristoval, not Cristóbal (*Columbiad*, 19); and that he was highly educated and at an early age had achieved great proficiency in geography, astronomy, and drawing. The truth about his education, according to Morison and other biographers, is not as benevolent. Lastly, the navigator's vision of the existence of another continent appears in a single anecdote in the introduction, based on the legend of the wooden stick:

> To corroborate the theory [Columbus] had formed of the existence of a western continent, his discerning mind, which knew the application of every single circumstance that fell in his way, had observed several facts which by others would have passed unnoticed. In his voyages to the African islands he had found, floating ashore after a long western storm, pieces of wood carved in a curious manner, canes of a size unknown in that quarter of the world, and human bodies with very singular features. (*Columbiad*, 4)

Barlow's lack of historical rigor notwithstanding, he depicts Columbus as an illustrious navigator, a prophet and man of great vision, a loyal Genoese, a genius with "every talent requisite to form and execute the greatest enterprises" (*Columbiad*, 3–4). He is compassionate and charitable and never experiences any regrets. About this larger-than-life, ahistorical symbol, Barlow chants:

> I sing the Mariner who first unfurl'd
>   An eastern banner o'er the western world,
> And taught mankind where future empires lay
>   In these fair confines of descending day;
> Who sway'd a moment, with vicarious power,
>   Iberia's sceptre on the new found shore,
> Then saw the paths his virtuous steps had trod
>   Pursued by avarice and defiled with blood,
> The tribes he foster'd with paternal toil
>   Snatched from his hand, and slaughter'd for their spoil.
>   (*Columbiad*, 23)

A self-serving poem full of patriotic excess, *The Columbiad* was written by a U.S. diplomat and intellectual who saw literature in the early Republic as an exalting, nationalistic activity devoted to enlightening the collective soul. His poem has a cadence, grandiloquence, and lyricism not without fault. The critic Roy Harvey Pearce sees the poem as unimportant in itself, but essential to an understanding of the overall development of North American literature: it was a fundamental step in the consolidation of the national epic, which eventually produced such outstanding works as Whitman's *Leaves of Grass* and William Carlos Williams's *Paterson* (1946–58).[9]

= The Solitary Romantic =

As discussed in chapter 4, Spain produced in the nineteenth century an overwhelming number of plays and poems about Columbus—most of them romantic and, like Joel Barlow's *The Columbiad*, patriotic.[10] Typical of this phenomenon is the work of Ramón de Campoamor, who, together with Rosalía de Castro, Gaspar Núñez de Arce, and Gustavo Adolfo Bécquer, is considered a leading figure in Iberian romanticism—a grimmer version of the movement that had such a major influence elsewhere, mainly in Germany in the craft of Sturm und Drang. In Spain romanticism was more nationalistic and sentimental.[11]

Famous for two early books, *Dies Irae* (1873) and *Doloras y Contares* (1846), Campoamor, a tormented loner, published in 1854, at the age of 65, while working in a government office in Valencia, a book-length poem with Catholic elements, entitled *Colón*. Influenced by Gustavo Adolfo Bécquer, it is not a very inspired lyrical piece. The text is made up of sixteen *cantos en octavas*—stanzas of eight lines with twelve syllables each. Narrating in a conventional first-person voice, Campoamor pictures Columbus and his crew from a distance against a beautiful natural landscape. The historical plot is packaged in an allegorical format with clear theological undertones: after departing from Palos, the Genoese, like Dante in the *Divine Comedy*, crosses first through Hell and then through Heaven. He is in search of a redemption that ultimately takes place on Judgment Day, a date following his encounter with the Americas. The poet attempts to call attention to the glorious past of Spain by narrating the life of the navigator and a tragic love story between two invented characters: Nuño and Zaida.

The symbolism is obvious even in a superficial reading. While sailing on his caravels, the mariner is tempted or comforted by anthropomorphized abstract values such as Charity, Hope, Idolatry, Envy, Ignorance, and so on. They condemn or encourage the sailor to achieve his task; they stop him or advise him of future disappointments. Canto 1, entitled "Departure from Palos," offers a portrait of Columbus while writing in his diary and celebrates his forthcoming odyssey. Here is a free translation of the opening verses:

> That's Palos.—Be quiet!—Can't you hear that in a hurry,
> Three boats protected by the night are departing?
> —It's Friday.—It's three o'clock.—The breeze is blowing.
> The clumsiest of all these boats is about to fly.
> Beyond Saltes one could see
> The first . . . the second . . . the third caravel.
> So who are the members of the crew?—Like the shadows,
> Allow me to keep the secret until later.[12]

Campoamor proceeds to tell the story as if it were a fairy tale. Canto 2 is about Zaida, a young Spanish girl, and her tragic passion for Nuño, a valiant crew member. Canto 3 introduces the theological concepts of Faith, Charity, and Hope, portraying them as entities standing ready to aid the voyage of Columbus. Canto 4 takes place on 24 August 1492, when the Genoese passes by Tenerife; here Campoamor describes Hell and Satan. Undoubtedly the most important Canto, at least for the purposes of this book, is canto 5, a microbiography of the navigator as told by himself to Don Elías, a member of the court who is close to Queen Isabella and King Ferdinand. Canto 6 continues the biographical account by describing the life of Beatríz Enríquez, the admiral's mistress and mother of his son Ferdinand. Canto 7 describes the first voyage; here Campoamor introduces the allegories of Ignorance, Envy, and Idolatry. Canto 8 returns to the love affair of Zaida. Canto 9 is a brief review of Spain's history. Canto 10 develops Seneca's concept of Antarctica as an Ultima Thule. Canto 11 conveys Columbus's reflections while on board his boat. Canto 12 takes place on 28 September 1492 and invokes many mythical and historical characters, such as Socrates and Muhammad. Canto 13 describes the mutiny against Columbus just before he reached Guanahaní. Canto 14, entitled "Land!" is a snapshot of his actual stepping onto the land of the Americas. Canto 15 covers the tragic death of Nuño after acknowledging the discovery of a new land, and the immediate sorrow of Zaida. And canto 16, "Judgment of the World," is a summary, in eschatological terms, of the impact of Columbus's voyage around the globe.

The final canto encapsulates the message of *Colón*. Structured as a symphonic dialogue between Charity and Hope, it examines the global dimension of Columbus's accomplishment. As a Christian, Campoamor perceives the admiral as an enlightened soul bringing faith and spirituality to ignorant unbelievers, a proselytizer in the Americas, a messiah,[13] a giant who projected the glories of Spain's religion beyond its national borders. At one point Charity says: "Forward, / with eternal sorrow, that seeing Columbus / advancing to defeat idolatry / his providential mission will be accomplished today" (*Colón*, 254).[14]

Columbus's biography is manipulated to accommodate the vision of a triumphant Spain. Little is said about his childhood. He was born, according to Campoamor, in the Spanish town of Liguria (*Colón*, 75). The first time he is in Lisbon, in full control of his faculties. We follow him through his relationship with the king of Portugal, his travels to Spain, his friendship with Martín Alonso Pinzón, his fund-raising efforts—up until the moment he is set to leave from Palos and suffers a setback in the Canary Islands. The story of Nuño and Zaida is similar to the affair between Luis de Bobadilla and Ozema in Cooper's *Mercedes of Castile*; but it is totally irrelevant to the plot—a sentimentalized addition.

Campoamor's portrait of Columbus is an example of Spanish romanticism, which was enamored of patriotic emblems: equating him with Hercules and Pormeteo, Campoamor sees the admiral as both genial and wise, a loner with a sometimes tenuous link to reality ("Some think he is a wise man, others a lunatic" [*Colón*, 31]).[15] He views Columbus's enterprise as a brave adventure that brought wealth and glory to the Catholic kings and the Iberian peninsula and never mentions the ecological and human holocaust perpetrated by the conquistadores. This omission can, of course, be explained by the historical period in which it was made. Having been one of the richest nations in the sixteenth century, Spain thereafter declined; from 1701 to 1714 the nations of Europe fought the War of the Spanish Succession. By 1808 Spain was occupied by French troops, and only four decades later it was torn by internal struggles—what historians call the Carlist Wars, after Don Carlos and his successors, who fought to make their claim to the throne. When *Colón* was published in 1854, the conservatives, supporting clerical views, wanted to promote Don Carlos's son, Conde de Montemolin, to power, and later his nephew; the internecine rivalries generated a civil war that consumed the national energy. What Spain needed, in Campoamor's eyes, was a reevaluation of its myths, a return to its historic roots. Placing the Genoese at center stage, he attempted a pious reexamination of a decisive if troublesome year in Spain's past: 1492, when Aragon and Castile were unified, and the Jews were expelled. In the poet's moral world, Love, Good, and Evil are determining forces. His Columbus is a marionette manipulated by the powers of destiny—Charity, Hope, Idolatry, Envy, Ignorance—a symbol of Spanish grandeur and illustriousness.

= Genoa Has Sunk =

Friedrich Nietzsche's perpetual attempt to understand the undercurrent of irrationality in humankind attracted him to the antichrist and Jesus, to Zarathustra and Schopenhauer, but not to Columbus. The admiral was too mellow a historic figure, a Christian subject to "slave morality," with one foot in the world to come; in Nietzsche's view, Columbus simply was not a "representative man," using the famous Emersonian category. Nothing in the Genoese's life attracted him, with one exception: Columbus's native Genoa. Sometime around 1892 Nietzsche wrote the following poem, entitled "The New Columbus":

> "Dearest," said Columbus, "never
>   Trust a Genoese again."
> At the blue he gazes ever,
>   Distance doth his soul enchain.
>
> Strangeness is to me too dear—
>   Genoa has sunk and passed—
> Heart, be cool! Hand, firmly steer!
>   Sea before me: land—at last?
>
> Firmly let us plant our feet,
>   Ne'er can we give up this game—
> From the distance what doth greet?
>   One death, one happiness, one fame.[16]

Nietzsche uses the navigator to illuminate Genoa's character. Thus, Columbus is a symbol of the Italian city. Superficially, this poem—only one small vignette in the writer's vast canon—gives a substantial portrait of Columbus: Europe is in the past while the Americas are in the future; Genoa, his birthplace, sinks below the horizon behind him; nothing matters except the possibility of overcoming death, and individual limitations, by stamping one's name in posterity. The portrait that emerges is that of a selfish man who is driven to accomplish his task because it has become impossible to return to his mother country. And what is the mariner looking for? A firm territory to stand on, a home. But he will find what almost all other humans do: his own death, a temporary happiness, perhaps fame. The new Columbus is an American, the old is a Genoese. As his portrait of the admiral makes clear, pessimism, the inevitability of fate, and the recycling of history are Nietzsche's trademarks. The mariner embodied these ideas forcefully, and the German thinker therefore could readily transform him into a philosopher's mask.

= The Doctor's View =

A completely different sort of writer is William Carlos Williams, a prolific and highly influential North American poet born in 1883 in Rutherford, New Jersey (the "Paterson" of his poetry). The mentor of Allen Ginsberg, the representative Beat voice of the 1960s, Williams was the son of a Puerto Rican mother and an English father who had been raised in the Caribbean.[17] His writing is deeply rooted in his multicultural background: it gave him a distinctive sensitivity to the varieties of cultural experience rather than the traditional monolithic perception of the United States.[18] Octavio Paz understands Williams's contribution in the following terms:

> In the first third of our century, a change occurred in the literatures of the English language which affected verse and prose, syntax and sensibility, imagination and prosody alike. The change—similar to those which occurred about the same time in other parts of Europe and in Latin America—was originally the work of a handful of poets, almost all of them American. In that group of founders, William Carlos Williams occupies a place at once central and unique: unlike Pound and Eliot, he preferred to bury himself in a little city outside New York rather than uproot himself and go to London or Paris; unlike Wallace Stevens and e. e. cummings, who also decided to stay in the United States but who were cosmopolitan spirits, Williams from the outset sought a poetic Americanism. In effect, as he explains . . . America is not a given reality but something we all make together with our hands, our eyes, our brains, and our lips. The American reality is material, mental, visual, and above all, verbal: whether he speaks Spanish, English, Portuguese, or French, American man speaks a language different from the European original. More than just a reality we discover or make, America is a reality we speak. (Paz 1986, 13–14)

Williams's *In the American Grain*, first published in 1925, is a collection of a handful of "narrative impressions" on crucial personalities and mythological figures and events that helped shape the continent's past. Williams refers to the pieces in the volume as "studies," but more than anything else they are personal accounts, dreamlike, subjective portraits. There are, for instance, pieces on Thomas Morton, Daniel Boone, Sir Walter Raleigh, Edgar Allan Poe, Benjamin Franklin, and Abraham Lincoln. But the collection opens with essays on Eric the Red, Columbus, Cortés, Moctezuma, Juan Ponce de León, and Hernando de Soto—a cast of "remarkable men" similar to Emerson's, but related to the Americas rather than to Europe. The background to such a photographic album is described by Thomas Whitaker:

> In 1920, D. H. Lawrence had addressed readers of *The New Republic* with these words: "America, Listen to Your Own." If Americans would fulfill their destiny, he said, they must turn for support not to the monuments of the European past, which have an "almost fatal narcotic, dream-luxurious effect upon the soul," but to what is "unresolved" and "rejected" in their dark continent. "That which was abhorrent to the Pilgrim Fathers and to the Spaniards, that which was called the Devil, the black Demon of savage America, this great aboriginal spirit the Americans must recognize again, recognize and embrace." Lawrence was asking for a "mysterious, delicate process" of psychic integration very like Williams's "descent." "Americans must take up life where the Red Indian, the Aztec, the Maya, the Inca left it off . . . ," he said. "They must catch the pulse of the life which Cortés and Columbus murdered." He urged that this theme, touched upon "uncannily, unconsciously," in the past, now become fully conscious. (58)

Williams was ready to embark on such a process. In an improvisation entitled *Kora in Hell*, published in 1920, he had already envisioned the fall of Tenochtitlán. In 1925, only two years after the publication of Lawrence's pioneering work of criticism, Williams's *In the American Grain* was a decisive attempt to revisit from within the whole history of the New World. Its immediate precursor was Williams's *The Great American Novel*, written in 1921, a 70-page experimental antinovel in which dialogues, philosophical reflections, dreams, and parodies are intertwined. In *In the American Grain*, Williams seems to often announce that everything is a subject of inquiry and, thus, ought to be reevaluated. Other sections display an Italo Calvino–like device of beginning stories and leaving them unfinished. Chapters 7 through 10 include descriptions of Columbus discovering the New World, Eric the Discoverer, Aaron Burr, Hernando de Soto, and the Mormon pioneers.

From the beginning of the second essay of *In the American Grain*, "The Discovery of the Indies," the Genoese acquires mythic stature:

> The New World, existing in those times beyond the sphere of all things known to history, lay in the fifteenth century as the middle of the desert or the sea lies now and must lie forever, marked with its own dark life which goes on to an immaculate fulfillment in which we have no part. But now, with the maritime success of that period, the western land could not guard its seclusion longer, a predestined and bitter fruit existing, perversely, before the white flower of its birth, it was laid bare by the miraculous first voyage.[19]

Williams's depiction of Columbus intertwines nonexistent quotes from Columbus's journals, letters he addressed to the Catholic kings, and third-person description of the mariner's adventures and misfortunes—all in the present tense. The characters parading through his pages are mostly crew members: Martín Alonso Pinzón, Peter Gutiérrez, Vincent Váñez Pinzón, Rodrigo de Triana, and others. Columbus openly discusses his confusion about the oceanic route of the *Niña, Pinta,* and *Santa María.* He has two faces: the fragile but stubborn pursuer of ethereal dreams in spite of earthly obstacles; and the puppet, the messenger of destiny. Since his cosmic duty is to open up a different reality, the Genoese is only the key to the door. Of Queen Isabella's uncertainty about promising her support for Columbus's enterprise, Williams writes:

> Unhappy talk. What power had such ridiculous little promise to stay a man against that terrific downpour on the brink of which they were all floating? How could a king fulfill them? Yet this man, this straw in the play of the elemental giants, must go blindly on. More and more he threw everything he had into the contest, his sons, his brothers, in the hope that his fortunes would be retrieved in the end. How could he have realized that against which he was opposed? . . . Heroically, but pitifully, he strove to fasten to himself that enormous world, that presently crushed him among its multiple small disguises. With its archaic smile, America found Columbus its first victim. This was well, even merciful. As for the others, who shall say?—when riding a gigantic Nature and when through her heat they could arrogate to themselves a pin's worth of that massive strength, to turn it against another of their own kind to his undoings,—even they are natural and as much a part of the scheme as any other. (*Grain,* 10–11)

This eloquent description is followed by an account of the events between the time Columbus went to the king of Portugal up until the three caravels traveled across the Atlantic Ocean to land in the unknown Americas on 12 October 1492. Williams logs the happenings on the three boats day by day. When setting foot on the newly approached continent, Columbus claims to have never seen such gorgeous scenery. "These're the most beautiful trees I ever saw. . . . The fauna and flora are stupendous. He does not include bestiaries of any sort in his epistolary description. The most bizarre creatures around this land, he assures his reader, are parrots and lizards (*Grain,* 25). Williams's description of the new landscape, unlike those of Pedro Henríquez Ureña and Alejo Carpentier, is neither surreal nor fantastic. On the contrary, its two major characteristics are plenitude and beauty within the realm of the concrete. "The Discovery of the Indies" ends with a piously Catholic passage in Latin, announcing the Kingdom of Heaven: "*Eia ergo, advocata nostra, illos tuos misericordes oculos ad nos converte. Et Jesum benedictum frectum ventris tui, nobis post hoc exsiliurn estrende. O clernens, o pia, o dulces Maria*" (*Grain,* 26). The Americas will become fertile, religious countries.

In the American Grain is an attempt to perceive history from a personal point of view—to make the past tangible, human. Williams is anxious to bring the individual perspective to the research of major historical events and personalities to make them more alive in the reader's imagination. "Dr. Williams," says the scholar Horace Gregory in his introduction to *In the American Grain*, "makes his discovery of his tradition with the insight of a man who walks into a brightly lighted room and there, for the first time, actually sees the things he has lived with all his life" (*Grain*, xviii). As a poet with a doctor's empirical point of view, Williams's historical research, at least as reflected in his narratives, is less a science than a compendium of instincts, tastes, and personal impressions.[20] After the cruelties of World War I, many artists were trying to regain lost ground by looking to understand human and natural behavior from a more individualistic perspective. Also, as Thomas Whitaker argues, Anglo-Saxon writers like D. H. Lawrence and Sherwood Anderson were ready to embark on pilgrimages into "the true soul" of the United States. Thus, Williams's portrait of Columbus and his version of other "American" myths are subjective, partial, incomplete. In *In the American Grain*, William does not pretend to take a comprehensive approach to world events; he gives us instead dreams of the past filtered through his own fantasy and intellect.

Williams's Columbus, like Joel Barlow's, has a mission: to open up the eyes of the blind to the beauties and glory of the United States. Yet their approaches could not be more different: Barlow makes the Genoese a meta-temporal prophet, a visionary who foresees future events, such as the French Revolution; Williams, on the other hand, portrays him as a victim of his contemporaries, a peon in nature, a small man with an outsized dream. Unlike Washington Irving or Ramón de Campoamor, Williams never gets into the mysterious, labyrinthine complications of Columbus's life; instead, he focuses on his subject's truest wisdom, turning Columbus into a metaphor for triumph, courage, and integrity. His mariner is a doctor investigating the soul of the Americas in order to offer a helpful diagnosis. Although Williams is interested in details about the Genoese, he gives him a large-scale, abstract stature—makes him, oxymoronically, into a small giant.

= Te Deum =

Written in a similar metaphorical vein are Paul Claudel's oratorio *The Book of Christopher Columbus* (1927) and Nikos Kazantzakis's play *Christopher Columbus* (1965). They belong here because, like Campoamor, their authors turned the mariner into a sort of messiah, a prophet. A dramatist, poet, translator, and diplomat, Claudel was born in 1868 in a small French village and moved to Paris during his adolescence. A fervent Catholic all his life, he rediscovered his faith at the age of 18 through the supernatural art of the symbolist Arthur Rimbaud, a prodigious poet who debauched himself in order to achieve transcendence through sin and suffering, and whose poetry was characterized by a dramatic, imaginative, sometimes hallucinatory, vision. In a service at Notre Dame Cathedral on Christmas Eve, Claudel decided he would permanently entrust himself to the teachings of the Church. His early work—*The City* (1890), for instance—was influenced by other symbolists besides Rimbaud. Yet Christian imagery was clearly his obsession: in *The Tiding Brought to Mary* (1912). *The Hostage* (1909), and in most of his other work, he reflects on the contemporary needs of the characters and the values of the New Testament.

Claudel's oratorio on the Genoese—in two parts (18 scenes in part 1, 8 scenes in part 2), and with a large cast of characters—is one of many poetic dramas he wrote about historical figures. *The Book of Christopher Columbus* was lavishly published in 1930 in English translation by Yale University Press with drawings and a tricolored design by the celebrated scholar, painter, and lithographer Jean Charlot.[21] It was accompanied by music by Darius Milhaud, a French composer who was a member of Les Six, whose mentor was Jean Cocteau, and who explored the possibilities of jazz style, polytonality, and Latin American music in his symphonic arrangements.

The piece, subtitled *A Lyrical Drama*, was staged in Paris, London, New York, and Buenos Aires in the late 1920s and 1930s and is intriguing for three reasons: its handling of modernist literary devices, its mix of Catholic images, and its view of world history. As described by Claudel, the scenery is full of ahistorical objects piled against each other. At the back of the stage, a white screen shows gigantic photographs—some realistic, others abstract—projected from the technician's booth behind the audience. The protagonist is a Columbus with a Pirandello-like split personality: an old, Whitmanesque admiral, mature and wise, engages in a dialogue with his young, adventurous self. (The device requires two actors.)[22] Another modernist gimmick is the Reader, an anonymous and solemn character who functions as a narrator of the plot. Not only does he organize and describe scene after scene by reading through the pages of a heavy, precious volume entitled *The Book of Christopher Columbus*, but he also tries to find meaning in the development of the allegorical plot: here and there the Reader reflects on the ultimate message of Columbus's action and on his spiritual power to open up the heavens. Other modernist tools used by Claudel are interrupting a scene with a flashback; monologues within the consciousness of characters (frequently Columbus himself); and linking anachronistic elements to make the plot atemporal. Although the immediate inspiration for these devices, by Claudel's own admission, was Rimbaud's *A Season in Hell* (1973)—a psychologically autobiographical prose poem describing the writer's tortured existence—they certainly fit the mood of the late 1920s: in theater Pirandello was experimenting with stages within stages, and in prose James Joyce and Virginia Woolf were exploring the possibilities of stream-of-consciousness, allusive, and other unconventional narratives.

Claudel structured his Columbus oratorio in such a way that the spectator takes an active, participatory role and the Catholic references are accessible.

A ring belonging to Isabella and a dove, two symbols of peace and love, are the leitmotivs. At the beginning of part 1, the Reader opens *The Book of Christopher Columbus*, setting the story in motion. He prays to the Almighty to grant him courage and competency to perform his task: narrating the true events of the admiral's life. The Genoese, sick and aged, is seen in Valladolid, the town where he would die. Confusion prevails onstage. Shortly after, a Greek-like chorus claims, in a biblical tone, "And the Earth was void and shapeless, and Darkness covered the face of the deep and the spirit of God hovered over the Waters."[23] Toward the end of part 2, while Columbus is trying to regain control of his crew on the three caravels, the chaos returns. Reference is constantly made to the Father, the Son, and the Holy Spirit in such a way as to suggest that the admiral's adventure in 1492 (only the first voyage and its aftermath are portrayed by Claudel) was a revival, a restaging, of the Passion.

Other characters are Isabella, members of the court, delegates and officers of the Spanish government, a cosmographer, the marshal of an Iberian palace. Actual people in Columbus's life, like Beatríz Henríquez de Arana and her son Diego, Luis de Santángel and Martín Alonso Pinzón, are absent here, replaced by common folk who can tell the navigator's story from the viewpoint of the average Iberian citizen. By today's standards, Claudel's sense of history is biased and nearsighted: as a believer in the proselytizing mission of the Church, and as an avant-garde intellectual writing before the Second World War, he pictures Europe as the only theater of human affairs, as the core of civilization. He portrays the pre-Columbian Mexican gods as bloodthirsty criminals anxious to stop the Genoese from discovering the New World. No support, no appreciation of their victimized situation, is ever offered. In scene 16 of part 1, the Reader says: "And now it is time to find out what is happening in America at the moment when the long night previous to its birth is drawing to a close and when the first ray of sun will give it back to Life and Humanity" (*Book*, 23). The position, clearly, is that of a European who believed the Americas were peripheral to history up until 1492. Although Claudel was aware that the natives were human, in *The Book of Christopher Columbus* the native American civilization is ridiculed by the Reader and other characters, mainly because of the exotic names of its gods and the strange customs of their worshipers.[24] Here is scene 16 of part 1, in which Huitchilopotzli, Quetzalcoatl, Tlaloc, and other Aztec deities discuss their fate and future.[25] Although they have plotted a sequence of natural accidents to stop Columbus from invading the Americas, they never succeed in accomplishing their goal:

> READER: And now it is time to find out what is happening in America
> at the moment when the long night previous to its birth is drawing
> to a close and when the first ray of sun will give it back to Life
> and Humanity. Hark! The underground thunder is rumbling, the

mountains are shaken! Hideous temples are crumbling! Vitzliputzli falls headlong! On the seashore are gathering the foul gory gods of darkness, the diseased and bloodthirty monsters. They look anxiously toward the East!

THE BEADLE: Huichtlipochtli!
HUICHTLIPOCHTLI: Here I am!
BEADLE: Quetzalcoatl!
QUETZALCOATL: Here!
BEADLE: Tlaloc!
TLOALOC: Here!
BEADLE: Ixtlipetzloc!
IXTLIPETZLOC: Here!
BEADLE: Where is Panchacamac?
IXTLIPETZLOC: He is manufacturing fog by frying glaciers at the end of the fork.
BEADLE: Where is Rxtxtchl—Krktxkchtl—the plague take them! Where the devil did they find names like that? (*He spits*) (*Book*, 23)

Claudel's central theological theme is the explicit equation between Jesus Christ and Columbus, who was also ignored and forgotten by his people during his lifetime and rejected by the emperors until it was too late.[26] As in Campoamor's *Colón*, the so-called discovery, at the end of part 1, is a re-creation of judgment Day. A crew member, after a violent mutiny, shouts "Land ho!" and others echo him: "Land! Land! Land! Land!" (*Book*, 33). In scene 18 the rising curtain reveals a tangled mass of palms, ferns, creepers, and dead trees in which monkeys and parrots are gamboling and pelicans are perching. Suddenly an enormous body appears, lying on the ground, behind which the ocean can be seen. From the right side of the stage emerges a two-faced colossal head built of corroded stones, overgrown with ferns and mangroves, and with a big snake coiled about it; one face is turned toward the sea, the other toward the audience. The Spanish sailors soon begin to shout around it, and a Te Deum begins to be heard off in the distance: *"Tibi Cherubim et Seraphim. . . . Incessabili voce proclamant:—Sanctus! Sanctus! Sanctus!"* (*Book*, 32–33). Part 2 deals with the return of Columbus to Spain, where disbelief about his achievement prevails among the population. In a soul-searching scene the navigator, alongside the Reader, splits his personality, looking for the deepest meaning of his oceanic adventure; but like Jesus, he is left defeated and dying. The oratorio tentatively ends in scene 6, but a dreamlike conclusion also appears in scenes 7 and 8. Queen Isabella, in Majorca, remembers her friend Columbus and tries to locate him through a messenger; when the Genoese refuses to acknowledge her inquiry, she asks for a mule. "On this poor animal," she says, "I will make my entry into the kingdom which Christopher has made ready for me by unfolding from one shore to a farther shore so splendid a carpet" (*Book*, 53). One of Charlot's drawings shows Queen Isabella riding on the entire new continent, as if

Western civilization—that is, Christianity—were making a triumphant entry onto the American stage.

The name Christopher is used by Claudel to suggest the admiral's celestial nature. Colombo, in Italian, means dove, another religious symbol used in the oratorio: in scene 13 Columbus promises to return to her a ring Isabella has given him, on the leg of a dove; the ring is a symbol of marriage, and the dove, as in the story of Noah's Ark, is a sign of peace and better times to come. Another biblical image appears at the conclusion of Claudel's play: a donkey brings Isabella to paradise, just as Jesus entered Jerusalem on a mule. Although Claudel does not quite equate the Genoese with Jesus Christ, he does portray the admiral as a man of vision—a redeemer ready to open a new path for humankind and bring salvation. Betrayed by his best men, his new road to paradise ignored, left alone and metaphorically crucified, Columbus remains loyal to his truth. And at the moment he is ready to depart this earth, others rediscover his revelation (*Book*, 50, 51).

Nikos Kazantzakis's last play, *Christopher Columbus: or, The Golden Apple*, published posthumously in 1969, is similar in tone and message to Claudel's oratorio. But his play is not an allegory but a drama focused on the individuals participating in the events of 1492. Also the author of *The Last Temptation of Christ* (1948) and *Zorba the Greek* (1946), Kazantzakis was born in Crete in 1883. A remarkable novelist and essayist with an interest in theater, his mentors were Nietzsche and the French thinker Henri Bergson, under whom he studied in his youth, and his role models were Jesus, Muhammad, and Buddha. Often nominated for the Nobel Prize (like Proust, Joyce, and Graham Greene, he never won it), his main spiritual interest was the dual nature of modern man, his lack of faith and the growth of his skepticism. Valuing freedom as an essential blessing, Kazantzakis was most concerned with the struggles between flesh and spirit, between Dionysius and Apollo. Although he never lost his faith in Christianity, it often troubled him.

Far from famous, his four-act Columbus play has a minimal role in Kazantzakis's posterity. Unlike Claudel's oratorio, *Christopher Columbus* has only 12 characters: Martín Alonzo Pinzón, Columbus, Queen Isabella, the sailors of the *Santa María*, a novice monk, two angels, and the disembodied voices of the Madonna and Christ. The scenes in acts 1 and 2 take place in different rooms of La Rábida, the Franciscan monastery near Palos where the admiral left his son Diego before traveling from Lisbon to Seville. Curiously enough, Kazantzakis, taking an artistic liberty, does not include the child Diego in his cast; his Columbus, alone, hungry, tired, and anxious to pray, is looking for shelter in the monastery. Act 3 takes place at the Alhambra in Granada, and act 4 in the middle of the ocean aboard the *Santa María*.

Other poetic liberties are also evident. At the heart of the play is the legend of the unknown pilot and the admiral's alleged knowledge of a fruitful territory across the ocean. The two protagonists are Captain Alonso and Columbus, who at first is simply recognized as "a stranger." In act 1 Pinzón offers a plan to the Abbot by which, with the monastery's support, he will sail to distant islands and bring back gold and wealth to the monks. As a member of the Franciscan sect (present in other Kazantzakis works, such as *The Odyssey: A Modern Sequel* [1938]), the Abbot is devoted to leading a humble, unpretentious life, poverty being his way to salvation. A few scenes later, a stranger asks permission to enter and pay tribute to the Madonna. When the Abbot and Pinzón talk to him, he explains that he is ready to sail across the Atlantic to a New World, and that he has in his possession a mysterious map revealing important information. Pinzón, an ambitious man, knows the truth: that Columbus is eager to pray, to confess his sins to the Madonna, because to obtain the map he killed the carrier, an unknown pilot.

In act 2 Columbus is praying to the Madonna and trying to convince Pinzón to accompany him on his voyage. When Pinzón is about to gain possession of the map, the admiral proudly burns it. The suspected murder remains unsolved. The Genoese claims he is a prophet endowed by God. Act 3, the shortest of all, includes a dialogue between Columbus and Queen Isabella, after which the queen hands him a cross. It is a present, a sign of her support and friendship. In act 4 Columbus, during the first voyage, controls his mutinous crew, led by Pinzón carrying a revengeful knife. Against all odds, his one and only objective is to become the Great Admiral of the Ocean, the Regent of India—to bring a new revelation to earth. But his problems increase, and he undergoes a mystical experience that brings him to paradise in the hands of mocking, sarcastic angels. At this point nobody trusts his enterprise, and his hallucination is but an disturbance of character. In the end a sailor screams "Land ho!" Everybody congratulates Columbus: he is a "Charioteer of God," a messiah.[27]

Thematically, *Christopher Columbus* is very similar to *The Last Temptation of Christ*, Kazantzakis's novel about Jesus having earthly, instinctual desires and already doubting his mission while on the Cross. As a redeemer, the Genoese is stubborn, impatient. He knows Pinzón is Judas Iscariot, and during his final hallucination he understands with the help of the angels, that for as much as he fights his enemy's animosity, his personal trophy will be taken away from him: Isabella will name others as regents of the newfound territories, and he, Columbus, will perish in poverty, forgotten.

Unlike Paul Claudel, Kazantzakis is not timid about equating the navigator with Jesus. In *Nikos Kazantzakis*, a useful biography by his widow, based on his letters, Helen Kazantzakis quotes a letter written to Börje Knös, a friend, on 15 November 1917 in Zurich—when he was living for a period outside of Greece—in which he explains his search for self-assurance and God.[28] The letter enables the biographer to reflect on her husband's philosophical views and intentions in the play, from which she quotes.

> Kazantzakis was to believe more and more in the omnipotence of the spirit: If one knows how to desire a thing, one obtains it. One even creates it out of the void—an idea frequently expressed in his work. For instance, in his tragedy [on Columbus]:

COLUMBUS [who is trying to persuade the Abbot of the monastery, Captain Alonso, and Captain Juan of the existence of the Madonna of the Atlantic]: Faithless generation, defiled, ungrateful, doomed to death. This generation mentions the earthly Paradise and bursts out laughing! Never, Captain Alonso, never Captain Juan. You will never find the new land—know this from me—because you do not have it within your own vitals. The new land is born first inside our own heart and only then emerges out of the sea. . . .

And to Isabella, who is skeptical, and refuses to believe Columbus's promises:

"Nonexistent" we call whatever we have not yet desired. . . . If the islands do not exist, then why was I born? They exist because I exist. Let him exist, my Queen, who preserves the dreams of the night by day, and struggles to put them into action! This is what youth means, this is the meaning of faith. Only in this way can the world grow. (67–68)

The same idea, the reader will recall, is developed by O'Gorman in *The Invention of America*: in order for the Americas to be discovered, Europe must have wanted it to exist. Kazantzakis, like Léon Bloy in *Revealer of the Globe* transforms this hypothesis into Columbus's theological justification for overcoming every obstacle in the way of his dream. Although his past might be colored with sin—namely, murder—his future, in Kazantzakis's eyes, is that of humankind: the Kingdom of Heaven.

= Embryo =

Carlos Fuentes, the Mexican diplomat, essayist, and fiction writer born in Washington, D.C., in 1926, is the author of *Christopher Unborn*, originally published in Spanish in 1987; this narrative about the Genoese is similar in technique and ludicrous approach to Stephen Marlowe's *The Memoirs of Christopher Columbus*. A true revisionist, Fuentes sees the vast history of world literature as an exquisite banquet from which to extract, duplicate, and refine ideas. His literary career has been a series of experiments with other texts and genres: *Aura* (1962) is a tribute to Henry James and Francisco Quevedo, *Where the Air Is Clear* (1958) to Émile Zola and Honoré de Balzac, and *A Change of Skin* (1967) to the French nouveau roman: *The Hydra Head* (1978) is a mediation on spy fiction structured as a collage of cinematic attitudes that incorporates literary references ranging from Shakespeare to John LeCarré and Robert Ludlum; and *Christopher Unborn*, his *roman comique*, closely imitates the gimmicks and verbose chapters, parodic devices, and graphic images of *Tristram Shandy*. A classic is written twice—by two authors, Fuentes and a precursor. Thus, different readings are required.

Based on an impossible literary premise, it describes the life and opinions of Columbus as an embryo during the nine-month gestation process. After a brief prologue ("I Am Created"), each of the nine chapters—"The Sweet Fatherland," "The Holy Family," "It's a Wonderful Life," "Festive Intermezzo," "Christopher in Limbo," "Columbus's Egg," "Accidents of the Tribe," "No Man's Fatherland," and "The Discovery of America"—recounts Columbus's precocious anatomical development by juxtaposing his comments on such diverse topics as psychology, metaphysics, philosophy, sex, politics, geography, and gastronomy. He judges and condemns, investigates and reflects, without compromising his privileged omniscient position. His interests range from pre-Columbian (mainly Aztec) mythology to the 1910 revolution, from show business to modern Mexican life. By placing a monologue in the mouth of an unborn child, Fuentes attempts to make reality unreal, to turn things upside down. The Genoese is seen as an unfinished creature, and thus is a target of ridicule. The details of his actual life are left out: he is only a symbol. Or as Wohryzeky argues, his is a name without a self—he is a mask without a face.

Instead of focusing on Columbus's own life, Fuentes sets his story in 1992 in Mexico, a country now under a totalitarian regime controlled by a bureaucratic machinery that victimizes the population. The cast includes the ethnologist Fernando Benítez, who is a real national figure, and the fictional characters Matamoros Moreno, and Homero Fagoaga. (A few names are obvious tributes: Christopher's parents are Isabella and Diego, who conceive him in Acapulco.) The government has sponsored a national contest in order to appoint a new leader: the child to be born on Columbus Day, at 12:00 A.M., will become the country's absolute ruler. The contest rules:

> TO WHOM IT MAY CONCERN: The male child born exactly at the stroke of midnight on October 12, and whose family name, not including his first name (it goes without saying the boy will be named Christopher), most resembles that of the illustrious navigator, shall be proclaimed PROGIDAL SON OF THE NATION. His education shall be provided by the Republic and on his eighteenth birthday he will receive the KEYS TO THE REPUBLIC, prelude to his assuming the position, at age twenty-one, of REGENT OF THE NATION, with practically unlimited powers of election, succession, and selection. Therefore, CITIZENS, if your family name happens to be Colonia, Colombia, Columbario, Colombo, Colombiano, or Columbus, not to say Colón, Colomba, or Palomo, Palomares, Palomar, or Santospirito, even—why not?—Genovese (who knows? perhaps none of the aforementioned will win, and in that case THE PRIZE IS YOURS), pay close attention: MEXICAN MACHOS, IMPREGNATE YOUR WIVES—RIGHT AWAY![29]

Fuentes seems to have a fondness for on-the-edge narrators—maniacs, physically transformed lunatics, or simply depraved crazies. *A Change of*

Skin, for example, has Freddy Lambert, a marginal character, describing the whole action while inside the trunk of a Lincoln. He is the creator and judge, opponent and executor, of the major protagonists, two of whom finally place him in an asylum in Cholula. *Terra Nostra* (1975) has a narrator who is also enchanted with religion, millenarianism, and resurrection. And in *The Hydra Head* the phantom Timón de Atenas controls his protagonists through sado-masochistic tricks. *Christopher Unborn* is the culmination of this kind of creativity: the embryo's thoughts are intense, disorganized, even difficult to follow; yet how can one ask for logic from a nonexistent entity?

Tristram Shandy, a narrative based on clear, logical premises, has a human protagonist who is alive, not a mere embryo. His discourse, neverthe-less, is also abrupt because Sterne was intentionally misrepresenting the conventional British novel. Samuel Richardson's *Pamela* (1740) and *Clarissa* (1747–48) and Henry Fielding's *Tom Jones* (1749), regarded in eighteenth-century England as masterpieces, became immensely popular. They realisti-cally reproduce the flow of human dialogue and thought, their plots are straightforward, and their technique is based on psychological insight. Sterne's characters, on the other hand, are uninterested in credibility, and they have no specific goals. They find simple, unimportant acts enlightening, and large historical events uninteresting. *Tristram Shandy* is a rebellious book: it defies realism and the progressive plot. Sterne stood against artificial-ity and created a tradition of parody and irreverence. Artificiality is the tone in *Christopher Unborn*: everything is "literary," unreal, an object of satire, and jokes (some of them Sterne's) are made mainly through tongue twisters and wordplay. Verbal fireworks, misquoted names, and other misquotations permit Fuentes to describe both the obvious inability of an embryo to write and the adaptability of the Spanish language in forming tongue twisters and narrative crossword puzzles. Words in *Christopher Unborn* become a Joycean labyrinth, a mirror reproducing the chaos of the outside world.[30]

Besides its debt to *Tristram Shandy*, *Christopher Unborn* is also a futuris-tic, anti-utopian novel that pays indirect tribute to Aldous Huxley and George Orwell. By 1992 Mexico has undergone several transformations: after the 1985 earthquake and a major unspecified disaster in 1990, a cleric-president of the right-wing National Action party rules with limited power. Political stagnation and corruption are still the same. Overpopulation is not discour-aged but approved. The nightmarish reality of *1984* (1949) and *Brave New World* (1932) prevails: an all-powerful government is embodied in Big Mother—represented by Nuestra Señora Mamadoc—who is ubiquitous yet untouchable, a combination of Eva Perón, Mae West, and the Virgin of Guadalupe.

The symbolism of Columbus as used by Fuentes is clear: he resurrects the soul of the Genoese, metamorphosed into an unborn child, to reevaluate and judge the "discovery" during the quincentennial. Although the Mexican does not attack the admiral as the sole perpetrator of all evils suffered by the New World, unlike Rubén Darío and other South Americans, he does make fun of Columbus's grandiose character, his naïve, foolish spirit. The final section of the novel, "The Discovery of America," opens with an epigraph quote from Gabriel García Márquez's *The Autumn of the Patriarch* (1975): "Why do I have to find you if I never lost you."[31] The Americas were happier before 1492. The discovery brought only sadness.

About to be born, Christopher ponders his grim future as a citizen of an "ugly," confused, and unresolved half-Aztec, half-Spanish reality. Five centuries after the Genoese first set foot in the Caribbean islands, the regions south of the Rio Grande are still hurting. "We are all Columbuses," says the embryo, "those of us who bet on the truth of our imagination to win" (*Unborn*, 522). In the last line of the novel, the newborn Christopher forgets everything: his dislocated narrative, his celebration of *Tristram Shandy*, his comments on Mexican art and life, past and future, soul and body—the new Columbus, according to Fuentes, is better off forgetting.

8

Conclusion: In Search of the Future

"Wake up, Alice dear!" said her sister. "Why, what a long sleep you've had!"

"Oh, I've had such a curious dream!" said Alice. And she told her sister, as well as she could remember them, all these strange Adventures of hers that you have just been reading about; and, when she had finished, her sister kissed her, and said, "It *was* a curious dream, dear, certainly; but now run in to your tea: it's getting late." And Alice got up and ran off, thinking while she ran, as well she might, what a wonderful dream it had been.

—Lewis Carroll,
Alice's Adventures in Wonderland (1865)

IN THE PREVIOUS CHAPTERS I HAVE TRIED TO SHOW HOW immediately after Christopher Columbus's death in Valladolid in 1506 his image began another crucial voyage, one beyond time and space. This new odyssey was across the realm of the human imagination. His caravel was the printed word, and readers were his most loyal crew. For five centuries, biographies, novels, short stories, plays, and poems for young and old alike,[1] describing his life and examining his legacy, have populated libraries world-wide in huge numbers and in almost every language. And as we have seen, the admiral was transformed into a mythical figure with three identities: the *conventional man*, fragile, feverish, and impatient, sometimes foolish and sometimes brave and wise; the *traitor* and *villain*, a diabolical, unmerciful creature; and the *hero* and *messiah*, a redeemer not only of the suffering but of the nearsighted.

The continent Columbus found does not carry his name but that of another navigator, Amerigo Vespucci.[2] Amending this injustice, monuments, cities, institutions, even nations, celebrate him by using his appellation.[3] In fact, Simón Bolívar, during the internecine battles of revolution in nineteenth-century South America, tried to unify the countries in the region (Venezuela, Colombia, Bolivia, and so on) into one "Great Colombia," in honor of the man he considered the true founder of the Americas.[4] But otherwise, history has approached Columbus tactlessly and ambiguously. Immediately after 1492 his achievements were ignored; in 1592, only a century later, his name was known to only a very timid few in Europe and the American colonies. But by 1892 he had been elevated to the stature of originator—a semipaternal figure in the United States and a role model for explorerers in the Europe of Voltaire and Rousseau. And today his memory is troublesome to many: his legacy has been associated with slavery, conquest, disease, and humiliation.

Literature, on the other hand, has been gentler: its tribute to Columbus has been made without bloodshed, without any physical suffering (although not without pain). Washington Irving and Friedrich Nietzsche, Walt Whit-man and Rubén Darío, Paul Claudel and Nikos Kazantzakis, James Fenimore Cooper and Alejo Carpentier—their various, magisterial artistic contributions are nothing but a proof of how life can be metamorphosed into fiction. Since fiction writers never presume to offer historical truth, the collective literary portrait of Columbus is a composite: we experience Columbus as both good and evil, intelligent and stupid, big and small in spirit. Ultimately, only the reader can judge Columbus.

Columbus's real-life adventure was in itself literary: his struggle to make it out of obscurity to glory, the suspense regarding the support of Queen Isabella and her court, his voyage of discovery as a rite of passage, his lone-some death. His existential plight seems at times to have been the creation of a talented Superior Author. He can remind us of three narrative characters who are equally sophisticated and rich in spirit and energy: Don Quixote of La Mancha, Robinson Crusoe, and Lemuel Gulliver.

Like Cervantes's protagonist in *Don Quixote*, Alonso Quijano—whose brains dried up because of his obsession with Amadís de Gaula, Tirant Lo Blanc, and other fictitious knights in his beloved chivalry books—Columbus was a victim of the act of reading. His fascination with Marco Polo's *The Book of Marvels* encouraged him to wander, to travel to unknown lands like Cathay and Cipangu, to find quasi-fantastic territories. And like Don Quixote, he dared the impossible: the geographers of his time were confident that the earth was a plane, horizontal and limited, but he navigated to the "end" of the world to prove that it was spherical and richer and more diverse than previously imagined. He encountered enormous obstacles yet remained loyal to his dream—or his lunacy, depending on who is telling the story. At the end he died misunderstood, lonely, and in misfortune; the entire world was laughing at him, and King Ferdinand had taken away the fruits of his achievement, thus jeopardizing his legacy. Like Don Quixote, Columbus opened up people's eyes to another dimension, another reality. He showed us a different way to read the book that is the universe. Indeed, recalling Bertrand Russell's argument, somebody else could have done what he did—but in fact it was Christopher Columbus, born in 1451 and dead at the age of 55, just 99 years before the first installment of *Don Quixote of La Mancha* was published, who took upon himself the role of discoverer and has thus generated, since his departure from this earth, just as monumental an amount of fabulation as Jesus Christ, Buddha, and William Shakespeare.

Daniel Defoe's Robinson Crusoe has been compared with the Genoese by V. S. Naipaul, the Oxford-educated novelist from Trinidad. In a book review first published in the *Listener* in 1967, Naipaul equates Columbus's odyssey with *The Life and Strange and Surprising Adventures of Robinson Crusoe* (1719). Both are stories of exploration and survival. Defoe's protagonist sails away, is wrecked, and finds himself on an island in the Orinoco River; altogether, he spends 24 years there. His industrious spirit, his ingenuity, and his reading of the Bible help him overcome the difficult first period. Crusoe then meets a native, Man Friday, whom he saves from the cannibals. Their friendship is a proof of courage, patience, and dedication. In the end they both return to England. Defoe's two-part novel is a parable of man against nature, a metaphor for human capabilities in extreme circumstances, a dissertation on the pros and cons of civilization.[6] In Naipaul's eyes, the journal of the first voyage is also a narrative of a pilgrimage into the unknown, an attempt to describe an exotic, foreign reality from a European perspective.

> *Robinson Crusoe*, in its essential myth-making middle part, is an aspect of the same fantasy [as the voyage of Columbus]. It is a monologue; it is all in the mind. It is the dream of being the first man in the world, of watching the first crop grow. Not only a dream of innocence: it is the dream of being suddenly, just as one is, in unquestionable control of the physical world, of possessing "the first gun that had been fired there since the creation of the world." It is the dream of total power.[7]

Finally, Columbus can be compared with Jonathan Swift's protagonist in *Several Remote Nations of the World, by Lemuel Gulliver*, known by its shortened title, *Gulliver's Travels*, and written in 1720 but published six years later. A work of early science fiction and children's fantasy, its central character is a physician who makes four voyages: one to Lilliput, another to Brodbingnag, a third to Laputa, and the last to Houyhnhnmland. On the first voyage he meets inhabitants who are six inches tall; in the second, giants; in the third, "wise men"; and in the last, he encounters the Yahoos and the Houyhnhnms. Like Columbus reacting to the natives in the Caribbean, the voyager is always perplexed by the size and nature of these creatures; he is often forced to deduce meanings where his understanding of the language and customs falls short. Criticizing abuses of power and human reason, the satirist Swift went against the status quo of his time by antagonizing politicians and institutions. Similarly, the Genoese traveled to islands where European culture does not exist and another culture, quite different in customs and language, reigns. The pilgrimages of Columbus and Gulliver are almost identical in one respect: they are parables of man's search for himself beyond the limits of civilization.

What literature will the next century produce about Christopher Columbus?

During his illustrious literary career, Jorge Luis Borges wrote masterful short stories. But he also enjoyed writing scholarly reviews of nonexistent books. "Pierre Menard, Author of the *Quixote*" is one example: in it Borges discusses the art of a nineteenth-century French symbolist who decided to rewrite word by word, but not copy, the masterpiece by Cervantes.[8] Menard is, of course, an invention, and so is his revisionist effort. Nevertheless, this literary device gives Borges the amazing ability, otherwise unattainable in a straightforward short story, to write nonfiction and fiction at the same time. Stanislaw Lem, a Polish essayist and science fiction novelist born in 1921, has also produced this type of semicritical invention. A couple of his books, *A Perfect Vacuum* (1971) and *One Human Minute* (1986), include metafictional pseudo-reviews of nonexistent titles, and a third, *Imaginary Magnitude* (1981), is a collection of introductions to fictitious volumes to be written sometime in the near future.[9]

Why not speculate, as Borges and Lem do, in this conclusion to *Imagining Columbus*? Why not attempt a description of forthcoming volumes on the Genoese? Why not suggest entries to the Columbian library of the future?[10] Most probably, by the time the twenty-first century is ending our ever-changing universe will no longer distinguish between Europe and the Americas as two separate realities. With the present fall of Marxism and the Balkanization of the former Soviet Union, mass media, foreign policy, and trade are likely to unify our overpopulated, ecologically sick planet into a homogeneous whole. Multiculturalism will no longer be only a sum of parts but a totality, a unity: everybody will be a mestizo—a mix of bloods and traditions. Yet the violent colonial past will not be buried. Rich international corporations hope to make outer space a fertile battlefield for technological power struggles, a stage for conquests and renewed domination of the haves over the have-nots. Will man repeat the mistakes of 1492 when expanding into the galaxy? No doubt.

What follows is a description of a handful of titles, some more intriguing than others, that could appear in the next 100 years. The first, Haromir Slomianski Swedenborg's *The Labyrinth of History*, published in Boston in 2011, centers on the life of one Darian Columbus, a lawyer undergoing a midlife crisis. After a troublesome divorce and the death of his only daughter, Columbus has a miraculous vision during a picnic at Hanging Rock, a bucolic site in Australia; afterwards he receives, in a transmigrational reversal of a similar vision in James Joyce's *Ulysses* (1922), not only the soul of his distant forefather Christopher but also that of the precursor of the civil rights movement, Fray Bartolomé de Las Casas. In dreams, the new, businesslike Columbus acknowledges the desire of the Genoese and the freedom-fighting priest to return to earth and proclaim the redemption of a kind of utopia they refer to as the Kingdom of Indies. Slomianski Swedenborg devotes little space to specifying what the utopia is really all about; instead, he concentrates on his protagonist's effort to convince the two most important leaders of the time, the president of the Confederation of Nations, Sir Jonathan Augenbraum, and the Jewish pope, Mosheus VIII, of the truthfulness of his celestial vision. But he is ignored, and the new Columbus, in a rampage of fury and religious passion, and emulating Henry David Thoreau, César Chávez, and Mahatma Gandhi, begins to perform acts of civil disobedience, such as obstructing traffic on busy highways and organizing marches and hunger strikes. To get attention, his mistress, the prostitute Judith Liweranth, videotapes him and mails the tape to TV stations and important trade magazines. People begin to notice. His activity escalates. Liberal groups, which have been active in debunking the prestige of Christopher Columbus, enjoy ridiculing him. In a final demonstration of heroic courage, Darian Columbus bombs crucial sites on the Iberian peninsula, kills thousands, and commits suicide. His last, ungranted demand is the restoration of his family legacy by the Confederation of Nations. He dies screaming, "The Americas are mine!" *The Labyrinth of History* ends with Judith in an asylum, talking to a dead Darian Columbus through dreams. He now inhabits his solipsistic Kingdom of Indies, where the wolf befriends the sheep, and the cat the bird.

A second invented title is *The Mind and the Pendulum*, a horror story by Joshua Hawthorne, about another direct descendant of Christopher Columbus, an anonymous biologist and archaeologist. One day he discovers, in a storage room of the Museo de Santo Domingo in the Dominican Republic, a sack of hair that belonged to his forefather, apparently saved by Don Diego, Columbus's son, immediately after his father's death. Attempting to revive the mariner in the bodies of other creatures, the scientist experiments with implanting cells in infants. Later, he arranges adoptions for the children, carefully selecting environments like that of Genoa in 1452, and parents similar in personality to Domenico Colombo and Susanna Fontanarossa. *The Mind and the Pendulum*, a tribute to Ira Levin's *The Boys from Brazil* (1976), has the number 3 as a leitmotiv. Divided into three parts of 33 chapters each, the book includes two other characters as important as the scientist—two children who look and think like Christopher Columbus and grow up to be exactly like him. Published in New Delhi in 2079, Hawthorne's book will be celebrated as a masterpiece in the tradition of Mary Shelley's *Frankenstein* (1818) and will eventually become a classic. Hawthorne, a professor at Yale, will also write a guide to the science fiction elements of the Old and New Testaments, a bilingual Spanish-English edition of the previously unknown poetry of Gabriel García Márquez, and a comprehensive study of Sigmund Freud and his Jewish perception of monotheism.

Another title—published in Istanbul in 2003, in the not so distant future—by one Yerosaphim Venatar Shafbanijör, a Chilean poet of Hindu origin, is a rewriting of Barlow's *The Columbiad* from a Hispanic American perspective. Set in Ultima Thule (Iceland), the protagonist, an unknown pilot, is known simply as the Ancient Mariner, a name recalling the poem by Samuel Coleridge. Still another forthcoming work, *Colum-Bus*, published in Tel-Aviv in 2017 and written by Daniel Yehuda ben Nahson, a Palestinian Israeli, is an anachronistic piece in which ultramodern technology puts Columbus in the wrong historical contexts: at the battle of Waterloo; in Tlatelolco, a neighborhood in Mexico City, during the student massacre of 1968; by the side of Theodor Herzel during the First World Jewish Congress in Basel; as a stepbrother of Ludwig von Beethoven; and as the true self of Judas Iscariot. Nahson ultimately suggests that Columbus was nothing but an impostor.

Although these plots may seem ludicrous, the chance that these nonexistent books might actually be published is not slim. The already immense library of works on the Genoese is likely to expand even more in both the near and distant future. As stated in the preface, the novels, poems, dramas, and biographies analyzed here are but a small fraction of the actual list of narrative explorations of Columbus, a list so abundant, so rich, its compilation is already a superhuman task.

This chapter's epigraph quote from *Alice in Wonderland* illuminates an undeniable fact of literature: even after a work of fiction has exhausted every trick and gimmick, the enjoyment it leaves in the reader's mind remains alive. From *Christopher Unborn* to "Prayer of Columbus," from *The Columbiad* to *The Harp and the Shadow*, from *Admiral of the Ocean Sea* to *The Conquest of Paradise*, the books in the parade I have organized are, and will go on being, a great source of pleasure for me. They are narratives about the mariner, but also something more: texts to be thoroughly enjoyed in themselves. The literary voyage by Christopher Columbus continues. Humans can be understood only in effigy, said the Portuguese poet Fernando Pessoa, "when affection no longer compensates the dead person for the disaffection he experiences when alive."[11] The miserable death of the Genoese in 1506, sad as it was, resulted in another birth—the rebirth of his true self. To paraphrase T. S. Eliot, in his end was his beginning.

CHRONOLOGY

The historical and literary repercussions of 1492 are practically innumerable. Only a small fraction of world and biographical events are listed here.

981	Eric the Red discovers Greenland.
1000	Leif Eriksson explores the Atlantic coast; during the next decade a Viking colony will be established in New England.
1271	Marco Polo, a Venetian traveler, begins his 24-year voyage to China, India, and Southeast Asia. His diary, *The Book of Marvels*, especially the passages about the Grand Khan of Cathay and the island of Cipangu, will capture the imaginations of future European discoverers, among them the young Columbus.
1451	Sometime between August and October, Christopher Columbus is born in Genoa, Italy. Domenico Columbus, his father, is a master weaver. His mother, Susanna Fontanarossa, about

whom little is known, is the daughter of a weaver from the Bisagno Valley.

1461–1470 Columbus becomes a mariner.

1469 Ferdinand and Isabel marry, uniting the kingdoms of Castile and Aragon.

1473–1476 He works as a business agent for Genoese entrepreneurs, traveling throughout the Mediterranean and to Africa.

1476 A shipwreck causes Columbus to visit Lisbon. He soon moves to Portugal.

1477 Columbus may have visited Iceland and, around this time, may have met the "unknown pilot."

1480 In Lisbon, he marries Dona Felipa Perestrello e Moniz, the daughter of a noble family. The Spanish Inquisition is established.

1482 Columbus's son Diego is born.

1485 Columbus leaves Portugal with his child, his wife having died unexplicably sometime before 1485. Already ambitious, but unsuccessful in gathering funds to finance his dreams, he goes to Spain. He may have left his son in the monastery of La Rábida. He begins courting Queen Isabella.

1488 The Portuguese explorer Bartholomeu Dias sails around the Cape of Good Hope. Ferdinand, the son of Columbus and Beatriz Enríquez de Arana, is born; he will become a man of wealth and one of his father's first biographers.

1489 Columbus is invited to the Spanish court. The Talavera report persuades the Catholic kings that his enterprise is not worth the risk.

1491 At La Rábida, to which he may be returning to pick up Diego, Columbus meets two important figures: Juan Pérez, a friar who is Queen Isabella's confessor, and Martín Alonso Pinzón, the owner and commander of the *Pinta*. Queen Isabella takes Columbus's requests seriously.

1492 With the queen's consent and funds finally gathered from financial backers, Columbus sails out of Palos on 3 August with three ships—the *Niña*, the *Pinta*, and the *Santa María*. The Portuguese navigator Vasco da Gama finds a sea route to India. Martin Behaim, a German, shows that the earth is spherical. Antonio de Nebrija publishes his grammar of the Castilian language. On 12 October, after a near-mutiny by the 26 men aboard the *Pinta*, Columbus arrives at Watlings Island, Bahamas (San Salvador, also called Guanahaní). In March Queen Isabella and King Ferdinand decree that the Jews be expelled from the Iberian peninsula, an event preceded by the prohibition of Moors in Andalusia. The kingdoms of Castile and Aragon are now unified, but collecting taxes is difficult for the Spanish government, which will soon see the Americas as a vast source of wealth, the ideal solution to the country's fiscal problems and thirst for power.

1493 Columbus's completes the journal of his first voyage. Later abstracted by Fray Bartolomé de Las Casas, the text will not be published for almost three centuries. With 17 ships, Columbus sails again, on his second voyage, this time discovering Dominica, San Juan Bautista, and the Leeward Islands. He also reaches Hispaniola, an island that will remain under his viceroyalty until 1500. He writes his "Letter to Luis de Santángel" in which he describes the fabulous land across the Atlantic to convince the Catholic kings that his was and still is a worthy enterprise.

1494 Columbus's brother Bartholomeo explores Haiti, and his crew makes inland expeditions to Cibao. Columbus discovers Juana and Jamaica.

1495 The Tainos in Hispaniola rebel.

1498 This time sailing from the Canary Islands, Columbus embarks on the third voyage and eventually reaches Trinidad. After making expeditions to Venezuela, he finally realizes he has found a huge terrain, perhaps a continent.

1499 Alonso de Hojeda and Amerigo Vespucci, with a few pilots and mapmakers, reach the Gulf of Paria, Aruba, Curaçao, and Maracaibo.

1500 Unsettled political and social conditions in Hispaniola force Queen Isabella and King Ferdinand to replace Columbus as governor. He is captured and returned to Spain in chains.

1502–1503 On his fourth and last voyage, Columbus discovers Nicaragua, Costa Rica, and other parts of Central America. After the loss of one ship and another mutiny, the trip ends up a financial disaster.

1504 Queen Isabella dies. Columbus writes a letter to the new pope, Julius II.

1506 Columbus dies in neglect, almost forgotten, on 20 May.

1509 King Ferdinand names Diego Columbus governor of Hispaniola.

1511 Peter Martyr d'Anghiera publishes *Of the New World*, a biography of Columbus that includes rumors about his dishonesty and spreads the rumor of his contact with the unknown pilot.

1513 Juan Ponce de León explores Florida. Vasco de Balboa discovers the Pacific Ocean at Panama.

1535 Gonzalo Fernández de Oviedo y Valdés publishes *A General*

	and Natural History of the Indies, the second biography of Columbus.
1541	Hernando de Soto explores the Mississippi River.
1571	After being harshly censored, an Italian version of Ferdinand Columbus's *Life of the Admiral Don Cristóbal Colón*, is published. A first-person biographical account of his father, Ferdinand's *Histoire*, as it has been known, is full of distortions and factual errors, according to some historians.
1589–1591	Galileo discovers the law of falling bodies.
1604	The Spanish playwright Lope de Vega unsuccessfully stages *The Discovery of the New World by Christopher Columbus: A Comedy in Verse*.
1605	Miguel de Cervantes, an obscure soldier, publishes the first part of *Don Quixote of La Mancha*, a parody of chivalry novels.
1615	After a huge success, the second part of *Don Quixote* is published.
1619	The first black slaves arrive in Jamestown, Virginia.
1620	The British Pilgrims land at Plymouth Rock.
1719	Daniel Defoe's *The Life and Surprising and Strange Adventures of Robinson Crusoe* is published.
1726	Jonathan Swift's *Gulliver's Travels* is published anonymously.
1776	The British colonies declare their independence. Adam Smith publishes *The Wealth of Nations*.
1788	Philip Freneau publishes "The Pictures of Columbus: The Genoese."
1789	The government organized under the U.S. Constitution is inaugurated; George Washington is chosen the first president.
1791	The Bill of Rights goes into effect in the United States.
1792	France becomes a republic, and Denmark abolishes the slave trade. The third centennial, unlike the first and second, is celebrated, but with only minor national events. Mary Wollstonecraft publishes *The Vindication of the Rights of Women*.
1807	Simón Bolívar frees sections of South America from Spanish rule.
1809	Joel Barlow publishes *The Columbiad*, an epic poem about the past and future of the United States.
1823	President James Monroe issues the Monroe Doctrine, setting forth the U.S. position against European interference in the affairs of the Western Hemisphere.
1825	The Spanish scholar Martín Fernández de Navarrete discovers biographical papers on Columbus.

1828   Washington Irving's monumental novelistic biography, *The Life and Voyages of Christopher Columbus*, is published. An adaption and rewriting of the Navarrete papers, the book is a commercial and literary success both in Europe and the United States.

1831   Nat Turner leads a slave rebellion in Virginia.

1840   James Fenimore Cooper publishes his historical novel *Mercedes of Castile*, about the love affair between a beautiful native Indian and a Spanish explorer. Critics attack the book as boring and inarticulate.

1844   The first telegraphic message is sent from Washington to Baltimore.

1848   Karl Marx and Friedrich Engels publish the *Communist Manifesto*.

1854   Ramón de Campoamor, with Gustavo Adolfo Bécquer, publishes the poem *Colón*, an allegorical and patriotic interpretation of the myth of Columbus.

1859   Charles Darwin publishes *On the Origin of Species*.

1861   The U.S. Civil War begins.

1863   President Abraham Lincoln issues the Emancipation Proclamation, abolishing slavery in the United States.

1865   The Civil War ends 9 April; Lincoln is assassinated 14 April. Walt Whitman writes "Prayer of Columbus," a poem that will be added to the 1876 edition of *Leaves of Grass*.

1872   Whitman's "Passage to India," which also refers to Columbus, is added to the fifth edition of *Leaves of Grass*.

1875   After a long delay due to lost manuscripts, Las Casas's *History of the Indies*, written between 1527 and 1563, is published.

1876   Alexander Graham Bell patents the telephone.

1892   Rubén Darío, on a trip to Spain sponsored by South American governments, writes "To Columbus," an attack on Columbus. International celebrations of the fourth centennial take place in France, Spain, Portugal, and the United States.

1895   Sigmund Freud develops his theories and techniques of psychoanalysis. Auguste Lumière introduces motion pictures.

1907   Darío's "To Columbus" is published in *The Wandering Song*.

1924   Franz Kafka's *The Trial* and Thomas Mann's *The Magic Mountain* are published.

1924   Joseph Stalin succeeds Vladimir Lenin as leader of the Soviet Union.

1925   William Carlos Williams publishes *In the American Grain*, a collection of vignettes on New World myths and symbols. It slowly becomes an underground best-seller. A new Chinese government is formed with Communist members.

1927   Paul Claudel stages his oratorio *The Book of Christopher Columbus*, in which he supports the theological idea that Columbus had divine powers. The first television transmission takes place in England.

1929   The German scholar Jacob Wassermann publishes *Christopher Columbus: Don Quixote of the Ocean*. In Spain Blasco Ibáñez publishes the chauvinistic novel *In Search of the Grand Khan*.

1939   World War II breaks out: Germany annexes Czechoslovakia; Francisco Franco captures Madrid; Italy invades Albania, and Germany invades Poland; Jews in Eastern and Central Europe are under siege, and anti-Semitic attacks prevail. The Spanish scholar Salvador de Madariaga publishes *Christopher Columbus: Being the Life of the Very Magnificent Lord Don Cristóbal Colón*, arguing that Columbus was Jewish.

1941   Japan attacks the U.S. base at Pearl Harbor in Hawaii.

1942   The United States joins the Allies. To celebrate the 450th anniversary of Columbus's voyage, Samuel Eliot Morison publishes his magisterial biography *Admiral of the Ocean Sea*, based on detailed oceanographic and historical research. Simultaneously, the Mexican diplomat and scholar Alfonso Reyes publishes his investigations of a possible encounter between Europe and the Americas prior to 1492, entitled *Ultima Tule*.

1945   World War II ends, as does the age of colonialism. New nations gain independence in Oceania, Asia, Africa, and Hispanic America. Europe, since ancient times a center of Western culture, loses authority. The Soviet Union and the United States are recognized as world powers.

1950   Octavio Paz publishes *The Labyrinth of Solitude*, an examination of the Mexican psyche and an early inquiry into Hispanic America's collective historic identity.

1958   Edmundo O'Gorman publishes *The Invention of America*, which asserts that the Americas were never "discovered" but rather "invented" by the European imagination. The United States launches the satellite *Explorer 1* into outer space. Charles de Gaulle becomes president of the Fifth Republic of France.

1959   Fidel Castro overthrows Fulgencio Batista and establishes a Communist government, beginning a new chapter in Cuban history.

1961   The United States breaks off diplomatic relations with Havana, which thwarts the U.S. Bay of Pigs invasion.

1964	Martin Luther King, Jr., wins the Nobel Peace Prize.
1965	Nikos Kazantzakis's play *Christopher Columbus* is written. Like Claudel four decades earlier, Kazantzakis suggests that Columbus was a prophet, almost a messiah. Malcolm X is assassinated. U.S. marines are sent to Vietnam and U.S. air strikes begin.
1967	Gabriel García Márquez publishes *One Hundred Years of Solitude*, a mythical account of Macondo, a fictitious town on the Caribbean coast of South America. It unexpectedly ignites a literary boom in the region, and for the first time Hispanic American authors will influence literati in Europe and the United States. The Beatles' *Sergeant Pepper's Lonely Hearts Club Band* is released.
1969	Neil Armstrong and Edwin Aldrin walk on the moon. Chicano activists gather in Texas to found the Raza Unida party.
1972	The Watergate in Washington, D.C., is broken into by Republican party operatives. Simon Wiesenthal publishes *Sails of Hope*, another work supporting the thesis that Columbus was a Jew.
1974	President Richard Nixon resigns in reaction to the Watergate scandal.
1975	Germán Arciniegas publishes *America in Europe*, an analysis of how the Old World was changed forever after 1492, not vice versa. Saigon falls to the Communists on 30 April, ending the Vietnam War.
1978	The United States votes to return the Canal Zone to Panama in the year 2000.
1979	Alejo Carpentier publishes his last book, *The Harp and the Shadow*, only one year before his death. It includes a first-person narration by Columbus, who confesses his true, selfish motives. The Three Mile Island nuclear power plant in Harrisburg, Pennsylvania, has a near-meltdown.
1982	The Falklands War is fought between England and Argentina. Tzvetan Todorov publishes his polemical *The Conquest of America*, an examination of why the Spanish conquerors never quite succeeded in appreciating the native inhabitants and beauty of the Americas.
1985	Abel Posse publishes *The Dogs of Paradise*, a rewriting of Columbus's adventure with Holocaust-Nazi references.
1987	Stephen Marlowe publishes *The Memoirs of Christopher Columbus*, a humorous portrait of Columbus with a Brooklyn accent. Mikhail Gorbachev becomes the leader of the Soviet Union. Carlos Fuentes publishes the monumental *Christopher Unborn*, an anti-utopian, Orwellian adventure set in 1992 and

narrated by an embryonic Columbus in the womb. The book attracts a cool response in Mexico and elsewhere in Hispanic America. The year before the space shuttle *Challenger* explodes moments after liftoff, killing the astronauts aboard.

1989   The Berlin wall comes down, along with Communist governments throughout Eastern and Central Europe.

1990   Kirkpatrick Sale publishes the controversial *The Conquest of Paradise*, igniting a widespread and sour debate about Columbus's true intentions.

1991   Michael Dorris and Louise Erdrich publish *The Crown of Columbus*, an adventure story that takes place in the Bahamas and at Dartmouth College. John Noble Wilford publishes *The Mysterious History of Columbus*, a revisionist biography. An attempted coup against Mikhail Gorbachev by Soviet Communist hard-liners fails. Inspired by the international recognition of Latvia, Lithuania, and Estonia as nations, nationalists press for independence in Catalonia and in the Basque country, asking to secede from Spain's central government; 500-year-old nation is on the verge of a major redefinition.

1992   While the quincentennial is celebrated in Europe and the United States with public and private events, museum exhibits, concerts, and book publications, south of the Rio Grande a sense of defeat and a lack of enthusiasm are felt; the so-called heroism of Columbus is called into question. Intellectuals and artists join forces to try to stop the festivities in Mexico, Argentina, and elsewhere in Latin America. They call 1492 the year of an "encounter," not a "discovery." The cultural identity of the United States undergoes redefinition under the banner of multiculturalism.

NOTES AND REFERENCES

Preface

1. Ralph Waldo Emerson, "Nominalist and Realist" [Boston, 1844], *Essays and Poemas* (London: Collins, 1954), 270.

Chapter 1

1. In *The Decline of the West* (2 vols. [Berlin: C.H. Beeck'schen Verlags-buchhandlung, 1919, 1922]), Oswald Spengler wonders what would have happened if France had funded the admiral rather than Spain. The irrefutable consequence, he thinks, would have been Charles V inheriting the Americas and Paris becoming the center of baroque European culture instead of Madrid. This speculative idea by the pessimistic German philosopher, shaped after World War I, might be absurd, but it offers a window onto the mentality of the time of Columbus. The fact that it was an Italian of obscure origin who settled in Portugal and traveled to Spain to gain the favor of the Catholic queen, that he was a disoriented sailor, with good fortune in Spain, who searched for another route to

the Indies, was not only instrumental but decisive in the shaping of the Americas. The Iberian peninsula was going through a period of artistic and intellectual expansion beyond its borders. Exploring the meaning of earthly matters, authors such as Lope de Vega, Francisco de Quevedo, Luis de Góngora, Garcilaso de la Vega, Tirso de Molina, and Miguel de Cervantes, with their conceptual, religious visions of the universe, offered a view of reality that was simultaneously labyrinthine and emblematic, limitless and abundant, self-projecting and beyond human control. England, the Flemish empire, and France, on the other hand, were already in the transitional stage to a new form of mercantile society that would eventually become capitalistic. These cultures were looking inward; their rigid social classes were beginning to lose strength and they were more concerned with their internal social dynamics than with territorial expansion. Therefore, the baroque artistic spirit in Iberian letters, Spengler claims, was strong and influential in encouraging voyagers to travel beyond set geographic limits. While Spain was incapable of maturing into a free-trade, upwardly mobile society, other nations in Europe were already taking the first steps toward such a goal. Hence, Columbus was a peon of the expansive Spanish national soul.

2. A stimulating discussion of the topic appears in Norman Cohn, *In Pursuit of the Millenium* (New York: Oxford University Press, 1970), 19–36.

3. See Andrew Delbanco, *The Puritan Ordeal* (Cambridge: Harvard University Press, 1989).

4. The term "Indian" is a result of Columbus's confusion: he thought he had found the Indies when he set foot on the Caribbean islands, which eventually became known as the West Indies. See Edmundo O'Gorman, *The Invention of America: An Inquiry into the Historical Nature of the New World and the Meaning of Its History* [1958] (Bloomington: Indiana University Press, 1961; reprint, Westport, Conn.: Greenwood Press, 1972), as well as Pedro Henriquez Ureña, *Literary Currents in Hispanic America* (Cambridge: Harvard University Press, 1945), the works of two Hispanic essayists devoted to the examination of the misconceptions surrounding 1492.

5. José Vasconcelos, *La Raza Cósmica. Misión de la raza iberoamericana* (Madrid: Aguilar, 1961).

6. Octavio Paz's legendary *The Labyrinth of Solitude* (translated by Lysander Kemp, Yara Milos, and Rachel Phillips Belash [New York: Grove-Weidenfeld, 1991]), offers many insights on the idiosyncratic approach of the Mexican psyche, and that of Hispanic America in general, to death, God, the inner self, and society. The opening chapter, a comparative study of Hispanic and Anglo-Saxon civilization, analyzes certain cultural and social types and patterns in Los Angeles, California, during the 1940s.

7. At the end of his life, Bartolomé de Las Casas wrote: "I believe that because of these impious, criminal and ignominious deeds perpetrated so unjustly, tyrannically and barbarously, God will vent upon Spain His wrath and His Fury, for nearly all of Spain has shared in the bloody wealth usurped at the cost of so much ruin and slaughter." *The Devastation of the Indies: Writings* (New York: Knopf, 1971), quoted in Tzvetan Todorov, *The Conquest of America* [1982], translated by Richard Howard (New York: Harper & Row, 1989), 245, hereafter cited in the text.

8. In essence, this thesis is promoted by Alan Riding in his portrait of the Mexicans, *Distant Neighbors* (New York: Knopf, 1985), xi.

9. For a summary of the controversy between "discovery" and "encounter" proponents, see Alessandra Stanley, "The Invasion of the *Niña*, the *Pinta*, and the *Santa María*," *New York Times*, 2 June 1991.

10. A complete collection of the opinions of Hispanic American intellectuals about the quincentennial, as well as of some U.S. and European liberals, is included in *Nuestra América frente al V Centenario: Emancipación e identidad en América Latina (1492–1992)* (Our America in Light of the Quincentennial: Emancipation and Identity in Latin America [1492–92]), edited by Arturo Peña (Mexico City: Joaquín Mortiz, 1989). Among the authors included are Noam Chomsky, Mario Benedetti, Augusto Roa Bastos, Roberto Fernández Retamar, and Fidel Castro.

11. See Robert Dahlin, "An Armada of Books Launched for Columbus's Quincentennial," *Publishers Weekly* (5 July 1991): 25–29.

12. See Kirkpatrick Sale, *The Conquest of Paradise: Christopher Columbus and the Columbian Legacy* (New York: Knopf, 1990), 349–53, hereafter cited in the text; and Garry Wills, "1492 vs. 1892 vs. 1992," *Time* (7 October 1991): 61, hereafter cited in the text.

13. The 7 October 1991 issue of *Time* also contains two other compelling articles: Paul Gray, "The Trouble with Columbus" (52–56), which discusses the opposing views of "discovery" and "encounter," and Robert Hughes, "Just Who Was That Man?" (58–59), about the many artistic portraits of the Genoese admiral painted since his death in 1506.

14. Karl E. Meyer, "Columbus Was Not Eichmann," *New York Times*, 27 June 1991.

15. Russell Baker, "Columbus Did It," *New York Times*, 16 July 1991.

16. In the same vein, José Pascual Buxó examines the implications of the so-called discovery in terms of the European imagination and its impact on the Americas. See his *La imaginación del nuevo mundo* (Imagination in the New World) (Mexico City: Fondo de Cultura Económica, 1988).

17. Germán Arciniegas, *America in Europe: A History of the New World in Reverse* [1975], translated by Gabriela Arciniegas and R. Victoria Arana (San Diego: Harcourt Brace Jovanovich, 1986), 25.

18. Winifred Sackville Stoner, Jr., *Facts in Jingles* (1923).

19. According to John Noble Wilford (*The Mysterious History of Columbus: An Exploration of the Man, the Myth, the Legacy* [New York: Knopf, 1991], *199–201*, hereafter cited in the text), that the new continent took Vespucci's name and not Columbus's is a testimony to the chaotic nature of the entire European enterprise of discovery in the fifteenth century. See also Carlos Sanz, *El nombre América: Libros y mapas que lo impusieron* (Madrid: Suárez, 1959).

20. See Leo Marx, *The Machine in the Garden: Technology and the Pastoral Ideal in America* (New York: Oxford University Press, 1965).

Chapter 2

1. Virginia Woolf, *Letters*, edited by Nigel Nicolson (New York: Harcourt Brace Jovanovich, 1975), vol. 6, 245.

2. Leon Edel, *Writing Lives: Principia Biographica* (New York: W. W. Norton & Co., 1984), 13–17, hereafter cited in the text.

3. Not a single female author has ever written a biography of Columbus.

The one work written by a woman is the novel *The Crown of Columbus* (1991), actually by the married couple Michael Dorris and Louise Erdrich; it is discussed in chapter 6.

4. Miguel de Cervantes, *Don Quixote of La Mancha*, part 2, chapter 3, quoted in Samuel Eliot Morison, *Admiral of the Ocean Sea: A Life of Christopher Columbus* (Boston: Atlantic-Little, Brown, 1942), hereafter cited in the text. Published on the occasion of the 450th anniversary of Columbus's first voyage, a revised edition appeared in 1982, with a foreword by David B. Quinn.

5. In Spanish the text is known as *Vida del Almirante Don Cristóbal Colón*; the English-language edition is *The Life of Admiral Christopher Columbus by His Son Ferdinand*, edited by Benjamin Keen (New Brunswick, N.J.: Rutgers University Press, 1959), hereafter cited in the text.

6. José Torre Revello, "Don Hernando Colón: Su vida, su biblioteca, sus obras" (Don Ferdinand Columbus: His Life, His Library, His Works) *Revista de Historia de América* 19 (June 1945): 45–52. See also two texts by Ramón Iglesia: the prologue to Fernando Columbus, *Vida del Almirante Don Cristóbal Colón* (Mexico City: Fondo de Cultura Económica, 1946), 7–19, and *El hombre Colón y otros ensayos* (Columbus the Man, and Other Essays) (Mexico City: El Colegio de México, 1944).

7. A few commentators have suggested that his nephew, Don Luis, the admiral's grandchild, wrote Ferdinand Columbus's book. But that would have been impossible. See Iglesia (1946, 15–17).

8. Bartolomé de Las Casas, *Historia de las Indias*, 3 vols., edited by André Saint-Lu (Caracas: Biblioteca Ayacucho, 1986), hereafter cited in the text, in my own translation. Only a selection is available in English: *History of the Indies*, translated and edited by Andree Collard (New York: Harper & Row, 1971).

9. See Marcel Brion, *Bartolomé de Las Casas, Father of the Indians* [1927], translated by Coley B. Taylor (New York: E. P. Dutton, 1929). Henry Raup Wagner, with the collaboration of Helen Rand Parish, *The Life and Writings of Bartolomé de Las Casas* (Albuquerque: University of New Mexico Press, 1967) is a critical edition with biographical information useful to specialists.

10. Under the *encomienda* system, each native family was commended to a Spaniard, who took care in converting its members to Christianity and in assimilating them to the economic reality of the colony; see Wilford (35). A history of the *encomienda* system in Mexico is to be found in Ramon Eduardo Ruíz's *Triumph and Tragedy: A History of the Mexican People* (New York: W. W. Norton, 1992).

11. Columbus delivered his journal to Isabella and Ferdinand, but when the queen died in 1504 it was lost. A copy made by a court scribe survived and was used by Ferdinand Columbus in his biography. According to Wilford, Las Casas must have borrowed it from the navigator's son. As editor, the priest persuasively tells us that he never exercised any sort of censorship, and that he left untouched the prologue and Columbus's letter addressed to the Catholic Kings; yet his style can be felt on every page. See Bartolomé de Las Casas, *Journal of First Voyage to America of Christopher Columbus*, introduction by Van Wyck Brooks (Freeport, Conn.: Books for Libraries Press, 1971; see also Bartolomé de Las Casas, *The Diario of Christopher Columbus's First Voyage to America. 1492–1493*, edited

by Oliver Dunn and James E. Kelley, Jr. (Norman: University of Oklahoma Press, 1989), hereafter cited in the text as Dunn and Kelley.

12. See the back-breaking edition edited by John Harmon McElroy, *The Life and Voyages of Christopher Columbus* (Boston: Twayne, 1981), which has 589 pages plus an appendix: in total, 1110 pages; hereafter cited in the text.

13. Washington Irving, *Diary: Spain 1828–1829*, edited by Clara L. Penney (New York: Hispanic Society of America, 1926), 181, hereafter cited as *Diary*.

14. His finances suffered a terrible setback after the collapse of speculative enterprises in South American mines in which he had invested. McElroy (xvii–xcvii) describes how Irving's biography was created as his plans for it evolved in his diaries and correspondence.

15. Martín Fernández de Navarrete, ed., *Colección de los viajes y descubrimientos que hicieron por mar los Españoles desde fines del siglo XV* (Collection of Voyages and Discoveries Made on Sea by Spaniards at the End of the Fifteenth Century) (Madrid: Imprenta Real, 1825).

16. Washington Irving, *Diary*, 90.

17. Marcelino Menéndez y Pelayo claims: "Today [circa 1892], unfortunately, books of this kind are no longer being written, because the majority of those who are opposed to a dramatic and picturesque historiography are by their opposition making a tacit confession of their own inability to write in this way." Quoted in McElroy (xcvii).

18. See Foster Provost, *Columbus: An Annotated Guide to the Scholarship on His Life and Writings, 1750–1988* (Providence, R.I.: John Carter Brown Library, 1991), 167–70, hereafter cited in the text.

19. The exact number is unknown. Some estimate that between 120,000 and 150,000 Jews were expelled. The actual decree had been issued months before, on 30 March 1492, but the deadline was 2 August 1492.

20. See my book review of Sale's *The Conquest of Paradise*, "Dreams of Innocence," *Hungry Mind* (Spring 1991): 6, 12.

21. Kirkpatrick Sale, "A Dark Record," letter to the editor of the *New York Times*, 25 July 1991.

22. An excerpt from Wilford, *The Mysterious History*—"Discovering Columbus"—that appeared in the *New York Times* magazine (11 August 1991) was accompanied by a colorful display of Columbus portraits, from one painted by Sebastiano del Piombo 13 years after the explorer's death, to one by Joaquín Sorolla y Bastida painted around 1900, and a 1984 likeness by Leonardo Lasansky.

23. James Russell Lowell, *Selected Library Essays* (Boston: Houghton Mitflin, 1914), 256.

24. Walt Whitman, *Leaves of Grass* [1855].

25. John Updike, *Hugging the Shore* (New York: Vintage Books, 1984), xviii.

26. Updike, xviii.

Chapter 3

1. I have made extensive use in this chapter of Samuel Eliot Morison's *Admiral of the Ocean Sea*.

2. Letter from Elizabeth Hawthorne to Richard Manning, Essex (April 12,

1876). Quoted in *Salem Is My Dwelling Place. A Life of Nathaniel Hawthorne* by Edwin Haviland Miller (Iowa City: University of Iowa Press, 1991), xvii.

3. The first treatise on this topic was James Davis Butler, *Portraits of Columbus: A Monograph* (1883), followed by works by William Eroy Curtis and Nestor Ponce de León. John Boyd Thacher devotes part 3 of his biography, *Christopher Columbus* (New York: Knickerbocker, 1903), to artistic representations of Columbus. See also chapter 4, "The Many Faces of Columbus," in Wilford (51–64).

4. Henry Vignaud, *A Critical Study of the Various Dates Assigned to the Birth of Christopher Columbus: The Real Date, 1451, with a Bibliography of the Question* (London: Stevens & Stiles, 1903). The date 1451 was not confirmed until the publication of Jacob Wassermann's biography, *Christopher Columbus: Don Quixote of the Ocean* [1929], translated by Eric Sutton (Boston: Little, Brown, 1930).

5. Some claim he was Majorcan, French, German, Catalan, Greek, and even Armenian (Morison, 8).

6. William of Ocean, *Tractatus Sacramento Altaris* (1516).

7. The spelling has been erratic: Colomo, Colom, and, in Spanish, Colón (Morison, 356–57).

8. On the topic of maps produced by the young navigator, as well as by Toscanelli, Henricus Martellus, Fra Mauro, Charles de la Ronciere, Martin Behaim, Piri Re'is, Juan de la Cosa, Bartholomeo Columbus, and others, see Provost (143–50).

9. Ramón Menéndez Pidal, *La Lengua de Cristóbal Colón: El estilo de Santa Teresa y otros estudios sobre el siglo XVI* (The Style of Santa Teresa, and Other Studies about the 16th Century), 4th ed. (Madrid: Espasa-Calpé, 1958), hereafter cited in the text. The sections on Columbus were originally published in *Bulletine Hispanique* 42 (1940): 5–27; *Correo Erudito* (1940): 98–101; and *Revista de Indias* I (1940): 153–56. Other important studies of his polyglotism, although at times outdated, are Cecil Jane, "The Question of the Literacy of Columbus in 1492," *Hispanic American Historical Review* 10 (1930): 500–516; V. I. Milani, *The Written Language of Christopher Columbus* (Buffalo, N.Y.: Forum Italicum, 1973); and the special issue of *Columbeis II* (Genoa: DARFICLET, 1987), with essays by Mario Damonte, Anna M. Mignone, Giorgio Bertoni, Stefano Pittalugo, and Rosanna Rocca.

10. Salvador de Madariaga, "Nota para la cuarta edición" (Note to the Fourth Edition), *Vida del Muy Magnífico Señor Don Cristóbal Colón* (Christopher Columbus: Being the Life at the Very Magnificent Lord Don Cristóbal Colón) (Buenos Aires: Sudamericana, 1959), 567–76. He disagrees with Morison and Menéndez Pidal.

11. Gustavo Pérez Firmat, "Dedication," *Los Atrevidos: Cuban American Writers* (Princeton, N.J.: Linden Lane Press, 1988), 158.

12. Robert Park, "Columbus as a Writer," *Hispanic American Historical Review* 8 (1928): 424–30.

13. Juan Gil, ed. and trans. *El Libro de Marco Polo anotado por Cristóbal Colón: El Libro de Marco Polo: Versión castellana [1503] de Rodrigo de Santiella* (The Book of Marco Polo Annotated by Christopher Columbus: The Book of Marco Polo: Spanish Version [1503] by Rodrigo de Santiella) (Madrid: Alianza, 1987).

14. Alejo Carpentier, *The Harp and The Shadow*, translated by Thomas Christensen and Carol Christensen (San Francisco: Mercury Press, 1990), 65–71, hereafter cited in the text as *Harp*.

15. An informative, well-structured article on the reputed affair between the navigator and Queen Isabella and other unsubstantiated rumors is Juan José Barrientos, "Colón, personaje novelesco" (Columbus as Novelistic Character) *Cuadernos Hispanoamericanos* 437 (November 1986): 45–62, hereafter cited in the text. I came across this article just as I began writing this book; it has been very valuable and inspiring.

16. Antoine Francois Félix Roselly de Lorges, *Christophe Colomb: Histoire de sa vie et de ses voyages* (Christopher Columbus: History of His Life and His Voyages) (Paris: Didier, 1856); Angelo Sanguineti, *La Canonizzazione di Cristoforo Colombo* (The Canonization of Christopher Columbus) (Genoa: Sardomuti, 1875).

17. Francisco Guerra, "The Problem of Syphilis," in *First Images of America*. vol. 2, edited by Fredi Chiappelli (Berkeley and Los Angeles: University of California Press, 1976), 845–51. Morison deals with the topic in "Home Is the Sailor" (359). The recognition of the infected crew member is offered by Emiliano Jos, "El Centenario de Fernando Colón y la enfermedad de Martín Alonso" (The Centennial of Ferdinand Columbus and the Sickness of Martin Alonso) *Revista de Indias* 3, no. 7 (1942): 96–101. See also Wilford (23,195).

18. See J. R. L. Anderson, *Vinland Voyage* (London: Eyre & Spottiswoode, 1967).

19. Thomas Pynchon uses this myth in his novel *Vineland* (Boston: Little, Brown, 1990), about life in northern California for a group of individuals who survived the 1960s. Morison does not believe the story to be true, while Madariaga does.

20. Kenneth Auchincloss, "When Worlds Collide," *Newsweek*, special issue to commemorate the Smithsonian's natural history exhibit, "Seeds of Change" (Fall–Winter 1991): 8. See also Eugene Lyon, "Search for Columbus," *National Geographic* 181, no. 1 (January 1992): 2–39.

21. Alfonso Reyes, *Ultima Tule* [1942], in *Obras completas de Alfonso Reyes*, vol. 11 (Mexico City: Fondo de Cultura Económica, 1960, 9–153. Some of his investigations into utopia are developed in *No hay tal lugar. . . .* (There Is No Such Place) in the same volume of *Obras completas*. Interestingly enough, around the same time Reyes's volume came out in Spanish, Vilhjalmur Strefansson published *Ultima Thule: Further Mysteries of the Arctic* (New York: Macmillan, 1940), Strefansson supports the idea that Columbus received crucial information during his visit to Iceland; see also Madariaga (567–76).

22. Jean Franco, *Spanish American Literature since Independence* (London: Ernest Been, 1973), *180–81*.

23. Seneca, *Medea*, act 3, verse 375. Morison thinks that because of the meteorological realities, the event is just impossible.

24. Two important books about the La Rábida story are Angel Ortega, *La Rábida: Historia documental crítica* (La Rábida: Critical and Documentary History), 4 vols. (Editorial de San Antonio, 1925–26), which details the relationship between the Franciscan friars and Columbus; and Antonio Rumeu de Armas, *La Rábida y el descubrimiento de América: Colón, Marchena, y Fray Juan Pérez* (La

Rábida and the Discovery of America: Columbus, Marchena, and Friar Juan Perez) (Edicións Cultural Hispánica, 1968), a text that claims that the admiral was never in the monastery, but that he did befriend Marchena.

25. A historical interpretation of the difficult relationship between Columbus and Pinzón can be found in Francisco Morales Padrón, "Las relaciones entre Colón y Martin Alonso Pinzón" (Relations between Columbus and Pinzón), *Revista de Indias* 31 (1961): 95–106; and in Juan Manzano Manzano and Ana María Manzano Fernández-Heredia, *Los Pinzones y el descubrimiento de América* (The Pinzóns and the Discovery of America), 3 vols. (Edición Cultural Hispánica, 1988).

26. A detailed examination of the admiral's charts, routes, ships, and marine knowledge appears in Robert Fuson, *The Log of Christopher Columbus* (Tab Books, International Marine Society, 1988), as well as in Morison's *The Voyage of Discovery 1492* (New York: Marlboro/Dorset Books, 1991).

27. Luis Marden, "The First Landfall of Columbus," *National Geographic* 170 (November 1986): 572–77.

28. Alastair Reid, a translator of Borges and a promoter of Latin American letters, describes from a personal viewpoint the past and present of the Dominican Republic in "Reflections: Waiting for Columbus," *New Yorker* (24 February 1992): 57–75.

29. See Juan Pérez de Guzmán, "Sobre el nombre de América y los demás que se dieron a las tierras occidentales descubiertas por Cristóbal Colón y los españoles" (About the Name of America and Others Given to the Western Lands Discovered by Christopher Columbus and the Spaniards), *El Centenario* (Madrid) 2 (1892): 249–69.

30. Besides his correspondence and journals, his writings include *Arte de Navegar* (The Art of Navigation), a treatise on sailing sent to the Catholic kings in letter form in 1502, and *The Book of Prophecies*, a 1501 attempt to persuade Queen Isabella of the grandiosity of his project that includes passages and quotes from the Bible and other religious texts to support the idea of discovering a new territory across the Atlantic (Morison, 577, 583). Says John Noble Wilford about this last title: "A remarkable document, prepared after his third voyage but long ignored by historians, reveals the depth and passion of Columbus's belief that he was God's messenger. This work can be read as compelling evidence that his spirituality was the force motivating his vision and sustaining him through years of ridicule, hardship, and achievement. At the very least, it outlined a framework for interpreting the discoveries of Columbus, as he wished the world and his monarch to understand them" (217).

31. Reprinted in Samuel Eliot Morison, ed. and trans., *Journals and Other Documents on the Life and Voyages of Christopher Columbus* (New York: Heritage, 1963). See also *Admiral of the Ocean Sea*, 644.

32. The original Spanish-language letter was printed in Barcelona only two weeks after the *Pinta* arrived back in Palos. Soon translations into Latin, Italian, and German began to circulate. A second Spanish printing of it was distributed in 1497; Consuelo Varela, ed., *Cristóbal Colón: Textos y documentos completos: Relaciones de viajes, cartas, y memorias* (Christopher Columbus: Complete Texts and Documents: Descriptions of Voyages, Letters, and Memoirs) 3rd ed. (Madrid: Alianza, 1986), hereafter cited in the text as Varela, in my own translation. On the same topic, see also Cecil Jane, "The Letter of Columbus Announcing the

Success of His First Voyage," *Hispanic American Historical Review* 10 (1930): 33–50.

33. Published as *Literary Currents in Hispanic America* (see chapter 1, note 4).

34. Published under the title "Questions of Conquest," *Harper's* 281, no. 1687 (December 1990): 45–53, and reprinted in Mario Vargas Llosa, *A Writer's Reality*, edited by Myron I. Lichtblau (Syracuse, N.Y.: Syracuse University Press, 1990). See my brief book review, "Scrutinizing the Scholar," *Bloomsbury Review* (March 1991): 3.

35. Stephen Greenblatt, *Marvelous Possessions: The Wonders of the New World* (Chicago: University of Chicago Press, 1991). In his book review, "Man of the Year" (*New York Review of Books* 38, no. 19 [21 November 1991]: 12–18), Garry Wills analyzes the book's defects, concluding that, "in a book arguing for the understanding of foreign cultures, [Greenblatt] makes himself almost willfully blind to meanings within Columbus's culture" (17). That, by the way, is the same fault to be found in Todorov's *The Conquest of America*.

36. See the companion book, *The Buried Mirror: Reflections on Spain and the New World* (Boston: Houghton Mifflin, 1992), 87

37. Several documents describing his death are examined in Cesáreo Fernández Duro, "Noticias de la muerte de don Cristóbal Colón y del lugar de enterramiento en Valladolid" (News of the Death of Don Christopher Columbus and The Place of Burial in Valladolid), *Boletín de la Real Academia de la Historia* (Madrid) 24 (1894): 44–46.

Chapter 4

1. Italo Calvino, *The Uses of Literature*, trans. Patrick Creagh (San Diego: Harcourt Brace Jovanovich, 1986), 81.

2. Kirkpatrick Sale devotes a good sixth of *The Conquest of Paradise* (324–70) to these repercussions.

3. David Castillejo, *Las cuatrocientas comedias de Lope de Vega* (The Four Hundred Comedies of Hope de Vega) (Madrid: Teatro Clásico Español, 1984). See also, *La decoverte du Nouveau Monde. Piece on trois actes sur Lope de Vega*, preface by Afranio Peixoto (Rio de Janeiro: Atlantica, 1944).

4. According to both Justin Winsor (*Christopher Columbus and How He Received and Imparted The Spirit of Discovery* [Boston: Houghton Mifflin, 1891]) and Henry Harrisse (*Cristophe Colomb* [Paris: E. Leroux, 1884]), it was in 1630 when the 78-page poem *Tyrall of Travell*, by the merchant Baptist Goodall, first appeared, containing the stanza: "Collumbus and Magellan Prowdly venetrd/ Then Drake, Vespucius and our forbish enterd."

5. According to John Noble Wilford (250), the Boston poet Phillis Wheatley, in 1775, was the first to use the name Columbia as a poetic representation of the aspirations of North Americans. Others, such as Timothy Dwight, a chaplain of the Connecticut brigade at Yale, followed.

6. See Octavio Paz's rich biography, *Sor Juana Inés de la Cruz: or, The Traps of Faith* [1982], translated by Helen Lane (Cambridge: Harvard University Press, 1989). Also, Jean Franco has examined her work and that of other nuns of the colonial period in *Plotting Women: Gender and Representation in Mexico* (New York: Columbia University Press, 1989), hereafter cited in the text.

7. Sor Juana Inés de la Cruz, "Pintura de la Excelentísima Señora Condesa de Galve, por comparaciones de varios héroes," (Portrait of the Very Excellent Señora Countess of Galve, Comparing Her to Various Heroes), *obras completas de Sor Juana Inés de la Cruz*, vol.1, *Lirica personal*, edited by Alfonso Méndez Plancarte (Mexico City: Fondo de Cultura Económica, 1951), 208, hereafter cited in the text as *Obras 3*, in my own translations. An important selection of Sor Juana's baroque work was translated into English by John Trublood, *A Sor Juana Anthology*, introduction by Octavio Paz (Cambridge: Harvard University Press, 1989). See also Luis Harss, ed. and trans., *Sor Juana's Dream* (New York: Lumen Books, 1986).

The Spanish original reads:

> Un Colón en su frente
> por dilatada,
> porque es quien su Imperio
> más adelantada.

8. "Loa para el auto intitulado 'El Mártir del Sacramento, San Hermene-gildo' " (Praise for the Allegorical Religious Play Entitled 'The Martyr of Sacramento, Saint Hermenegildo'), (*Obras 3*, 106–7).

The Spanish original reads:

> ¡Fértil España, que ya
> tus rubias arenas beso,
> vencidos de tantos mares
> los peligros y los riesgos!
> ¡Gracias te doy, oh gran Dios,
> que mi derrotado leño
> la gran empresa fiaste,
> libraste el honroso empeño
> de pasar la Equinoccial
> al término contrapuesto!
> ¡Albricias, Europa, albricias!
> ¡Más Mundos hay, más Imperios,
> que tus armas avasallen
> y sujeten tus alientos!
> ¡Sál de aquel pasado error,
> que tus Antiguos tuvieron,
> de que el término del Mundo
> no pasaba del Estrecho!
> ¡Oh Hércules! de tus Columnas
> borra el rótulo soberbio
> del *Non plus ultra*, pues ya
> rompió mi timón el sello
> que Abila y Calpe cerrado
> tuvieron tan largos tiempos!
> Y vosotros, mis felices
> animosos compañeros,
> que tan dilatados Mundos

descubridores primeros,
con los clarines y cajas
publicad, en dulces ecos,
¡que hay más Mundos, que hay *Plus ultra*.
y que ya venís a verlo!
  Y porque todos lo escuchen,
diga el militar estruendo:
¡La Tórrida es habitable
a beneficios del Cielo!
    ¡*Plus Ulta*! ¡Más Mundos hay,
y ya venimos a verlos!

9. See John Barth, "The Literature of Replentishment," *The Friday Book* (New York: Perigee Books, 1984), 193–206.

10. Moses M. Nagy, "Christopher Columbus in the Eighteenth and Early Nineteenth Century French Drama," *Claudel Studies* 15, no. 2 (1988): 8.

11. Friedrich Nietzsche, *Complete Works*, vol. 17, edited by Oscar Levy, translated by Herman Scheffaver (London: T. N. Fovlis, 1911), 162–63.

12. Throughout his life, the Dominican Republic scholar Pedro Henríquez Ureña studied, sometimes in great detail, the Columbus works by José Joaquín Pérez, Rafael María Baralt, Narciso Foxá y Lecanda, Rubén Darío, José Martí, and Fray Fernando Portillo y Torres; see *Obra crítica de Pedro Henríquez Ureña* (Mexico City: Fondo de Cultura Económica, 1960).

13. Translated into English in 1802 as *A Tale of Mystery*. About Thomas Morton, see Allerdyce Nicoll, *History of Early Nineteenth Century Drama, 1800–1850*, 2 vols. (Cambridge: Cambridge University Press, 1930), 50, 101, 288–9.

14. Peter Brooks, *The Empty Space* (New York: Atheraum, 1983), 9.

15. Nathaniel Hawthorne, *The House of the Seven Gables*, edited by Seymour L. Gross (New York: W. W. Norton, 1967), 1.

Chapter 5

1. Quoted in *The Poems of Philip Freneau: Poet of the American Revolution*, vol. 1, edited by Fred Lewis Pattee (Princeton, N.J.: The University Library, 1902–1907.), v, hereafter cited in the text as *Freneau*.

2. Mary Weatherspoon Bowden, *Philip Freneau* (Boston: Twayne, 1976), 173, hereafter cited in the text.

3. Jorge Luis Borges, in collaboration with Esther Zemborain de Torres, *An Introduction to American Literature* [1967], translated and edited by L. Clark Keating and Robert O. Evans (Lexington: University Press of Kentucky, 1971), 10–11. The Argentine does not include this passage in his *Obras completas en colaboración*, vol. 2 (Buenos Aires: Emecé, 1972; Madrid: Alianza, 1983).

4. See Justin Kaplan, *Walt Whitman: A Life* (New York: Simon and Schuster, 1980); and Ilan Stavans, "Walt Whitman en persona" *La Nueva España* (10 May 1991): 10.

5. Walt Whitman, *Leaves of Grass* [1891–92], introduction by Gay Wilson Allen (New York: New American Library, 1955), 7, hereafter cited in the text as

Leaves [1891–92]. The first edition, available with a preface by Malcolm Cowley (New York: Penguin, 1959), includes the long introduction by Whitman; hereafter cited as *Leaves* [1855].

6. An admirer of Columbus, Emerson did not include him in his 1850 *Representative Men*, in which Plato, Swedenborg, Montaigne, Shakespeare, Napoleon, and Goethe are featured. See Ralph Waldo Emerson, *Essays and Poems*, edited by G. F. Maine (London: Collins, 1954), 311–435.

7. Octavio Paz, *On Poets and Others* [1943], translated by Michael Schmidt (New York: Arcade, 1986), 8, hereafter cited in the text.

8. *Harper's Monthly* 48 (February 1874): 366–67.

9. Alfred Kazin, *An American Procession: The Major American Writers from 1830 to 1930: The Crucial Century* (New York: Knopf, 1984), 124.

10. Gay Wilson Allen, *The Solitary Singer: A Critical Biography of Walt Whitman* (New York: New York University Press, 1967), 458–59.

11. The same feeling is clearly expressed in Whitman's "Song of the Redwood Tree" (*Leaves*, 328–30).

12. See Ilan Stavans, "Walt Whitman, Cristóbal Colón, Rubén Darío," *La Jornada Semanal* 150 (26 April 1992): 30–33.

13. Among others, by Henry Nash Smith, *Virgin Land: The American West as Symbol and Myth*. (Cambridge: Harvard University Press, 1950), 47.

14. James Fenimore Cooper, *Letters and Journals*. Edited by James Franklin Beard (Cambridge: Belknap Press of Harvard University Press, 1960–1968), vol. 3, 38.

15. When translated into Spanish, the novel had a tremendous impact on Iberian literature, especially the theater. See Patricia Perutti, *Cristofo Colombo nella lettera spagniola* (Christopher Columbus in Spanish Literature) (Naples: Instituti d'Informatica de Torino, 1988); she examines nineteenth-century playwrights such as A. Ribot y Fonseré (*Cristóbal Colón o las glorias de España*, [Christopher Columbus: O, The Glories of Spain] 1840), Eugenio Sánchez de Fuentes (*Colón y el judío errante*, [Columbus and the Wandering Jew], 1845), and Victor Balaguer (*La última hora de Colón* [The Last Hour of Columbus], 1868).

16. Donald A. Ringe *James Fenimore Cooper* (Boston: Twayne, 1962), 80, hereafter cited in the text.

17. James Fenimore Cooper, *Mercedes of Castile: or, The Voyage to Cathay* (New York: D. Appleton & Co., 1959), 5, hereafter cited in the text as *Mercedes*.

18. Washington Irving is a natural source for Cooper to have used, yet Prescott, who authored dramatic histories of the conquest of Mexico (1843) and Peru (1847), would have been of dubious utility. Although a scholar of the reigns of Ferdinand and Isabella and Philip the Second, Prescott was not a biographer of Christopher Columbus.

19. Francisco de Bobadilla was sent to Santo Domingo by the Catholic kings in 1500 to replace Columbus as governor of the Indies.

20. In Umberto Eco [1963], *Name and Tears, and Other Stories*, edited and translated by Katherine Jason (St. Paul, Minn.: Graywolf Press, 1990), 62, hereafter cited in the text as "Discovery."

21. According to Katherine Jason, *Belin* is an obscenity in Genoese dialect.

22. "The Discovery of America" resembles Todorov's *The Conquest of America* and Greenblatt's *Marvelous Possessions*: besides the fact that all three

works are by literary critics, they are all concerned with the lack of communication between cultures and the sense of superiority of one vis-à-vis the other. Umberto Eco's piece is unique in that it explores this theme through fiction, not expository writing.

23. Salman Rushdie, "Christopher Columbus and Queen Isabella of Spain Consummate Their Relationship, Santa Fé, January, 1492," *New Yorker* (17 June 1991): 32, hereafter cited in the text as "Columbus."

24. The gimmick has been popular since Cervantes, who claimed not to have authored *Don Quixote of La Mancha*. Instead, he "confessed" to having copied the manuscript from an Arabic original by one Cide Hamette Benegueli. In *The Traveler Disguised* (New York: Schocken Books, 1973), Dan Miron studies the device in Yiddish literature. And in my essay, "The Ventriloquist and the Name: Forays into Philip Roth's Contemporary Modernism" (*Review of Contemporary Fiction* 19, no. 2 [Fall 1993], forthcoming), I examine its implications in contemporary modernist writers.

25. Another humorous book is Robert Wechsler, *Columbus à la Mode* (New York: Catbird Press, 1992), which is made up of experimental segments narrated in the style of John Updike, Kurt Vonnegut, Anne Tyler, Art Buchwald, Dr. Seuss, and others.

26. C. V. Wedgwood, *Truth and Opinion: Historical Essays* (New York: Macmillan, 1960).

27. Stephen Marlowe, *The Memoirs of Christopher Columbus* (New York: Scribner's, 1987), 238–239, hereafter cited in the text as *Memoirs*.

Chapter 6

1. José Enrique Rodó, *Hombres de América* (American Men) (Mexico: Editorial Novaro, 1957), 137.

2. The confusion in terminology has been analyzed by, among other critics, Earl E. Fitz in his book *Rediscovering the New World: Inter-American Literature in a Comparative Context* (Iowa City: University of Iowa Press, 1991), 121–145, hereafter cited in the text.

3. Octavio Paz, "Translation and Metaphor," in *Children of the Mire* (Cambridge: Harvard University Press, 1974), 115–41.

4. The best biographical and critical essays on Darío are by José Enrique Rodó, "Rubén Darío" [1899], in *Obras completas de José Enrique Rodó*, edited by Emir Rodríguez Monegal (Madrid: Aguilar, 1967); and by Octavio Paz, "El caracol y la sirena [R.D.]" (The Snail and the Syren), *Cuadrivio* (Mexico City: Joaquín Mortiz, 1965). Also valuable are Ricardo Gullón, *Páginas escogidas* (Selected Writing) (Madrid: Cátedra, 1984), with a chronology and selected bibliography; Ivan A. Schulman and Manuel Pedro González, *Martí, Darío, y el modernismo* (Marti, Darío, and *Modernismo*) Lily Lutwak, ed., (Madrid: Gredos, 1969); and *El Modernismo* (Madrid: Taurus, 1975).

5. See Homero Castillo, ed., *Estudios críticos sobre el modernismo* (Critical Studies on *Modernismo*) (Madrid: Gredos, 1968); and Raúl Silva Castro, ed., *Antología crítica del modernismo* (*Modernismo*: A Critical Anthology) (New York: Las Américas Publishing, 1963).

6. Rubén Darion, *El canto errante* (The Wandering Song) [1907] (Mexico City: Nueva Visión, 1977), 27–29. The Spanish original reads:

¡Desgraciado Almirante! Tu pobre América,
tu india virgen y hermosa de sangre cálida,
la perla de tus sueños, es una histérica
de convulsivos nervios y frente pálida.

Un desastroso espíritu posee tu tierra:
donde la tribu unida blandió sus mazas
hoy se enciende entre hermanos perpetua guerra,
se hieren y destrozan las mismas razas.

Un ídolo de piedra reemplaza ahora
el ídolo de carne que se entroniza,
y cada día alumbra la blanca aurora
en los campos franternos sangre y ceniza.

Desdeñando a los reyes, nos dimos leyes
al son de los cañones y los clarines,
y hoy al favor siniestro de negros beyes
fraternizan los Judas con los Caínes.

Bebiendo la esparcida savia francesa
con nuestra boca indígena semi-española,
día a día cantamos la *Marsellesa*
para acabar danzando la *Carmañola*.

Las ambiciones pérfidas no tienen diques,
soñadas libertades yacen deshechas.
¡Eso no hicieron nunca nuestros Caciques,
a quienes las montañas daban las flechas!

Ellos eran soberbios, leales y francos,
ceñidas las cabezas de raras plumas;
¡iojalá hubieran sido los hombres blancos
comos los Atahualpas y Moctezumas!

Cuando en vientres de América cayó semilla
de la raza de hierro que fue de España,
mezcló su fuerza heróica la gran Castilla
con la fuerza del indio de la montaña.

¡Plugiera a dios las aguas antes intactas
no reflejaran nunca las blancas velas;
ni vieran las estrellas estupefactas
arribar a la orilla tus carabelas!

Libres como las ágilas, vieran los montes
pasar los aborígenes por los boscajes,
persiguiendo los pumas y los bisontes
con el dardo certero de sus carcajes.

Que más valiera el jefe rudo y bizarro
que el soldado que en fango sus glorias finca,
que ha hecho gemir al Zipa bajo el carro
o temblar las heladas momias del Inca.

La cruz que nos llevaste padece mengua:
y tras encanalladas revoluciones,
la canalla escritora mancha la lengua
que escribieron Cervantes y Calderones.

Cristo va por las calles flaco y enclenque,
Barrabás tiene esclavos y charreteras,
y las tierras de Chibcha, Cuzco y Palenque
han visto engalonadas a las panteras.

Duelos, espantos, guerras, fiebre constante
en nuestra senda ha puesto la suerte triste:
¡Cristóforo Colombo, pobre Almirante,
ruega a Dios por el mundo que descubriste!

7. See Stavans "Whitman, Colón, Darío."

8. Carpentier finished the manuscript on 10 September 1978.

9. Roberto González Echeverría, *Alejo Carpentier: The Pilgrim at Home* (Ithaca, N.Y.: Cornell University Press, 1977), 214, and especially 215–20. This book came out two years before the publication in Spanish of *The Harp and the Shadow*; thus it does not contain an examination of that novel. Yet González Echeverría's analysis of most of the Cuban novelist's narratives is not only compelling but essential to anyone beginning the ardous project of reading it.

10. Independent of the Vatican investigation, Hispanic America also felt the controversy—primarily, during the ten-year period of religious examination, in the research of the investigators combing the records of every country from the Dominican Republic and Puerto Rico to South America, but also in theological debates and literature. By 1935, David Vela, with Church approval, was still publishing on the subject. His text, "El mito de Cristóbal Colón" (The Myth of Christopher Columbus) (*Publicaciones de la Academia Guatemalteca* [November 1935]: 5–154), one of the last in a long list, promotes Columbus as a preromantic spirit and an inspirational figure. His work was preceded and followed by a number of texts with ecclesiastical approval, including Enrique Bayerri y Bertomeu's *Colón tal cual fue* (Columbus The Way He Was) (Madrid: Manuel, Obispo de Tortosa, 1961).

11. Juan José Barrientos in Colón personaje novelesco," perceives part 2 of *The Harp and the Shadow* as an autobiographical account along the same lines as Robert Graves's *l, Claudius* (1934). He discusses Carpentier's novel vis-à-vis Blasco Ibáñez's *En Busca del Gran Kan* ([In Search of the Grand Khan] [1929] Barcelona: Plaza & Janés, 1978) and comments on Columbus's secrets, his origins, his marital and love affairs, his dishonest purposes, and his vision of the natives.

12. Abel Posse, *The Dogs of Paradise* [1985], translated by Margaret Sayers Peden (New York: Atheneum, 1989), 78–79, hereafter cited in the text as *Dogs*.

13. Michael Dorris and Louise Erdrich, *The Crown of Columbus* (New York: HarperCollins), 81, hereafter cited in the text as *Crown*.

14. Dorris and Erdrich quote Dunn and Kelley's *Diary* (see chapter 2, note 11) and reprint Columbus's letter to Prince John from *Select Letters of Christopher Columbus, with Other Original Documents Relating to His Four Voyages to the New World*, 2d ed., translated and edited by R. H. Major (London: Hakluyt Society, 72–107). They also quote from his diary as it appears in Fuson, *Log of Columbus*.

15. See Paul Claudel, *The Book of Christopher Columbus* [1927] (New Haven: Yale University Press, 1930, hereafter cited in the text as *Book* for a similar premise.

Chapter 7

1. Léon Bloy, *Le Révélateur du globe* (The Revealer of the Globe). 3 vols. (Paris: Médecins Bibliophiles, 1889), quoted in Carpentier (140).

2. Derived from the Greek verb *symballien*, the term *symbol* means "to put together" when used as an adjective; as a noun it connotes "sign" "token," or "mark." Understood as a metaphor in the sense that it replaces a certain object by analogy, a symbol is a figure of speech that substitutes a representation for the real item, thus calling attention to some of the item's qualities. Its aesthetic beauty depends on the reader finding its connection to what it represents; if the transition is too mechanical, the symbol can be simplistic and superficial. See Alex Preminger, ed., *Princeton Encyclopedia of Poetry and Poetics*, enlarged edition (Princeton, N.J.: Princeton University Press, 1974), 833–36.

3. Barlow is one of those obscure U.S. writers about whom not much has been written; John Dos Passos praises his democratic spirit in *The Ground We Stand On* (1941), but most of his compatriots have ignored him. Nevertheless, there are valuable biographies and commentaries on his writing, among them: Charles B. Todd, *Life and Letters of Joel Barlow* (New York: [G. P. Puttman's,] 1886); Theodore Zunder, *The Early Days of Joel Barlow* (New Haven: Yale University Press, 1934); and Arthur L. Ford, *Joel Barlow* (New York: Twayne, 1971, especially 46–67 on *The Vision of Columbus*), hereafter cited in the text.

4. James Woodress, *A Yankee's Odyssey: The Life of Joel Barlow* (Philadelphia: J. B. Lippincott Co., 1958), 85–86.

5. Joel Barlow, *The Vision of Columbus*. 5th ed. (Paris: English Press, 1793), 121, hereafter cited in the text as *Vision*.

6. Ford (48–62) offers a coherent, organized synthesis.

7. Joel Barlow, *The Columbiad*, 2 vols. (Philadelphia: C. and A. Conrad & Co., 1809), 1:xiii, hereafter cited in the text as *Columbiad*.

8. See chapter 3, note 4.

9. Roy Harvey Pearce, *The Continuity of American Poetry* (Middletown, Conn: Wesleyan University Press, 1987), 59–61.

10. In Ibáñez's *In Search of the Grand Khan* most of these defects are still stubbornly present. The plot revolves around the first voyage, and the subtext is a glorification of Spain for having produced such an outstanding personality. See Barrientos, "Colón, personaje novelesco."

11. On the vicissitudes of romanticism in Spain and Hispanic America, see Octavio Paz's illuminating essay, "Translation and Metaphor," in his Charles

Eliot Norton lectures published as *Children of the Mire* (Cambridge: Harvard University Press, 1974), 115–41. My introduction to the bilingual edition of Felipe Alfau's *La poesía cursi/Sentimental Songs* (Naperville, Ill.: Dalkey Archive, 1992) elaborates on the use of Spanish romantic poetry by twentieth-century authors.

12. Ramón de Campoamor with Gustavo Adolfo Bècquer, *Colón* (Madrid: Luis Navarro Editor, 1882), 24, hereafter cited in the text as *Colón*, in my own translation. The Spanish original reads:

> Ese es Palos.—Callad.—No oigan que aprisa
> Tres buques zarpan que la noche vela.
> —Es viernes.—Dan las tres.—Sopla la brisa,
> Y la más torpe de las tres naves vuela.
> Ya más allá de Saltes se divisa
> Una . . . dos . . . la tercera carabela.
> ¿Que quiénes son?—Dejad que hasta más tarde
> Yo, cual las sombras, el secreto guarde.

13. "Si la tierra no halláis, loco profundo: / Si halláis la Tierra, redentor del mundo" (If you don't find land, you'll be a profound lunatic: / If you do find land, you'll be a redeemer) (*Colón*, 47).

14. The Spanish original reads:

> Después la Caridad repite:—"Avanza,
> Con eterno pesar, á Colón viendo
> Que á derrotar la idolatría avanza
> Hoy su mission providencial cumpliendo."

15. The Spanish original reads: "Unos dicen que es un sabio, otro que un loco."

16. Seen *Masquerade*, Note 11.

17. See William Carlos Williams, *Yes, Mrs. Williams* (New York: New Directions, 1973). An interesting essay on Williams's linguisitic education and his mother's role in his childhood is Julio Marzán's "Mrs. Williams's William Carlos," *Reinventing the Americas: Comparative Studies of Literature of the United States and Spanish America*, edited by Bell Gale Chevigny and Gari Laguardia (Cambridge: Cambridge University Press, 1986), 106–21.

18. For a valuable study, see Thomas R. Whitaker *William Carlos Williams* [1968] (Boston: Twayne, 1989), hereafter cited in the text.

19. William Carlos Williams, *In the American Grain* [1925] (New York: New Directions, 1956), 7, hereafter cited in the text as *Grain*.

20. The attitude of major critics toward Williams's oeuvre is complex. Edmund Wilson, after an extensive discussion of H. D., Carl Sandburg, and e. e. cummings in *The Shores of Light* (Evanston, Ill.: Northwestern University Press, 1985), claims, "W. C. Williams and Maxwell Bodenheim I have tried my best to admire, but I have not been able to believe in them" (240). And in *On Native Grounds: An Interpretation of Modern American Prose Literature* (New York: Reynal & Hitchcock, 1942) and *An American Procession*, Alfred Kazin ignores him completely.

21. For another facet of Jean Charlot as influential experimentalist close

friend of Mexicans like Diego Rivera, see my essay, "José Guadalupe Posada, Lampooner," *Journal of Decorative and Propaganda Arts* 16 (Summer 1990): 54–71.

22. See Patrick Lobert, "Spectatorhood and Transaction in Claudel's *Livre de Christophe Colomb*," *Claudel Studies* 15, no. 2 (1988):49–57.

23. The Yale English-language edition does not credit the translator.

24. See Moses M. Nagy, "The Concept of History in *The Book of Christopher Columbus* by Paul Claudel," *Claudel Studies* 15, no. 2 (1988):23–36.

25. For a study of how *The Book of Christopher Columbus* influenced Carpenter's *The Harp and the Shadow*. See Klaus Muller-Berg, "The Perception of the Marvelous: Paul Claudel and Carpentier's *El arpa y la sombra*," *Comparative Literature Studies* 24, no. 2 (1987):165–91.

26. See Jacques Houriez, "Inspiration scripturaire et écriture dramatique dans *Le Livre de Christophe Colomb*" (Biblical Inspiratior and Dramatic Writing in *The Book of Christopher Columbus*), *Claudel Studies* 15, no. 2 (1988): 37–48.

27. Nikos Kazantzakis, *Christopher Columbus*, translated by Athena Gianakas Dallas, in *Three Plays* (also includes *Melissa* and *Kouros*) (New York: Simon and Schuster, 1969), 92. The subtitle, *The Golden Apple*, was lost in translation.

28. Helen Kazantzakis, *Nikos Kazantzakis: A Biography Based on His Letters* [1965], translanted by Amy Mims (New York: Simon and Schuster, 1968), 66–67, hereafter cited in the text.

29. Carlos Fuentes, *Christopher Unborn* [1987], translated by Alfred MacAdam, in collaboration with the author (New York: Farrar, Straus & Giroux, 1989), 6, hereafter cited in the text as *Unborn*.

30. Although well done, the English translation does reshape the original *Cristóbal nonato*. Both versions are extravaganzas written for the academic reader. An in-depth analysis comparing them has yet to be written, but a superficial look at their tables of contents reveals some of their differences: the English version is shorter, more versatile, and dynamic; it eliminates some chapters and some tangential passages.

31. Gabriel García Márquez, *The Autumn of the Patriarch*, translated by Gregory Rabassa (New York: Harper & Row, 1976), 87.

Chapter 8

1. Books for children and young adults have also embraced the Genoese navigator as a protagonist. Among the most outstanding: Peter Sis, *Follow the Dream*, ages 5–10 (New York: Knopf, 1991); Deino C. West and Jean M. West, *Christopher Columbus: The Great Adventure and How We Know about It*, ages 10–14 (New York: Atheneum, 1991); Miriam Schlein, *I Sailed with Columbus*, illustrated by Tom Newsom, ages 8–12 (New York: HarperCollins, 1991); Barbara Brenner, *If You Were There in 1492*, ages 8–12 (New York: Bradbury Press, 1990); Milton Meltzer, *Columbus and the World around Him*, ages 12 and up (London: Franklin Watts, 1990); Jean Marzollo, *In 1492*, ages 4–8 (New York: Scholastic, 1990); Ken Hill, *Voyages of Columbus*, illustrated by Paul Wright, ages 8–12 (New York: Random House, 1991); Stephen C. Dodge, *Christopher Columbus and the First Voyages to the New World*, ages 12 and up (London: Chelsea House, 1991); Susan Martin, *I Sailed with Columbus: The Adventures of a Ship's Boy*, illustrated by Tom La Padula, ages 10 and up (Woodstock, N.Y.:

Overlook Press, 1991); Olga Litowinsky, *The High Voyage: The Final Crossing of Christopher Columbus*, ages 10–14 (New York: Delacorte Press, 1991); Kathy Pelta, *Discovering Christopher Columbus: How History Is Invented*, ages 8–12 (Minneapolis: Lerner Publications, 1990); Betsy and Giulio Maestro, *The Discovery of the Americas*, ages 6–10 (London: Lethrop, Less & Shepard Books, 1990).

2. See chapter 1, note 19. On the relationship between Vespucci and Columbus, see Ilaria Luzzana Caraci, *Colombo e Amerigo Vespucci* (Genoa: Edizioni Culturali Internazionali Genova, 1987).

3. Here is a partial and very limited inventory of such places, holidays, institutions, and monuments: Columbus, Ohio; Columbus Circle, N.Y.; Columbia University in New York; Colombia, South America; El Dia de la Raza in Mexico; Columbus Day in the United States; the 1893 Columbian Exposition in Chicago; Colombo, Sri Lanka; British Columbia, Canada; Washington, District of Columbia. Kirkpatrick Sale lists and describes these places at great length in *The Conquest of Paradise* (296–364). John Noble Wilford, in *The Mysterious History of Columbus*. is also interested in Columbus's geographical and architectural posterity.

4. Gabriel García Márquez made Simón Bolívar's revolutionary dreams, his individual and political collapse, and his final days on the Magdalena River the subject of his novel *The General in His Labyrinth* [1989], translated by Edith Grossman (New York: Knopf, 1990).

5. Also comparing the mariner to the man of La Mancha are Jacob Wassermann, in *Christopher Columbus: Don Quixote of the Ocean*, and Gianni Granzotto (*Christopher Columbus*. translated by Stephen Sartarelli [New York: Doubleday, 1985]), who asserts: "Columbus and Don Quixote, each in his own way, extended these limits [of reality], expanded the minds of other men. They gave others a glimpse of new freedoms attainable only through a rejection of common sense" (151).

6. See Ian P. Watt, *The Rise of the Novel: Studies in Defoe, Richardson, and Fielding* (Hardmondsworth: Penguin, 1963).

7. V. S. Naipaul, *The Overcrowded Barracoon* (New York: Vintage, 1984), 206. See also Guillermo Schmidhuber, "La hispanidad y el personaje teatral de Cristóbal Colón" (The Hispanic World and Christopher Columbus as a Dramatic Character, *Ideas '92* 5 [Fall 1989]:35–43).

8. Jorge Luis Borges, "Pierre Menard, Author of the *Quixote*," *Sur* (May 1939).

9. See my analysis of both Borges and Lem in "Borges and the Future," *Science-Fiction Studies* [17, 1] (March 1990):77–83.

10. Darko Suvin, in *Metamorphosis of Science Fiction* (New Haven, Conn.: Yale University Press, 1979), 6, 22, 59, briefly comments on the utopian views of Columbus and his affinity with science fiction.

11. Fernando Pessoa, *The Book of Disquiet*, trans. Alfred MacAdam (New York: Pantheon, 1991), 139.

SELECTED BIBLIOGRAPHY

Primary Works

Listed below are the novels, plays, short stories, children's and young adult books, and poems discussed or referred to in the preceding pages, as well as the versions available of Columbus's own journals and correspondence. When available, English translations of non-English-language works are cited, but important foreign editions are also noted.

Aridjis, Homero. *1492: The Life and Times of Juan Cabezón of Castile*. Translated by Betty Ferber. New York: Summit Books, 1991. [*1492: Vida y tiempos de Juan Cabezón de Castilla*. Mexico City: Siglo XXI Editores, 1985.]
Barlow, Joel. *The Columbiad*, 2 vol. Philadelphia: C. and A. Conrad & Co.,1809.
———. *The Vision of Columbus*. 5th Edition. Pans: English Press, 1793.
Benítez, Fernando. *Cristóbal Colón: Misterio en un prólogo y cinco escenas*. Illustrated by Julio Prieto. Mexico City: Tezontle, 1951.
Brenner, Barbara. *If You Were There in 1492*. New York: Bradburg Press, 1990.
Campoamor, Ramón de. *Colón* [1854]. Madrid: Luis Navarro Editor, 1882.

Carpentier, Alejo. *The Harp and the Shadow*. Translated by Thomas Christensen and Carol Christensen. San Francisco: Mercury Press, 1990. [*El arpa y la sombra*. Havana: Editorial Letras Cubanas, 1979.]

Claudel, Paul. *The Book of Christopher Columbus*. [No translator cited.] Illustrated by Jean Charlot. New Haven: Yale University Press, 1930. [*Le Livre du Christophe Colomb*. Paris: Librairie Klicksieck, 1927.]

Columbus, Christopher. *Journals and Other Documents on the Life and Voyages of Christopher Columbus*. Edited and translated by Samuel Eliot Morison. New York: Heritage, 1963.

Cooper, James Fenimore. *Mercedes of Castile: or, The Voyage to Cathay* [1840], vol. 25, *Cooper's Novels*. New York: D. Appleton & Co., 1959.

Darío, Rubén. *El canto errante* (The Wandering Song) [1907]. Mexico City: Nueva Visión, 1977.

Dodge, Stephen C. *Christopher Columbus and the First Voyages to the New World*. London: Chelsea House, 1991.

Dorris, Michael, and Louise Erdrich. *The Crown of Columbus*. New York: HarperCollins, 1991.

Duboccage, Madame. *La Colombiade: ou, La Foi portée au nouveau monde: Poéme* (The Columbiad: or, Faith Transported to the New World). Paris: J. F. Bassompierre & Fils, Librairies à Liège, 1758.

Eco, Umberto. "The Discovery of America" [1963], in *Name and Tears, and Other Stories*, edited and translated by Katherine Jason. St. Paul, Minn.: Graywolf Press, 1990.

Freneau, Philip. *The Poems of Philip Freneau, Poet of the American Revolution*. Edited by Fred Lewis Pattee. Princeton, N.J.: The N.J University Library, 1902–1907.

Frohlich, Newton, *1492: A Novel of Christopher Columbus and His World*. New York: St. Martin's 1990.

Fuentes, Carlos. *Christopher Unborn*. Translated by Alfred J. MacAdam, in collaboration with the author. New York: Farrar, Straus & Giroux, 1989. [*Cristóbal Nonato*. Mexico City: Fondo de Cultura Económica, 1987.]

———. *The Buried Mirror: Relections on Spain and the New World*. Boston: Houghton Mifflin, 1992.

Hill, Ken. *Voyage of Columbus*. Illustrated by Paul Wright New. New York: Random House, 1991.

Ibáñez, Blasco. *En busca del Gran Kan* (In Search of the Grand Khan) [1929]. Barcelona: Plaza & Janés, 1978.

Irving, Washington. *The life and Voyages of Christopher Columbus* [1828]. New York: G. P. Putnam, 1863.

———. *The Companions of Columbus*. New York. G. P. Putnam, 1863.

———. *Diary: Spain 1828–1829*. Edited by Clara L. Penney. New York: Hispanic Society of America, 1962.

Kazantzakis, Nikos. "Christopher Columbus: or, The Golden Apple." In *Three Plays*, translated by Athena Gianakas Dallas. New York: Simon and Schuster, 1969.

La Cruz, Sor Juana Inés de. *Obras completas de Sor Juana Inés de La Cruz* (Complete Works of Sister Juana Inés de La Cruz), vols. 1 and 3 edited by Alfonso Méndez Plancarte. Mexico City: Fondo de Cultura Económica, 1955.

Las Casas, Fray Bartolomé de. *The Diary of Christopher Columbus's First Voyage to America, 1492–1493.* Edited by Oliver Dunn and James E. Kelley, Jr. Normari: University of Oklahoma Press, 1989. [A Previous edition is *Journal of First Voyage to America of Christopher Columbus,* introduction by Van Wyack Brooks. Freeport, N.Y. Books for: Libraries Press, 1971. *Obras completas,* vol. 14. *Diario del primer y tercer viaje de Cristóbal Colón,* edited by Consuelo Varela. Madrid: Alianza Editorial, 1989.]

————. *History of the Indies* (selection). Translated and edited by Andree Collard. New York: Harper & Row, 1971. [*Historia de las Indias* (1875) 3 vol., edited by Agustín, 1951; see also, *Historia de las Indias,* 3 vol., edited by André Saint-Lu. Caracas: Biblioteca Ayacucho, 1986.]

————. *The Devastation of the Indies: Writings.* New York: Knopf, 1971.

Lernercier, Népomucène Louis. *Christophe Colomb: ou, La Déuverte du Nouveau Monde* (The Discovery of the New World). Paris: Didot Jaune, 1809.

Litowinsky, Olga. *The High Voyage: The Final Crossing of Christopher Columbus.* New YorkL Delacorte, 1991.

Maestro, Bestsy, and Giulio Maestro. *The Discovery of the Americas.* London: Lothrop, Less & Shepard Books, 1990.

Marlowe, Stephen. *The Memoirs of Christopher Columbus.* London: Jonathan Cape, 1987.

Martin, Susan. *I Sailed with Columbus: The Adventures of a Ship's Boy.* Illustrated by tom La Padula. Woodstock, N.Y.: Overlook Press, 1991.

Marzollo, Jean. *In 1492.* New York: Scholastic, 1990.

Meltzer, Milton. *Columbus and the World Around Him.* London: Franklin Watts, 1990.

Morton, Thomas. *Columbus, or, A World Discovered.* London: W. Willer, 1792.

Nietzsche, Friedrich. *Complete Works,* vol. 17. Edited by Oscar Levy, translated by Herman Scheffauer. London: T.N. Foulis, 1911.

Pelta, Kathy. *Discovering Christopher Columbus: How History Is Invented.* Minneapolis: Lerner Publications, 1990.

Pixerécourt, Guilbert de. *Christophe Columb: ou, La, Découverte du nouveau monde* (Christopher Columbus: or, The Discovery of the New World). Paris: Chez Barba, Librairie, Palais-Royal, no. 5, 1815.

Posse, Abel. *The Dogs of Paradise.* Transcribed by Margaret Sayers Peden. New York: Atheneum, 1989. [*Los perros del paraíso.* Buenos Aires: Sudamericana, 1985.]

Raymond, George Lansing. *The Aztec God, and Other Dramas,* 3d ed. abridged. London: G. P. Puttman's Sons, 1908.

Rushdie, Salman. "Christopher Columbus and Queen Isabella of Spain Consummate Their Relationship, Santa Fé, January, 1492." *New Yorker* (17 June 1991): 32–34.

Sabatini, Rafael. *Columbus: A Romance.* Boston: Houghton Mifflin, 1942.

Schlein, Miriam. *Sailed with Columbus.* Illustrated by Tom Newsom. New York: HarperCollins, 1991.

Sis, Peter. *Follow the Dream.* New York: Knopf, 1991.

Varela, Consuelo, ed. *Cristóbal Colón: Textos y documentos completos: Relaciones de viajes, cartas, y memorias* (Christopher Columbus: Complete Texts and Documents: Descriptions of Voyages, Letters and Memoirs) 3d ed. Madrid: Alianza, 1986.

Vega, Lope de. *The Discovery of the New World by Christopher Columbus: A Comedy in Verse* [1604] Translated by Frieda Fligelman. Berkeley, Calif.: Gillick Press, 1950. [*El Nuevo Mundo descubierto por Colón*, in *Obras de Lope de Vega*, edited by Marcelino Menéndez y pelayo. Madrid: Real Academia Española, 1900.]

Walker, Alice Johnstone. *La Fayette, Christopher Columbus, The Long Knives of Illinois: Brief Plays for the Young.* New York: Henry Holt and Co., 1919.

West, Deino C., and Jean M. West. *Christopher Columbus: The Great Adventure and How We Know about It.* New York: Atheneum, 1991.

Whitman, Walt. *Leaves of Grass* [1891–92]. Introduction by Gay Wilson Allen. New York: New American Library, 1955. [See also the first edition (1855), edited and with an introduction by Malcolm Cowley. New York: Penguin, 1959.]

Wilhem, Ida Mills. *The Son of Dolores.* New York: Field-Doubleday, 1945.

Williams, William Carlos. *In the American Grain* [1925]. New York: New Directions, 1956.

Secondary Works

Listed below are important biographies, critical studies by the authors examined in this volume, and works on the life and legacy of Columbus. Also included are literary and historical essays on the fate of the Americas since 1492, specifically on the distinctions between the United States and the countries south of the Rio Grande.

Allen, Gay Wilson. *The Solitary Singer: A Critical Biography of Walt Whitman.* New York: New York University Press, 1967.

Arciniegas, Germán. *America in Europe: A History of the New World in Reverse* [1975]. Translated by Gabriela Arciniegas and R. Victoria Arana. San Diego: Harcourt Brace Jovanovich, 1986.

Arsenio y Toledo, José M. *Cristóbal Colón: Su vida, sus viajes, sus descubrimientos* (Christopher Columbus: His Life, His Voyages, His Discoveries). Barcelona: Espasa y Compañía, 1888.

Attali, Jacques. *1492.* Paris: Fayard, 1990.

Baker, Russell. "Columbus Did It." *New York Times*, 16 July 1991.

Barrientos, Juan José. "América: El paraíso perdido" (America: Paradise Lost) *Humboldt* 27, no. 89 (1986): 19–22.

————. "Colón, personaje novelesco" (Columbus: Novelistic Character) *Cuadernos Hispanoamericanos* 437 (November 1986): 45–62.

Bayerri y Bertomeu, Enrique. *Colón tal cual fue* (Columbus the Way He Was). Madrid: Manuel, Obispo de Tortosa, 1961.

Bedini, Silvio, ed. *The Columbus Encyclopedia.* New York: Simon and Schuster, 1992.

Bien, Peter. "*Christopher Columbus*: Kazantzakis's Final Play." *Journal of the Hellenistic Diaspora* 10, no. 4 (Winter 1983): 21–30.

Bloy, Léon. *Le Révélateur du globe* (Revealer of the Globe), 3 vol. Paris: Médecin Bibliophiles, 1889.

Boorstin, Daniel J. *The Discoverers.* New York: Random House, 1983.

Borges, Jorge Luis. *Borges: A Reader.* Edited by Emir Rodríguez Monegal and Alastair Reid. New York: E. P. Dutton, 1981.

————. *Other Inquisitions (1937–1952)*. Translated by Ruth L. C. Simms. Austin: University of Texas Press, 1964.

Borges, Jorge Luis, in collaboration with Esther Zemborain de Torres. *An Introduction to American Literature* [1967]. Translated and edited by L. Clark Keating and Robert O. Evans. Lexington: University Press of Kentucky, 1971.

Brion, Marcel. *Bartolomé de Las Casas, Father of the Indians* [1927]. Translated by Coley B. Taylor. New York: E. P. Dutton, 1929.

Brooks, Van Wyck. *The Times of Melville and Whitman*. New York: E.P. Dutton, 1947.

Browden, Mary Weatherspoon. *Washington Irving*. Boston: Twayne, 1981.

Buxó, José Pascual. *La imaginación del nuevo mundo* (The Imagination of the New World). Mexico City: Fondo de Cultura Económica, 1988.

Cachey, Jr., Theodore J. "The Earliest Literary Response of Renaissance Italy to the New World Encounter." In Paolucci and Paolucci, *Columbus*, 24–35.

Caraci, Ilaria Luzzana. *Colombo vero e falso* (Columbus, True or False). Genova: Sagep, 1989.

Cardini, Franco. *Europe 1492: Portrait of a Continent Five Hundred Years Ago*. New York: Facts on File, 1989.

Castillejo, David. *Las cuatrocientas comedias de Lope de Vega*. (The Four Hundred Comedies of Lope de Vega). Madrid: Teatro Clásico Español, 1984.

Castillo, Homero, ed. *Estudios críticos sobre el modernismo* (Critical Studies on Modernismo). Madrid: Gredos, 1968.

Chevigny, Bell Gale, and Gari Laguardia, eds. *Reinventing the Americas: Comparative Studies of Literature of the United States and Spanish America*. Cambridge: Cambridge University Press, 1986.

Cohn, Norman. *The Pursuit of the Millenium*. Oxford: Oxford University Press, 1970.

Columbeis 1. Genoa. Instituto di Filologia Classica e Medievale, 1986.

Columbeis 2. Genoa: DARFICLET, 1987.

Columbus, Ferdinand. *The Life of Admiral Christopher Columbus by His Son Ferdinand* [1571]. Edited by Benjamin Keen. New Brunswick, N.J.: University Press, 1959. [*Vida del Almirante Don Cristóbal Colón escrita por su hijo Don Hernando*, edited by Ramón Iglesia, Mexico City: Fondo de Cultura Económica, 1947.]

D. Cooper, James Fenimore. *Letters and Journals*. Edited by James Franklin Beard. Cambridge: Belknap Press of Harvard University Press, 1960–1968.

Crosby, Alfred. *The Columbian Voyages, the Columbian Exchange, and their Historians*. Washington, D.C.: American Historical Association, 1987.

Curtis, William Eleroy. *The Capitals of Spanish America*. New York: Harper, 1888.

Dahlin, Robert. "An Armada of Books Launched for Columbus's Quincentennial." *Publishers Weekly* (5 July 1991): 25–29.

Delbanco, Andrew. *The Puritan Ordeal*. Cambridge: Harvard University Press, 1989.

De Vorsey, Louis, Jr., and John Parker. *In the Wake of Columbus: Islands and Controversy*. Detroit: Wayne State University Press, 1985.

Dyson, John. *Columbus: For Gold, God, and Glory*. Photos by Peter Christopher. New York: Simon and Schuster, 1991.

Edel, Leon. *Writing Lives: Principia Biographica.* New York: W. W. Norton & Co., 1984.

Fernández-Armesto, Felipe. *Columbus.* Oxford: Oxford University Press, 1990.

———. *Columbus and the Conquest of the Impossible.* New York: Saturday Review Press, 1974.

Fernández de Navarrete, Martín, ed. *Colección de los viajes y descubrimientos que hicieron por mar los Españoles desde fines del siglo XV* (Collection of Voyages and Discoveries Made on Sea by Spaniards at the End of the Fifteenth Century). Madrid: Imprenta Real, 1825.

Fernández Duro, Cesáreo. "Noticias de la muerte de don Cristóbal Colón y del lugar de enterramiento en Valladolid" (News of the Death of Don Christopher Columbus and the Place of His Burial in Valladolid), *Boletín de la Real Academia de la Historia* [Madrid] 24 (1894):44–46.

Fitz, Earl E. *Rediscovering the New World: Inter-American Literature in a Comparative Context.* Iowa City: University of Iowa Press, 1991.

Ford, Arthur L. *Joel Barlow.* New York: Twayne, 1971.

Franco, Jean. *Plotting Women: Gender and Representation in Mexico.* New York: Columbia University Press, 1989.

———. *Spanish American Literature since Independence.* London: Ernest Been, 1973.

Fuson, Robert. *The Log of Christopher Columbus*: New York: Tab Books, International Marine Society, 1988.

Gil, Juan, ed. and trans. *El Libro de Marco Polo anotado por Cristóbal Colón: El Libro de Marco Polo: Versión castellana [1503] de Rodrigo de Santiella* (The Book of Marco Polo annotated by Christopher Columbus: The Book of Marco Polo: Spanish Version by Rodrigo de Santella). Madrid: Alianza, 1987.

González Echeverría, Roberto. *Alejo Carpentier: The Pilgrim at Home.* Ithaca, N.Y.: Cornell University Press, 1977.

Granzotto, Gianni. *Christopher Columbus.* Translated by Stephen Sartarelli. New York: Doubleday, 1985.

Greenblatt, Stephen. *Marvelous Possessions: The Wonder of the New World.* Chicago: University of Chicago Press, 1991.

Gullón, Ricardo, ed. *Páginas escogidas de Rubén Darío* (Selected Writing of Rubén Darío). Madrid: Cátedra, 1984.

———. *Diccionario del modernismo* (A Dictionary of *Modernismo*). Madrid: Gredos, 1964.

Harrisse, Henry. *Christophe Colomb devant l'histoire* (Christopher Columbus in History). Paris, 1892.

———. *Cristophe Colomb: Son origine, sa vie, ses voyages, sa famille et ses descendants, d'apres des documents inèdits tirès des archives de Génes, de Savone, de Séville et de Madrid* (Christopher Columbus: His Origins, His Life, His Voyages, His Family and His Descendants. With Unpublished Documents in the Archives of Geneva, Savone, Seville and Madrid). Paris: E. Leroux, 1884.

Henríquez Ureña, Max. *Breve historia del modernismo.* (Brief History of *Modernismo*). Mexico City: Fondo de Cultura Económica, 1954.

Henríquez Ureña, Pedro. *Obra crítica de Pedro Henríquez Ureña* (Critical Works of Pedro Henríquez Ureña). Mexico City: Fondo de Cultura Económica, 1960.

————. *Literary Currents in Hispanic America*. Cambridge: Harvard University Press, 1945.

Houriez, Jacques. "Inspiration scripturaire et écriture dramatique dans *Le Livre de Christophe Colomb*" (Biblical Inspiration and Dramatic Writing in *The Book of Christopher Columbus*), *Claudel Studies* 15, no. 2 (1988): 37–48.

Humbolt, Alexander Freiherr von. *Examen critique de l'histoire et de la géographie du nuveau continent et des progrès de l'astronornie nautique aux quinzème et seizième siècles*. (Critical Examination of the History and Geography of the New World, and the Progress of Oceanic Astronomy in the Fifteenth and Sixteenth Centuries). Paris: Gide, 1836–39.

Iglesia, Ramón. "Prólogo." In Fernando Columbus, *Vida del Almirante Don Cristóbal Colón*. Mexico City: Fondo de Cultura Económica, 1947.

————. *El hombre Colón y otros ensayos*. (The Man Columbus, and Other Essays). Mexico City: El Colegio de México, 1944.

Jane, Cecil. "The Question of the Literacy of Columbus in 1492." *Hispanic American Historical Review* 10 (1930): 500–516.

Jiménez, José Olivio, ed. *Antología crítica de la poesía modernista hispanoamericana* (Critical Anthology of Hispanic American *Modernista* Poetry). Madrid: Hiperión, 1985.

Kaplan, Justin. *Walt Whitman: A Life*. New York: Simon and Schuster, 1980.

Kazantzakis, Helen. *Nikos Kazantzakis: A Biography Based on His Letters* [1965]. Translated by Amy Mims. New York: Simon and Schuster, 1968.

Kazin, Alfred. *An American Procession: The Major American Writers from 1830 to 1930: The Crucial Century*. New York: Knopf, 1984.

————. *On Native Grounds: An Interpretation of Modern American Prose Literature*. New York: Reynal & Hitchcock, 1942.

Landström, Bjorn. *Columbus. The Story of Don Cristóbal Colón. Admiral of the Ocean Sea, and His Four Voyages Westward to the Indies. According to Contemporary Sources*. Translated by Michael Phillips and Hugh W. Stubbs. New York: Macmillan, 1967. [*Historien om Amiralen över Oceanen Don Cristóbal Colón*. Stockholm: Borkförlaget Forum, 1966.]

Lerner, John. "The Certainty of Columbus: Some Recent Studies." *History* [London] 73, no. 237 (February 1988): 3–23.

Levenson, Jay A., ed. *Circa 1492: Art in the Age of Exploration*. New Haven: Yale University Press, 1991.

Litvak, Lily, ed. *El Modernismo*. Serie "El Escritor y La Crítica." Madrid: Taurus, 1975.

Lobert, Patrick. " 'Spectatorhood' and Transaction in Claudel's *Livre de Christophe Colomb*." *Claudel Studies* 15, no. 2 (1988): 49–57.

Lyon, Eugene. "Search for Columbus," *National Geographic* 181, no. 1 (January 1992): 2–39.

Madariaga, Salvador de. *Christopher Columbus: Being the Life of the Very Magnificent Lord Don Cristóbal Colón*. Cambridge: Cambridge University Press, 1939.

Martyr d'Anghiera, Peter. *De orbe novo* (The New World) [1511].

Marx, Leo. *The Machine in the Garden: Technology and the Pastoral Ideal in America*. New York: Oxford University Press, 1965.

Marzán, Julio. "Mrs. Williams's William Carlos." In Chevigny and Laguardia, *Reinventing the Americas*, 106–21.

Menéndez y Pelayo, Marcelino. "De los historiadores de Colón" (Columbus's Historians), *El Centenario* [Madrid] 2 (1892): 433–53; 3 (1893): 51–57.

Menéndez Pidal, Ramón. *La lengua de Cristóbal Colón: El estilo de Santa Teresa y otros estudios sobre el siglo XVI* (The Language of Christopher Columbus: The Style of Santa Teresa, and Other Studies about the Sixteenth Century). 4th ed. [1942]. Madrid: Espasa-Calpé, 1958.

Merrie, Jean. *Christopher Columbus: The Mariner and the Man*. London: Odham Press, 1958.

Meyer, Karl E. "Columbus Was Not Eichmann." *New York Times*, 27 June 1991.

Milani, V. I. *The Written Language of Christopher Columbus*. Buffalo, N.Y. Forum Italicum, 1973.

Morison, Samuel Eliot. *Admiral of the Ocean Sea: A Life of Christopher Columbus*. Illustrated by Bertram Greene. Boston: Atlantic-Little, Brown, 1942; revised edition, Boston: Atlantic-Little, Brown, 1982.

———. *Christopher Columbus, Mariner*. Boston: Little, Brown, 1955.

Muller-Berg, Klaus. "The Perception of the Marvelous: Paul Claudel and Carpentier's *El Arpa y la sombra*." *Comparative Literature Studies* 24, no. 2 (1987): 165–91.

Nagy, Moses M. "Christopher Columbus in the Eighteenth and Early Nineteenth Century French Drama." *Claudel Studies*" 15, no. 2 (1988): 6–14.

———. "The Birth of a Biography: *The Life and Voyages of Christopher Columbus*, by Washington Irving." *Claudel Studies* 15, no. 2 (1988): 14–22.

———. "The Concept of History in *The Book of Christopher Columbus*, by Paul Claudel." *Claudel Studies* 15, no. 2 (1988): 23–36.

Naipaul, V. S. *The Overcrowded Barracoon* [1973]. New York: Vintage Books, 1984.

Nicoll, Allerdyce. *History of Early Nineteenth Century Drama, 1800–1850*, 2 vols. Cambridge: Cambridge University Press, 1930.

Obregón, Mauricio. *The Columbus Papers*. New York: Macmillan, 1991.

O'Gorman, Edmundo. *The Invention of America: An Inquiry into the Historical Nature of the New World and the Meaning of Its History* [1958]. Bloomington: Indiana University Press, 1961; Westport, Conn.: Greenwood Press, 1972. [*La idea del descubrimiento de América: Historia de esa interpretación y crítica de sus fundamentos*. Mexico City: Centro de Estudios Filosóficos, 1951; *La invención de América: El universalismo de la cultura de occidente*. Mexico City: Fondo de Cultura Económica, 1958.]

Oriedo y Valdés, Gonzalo Fernández de. *Historia general y natural de las Indias* (General and Natural History of Indies) [1535]. Madrid: Ediciones Atlas, 1959.

Paolucci, Anne, and Henry Paolucci, eds. *Columbus*. New York: Griffton House, 1989.

Park, Robert. "Columbus as a Writer." *Hispanic American Historical Review* 8 (1928): 424–30.

Parlakian, Nishan. "Lope de Vega's Christopher Columbus Play (Re)Discovered." In Paolucci and Paolucci, *Columbus*, 36–41.

Paulmier, Hilah, and R. H. Schauffer. *Columbus Day: Prose and Verse on Christopher Columbus*. New York: Dodd-Mead, 1938.

Pavese, Cesare. "Interpretation of Walt Whitman, Poet." In *American Literature: Essays and Opinions*, translated and introduced by Edwin Fussell, 117–41. Berkeley: University of California Press, 1970.

———. *The Labyrinth of Solitude* [1950]. Translated by Lysander Kemp, Yara Milos, and Rachel Phillips Belash. New York: Grove-Weidenfeld, 1991.

———. *On Poets and Others* [1943]. Translated by Michael Schmidt. New York: Arcade, 1986.

———. "El caracol y la sirena (R.D.)" (The Snail and the Syren) In *Cuadrivio*. Mexico City: Joaquín Mortiz, 1965.

———. "Translation and Metaphor." In *Children of the Mire*. Cambridge: Harvard University Press, 1974.

Paz, Octavio. *Sor Juana: or, The Traps of Faith*. Translated by Margaret Sayers Peden. Cambridge: Harvard University Press, 1988. [*Sor Juana Inés de la Cruz: o, Las trampas de la fe*. Mexico City: Fondo de Cultura Económica, 1982.]

Pearce, Roy Harvey. *The Continuity of American Poetry*. Middletown, Ct: Wesleyan University Press, 1987.

Peña, Arturo, ed. *Nuestra América frente al V Centenario. Emancipación e identidad en América Latina (1492–1992)* (Our America and the Quincentennial. Emancipation and Identity in Latin America [1492–1992]). Mexico City: Joaquín Mortiz, 1989.

Pérez-Firmat, Gustavo, ed. *Do the Americas Have a Common Literature?* Durham N.C.: Duke University Press, 1990.

Phillips, Jr., William D., and Carla Rahn Phillips. *The Worlds of Christopher Columbus*: Cambridge: Cambridge University Press, 1992.

Polo, Marco. *El Libro de Marco Polo anotado por Cristóbal Colón. El Libro de Marco Polo: Versión castellana [1503] de Rodrigo de Santiella* (The Book of Marco Polo Annotated by Christopher Columbus. The Book of Marco Polo: Spanish Edition [1503] by Rodrigo de Santiella). Edited and translated by Juan Gil. Madrid: Alianza, 1987.

Provost, Foster. *Columbus: An Annotated Guide to the [Scholarship of] His Life and Writings, 1750–1988*. Providence, R.I.: John Carter Brown Library, 1991.

Reid, Alastair. "Reflections: Waiting for Columbus." *New Yorker* (24 February 1992): 57–75.

Revello, José Torre. "Don Hernando Colón: Su vida, su biblioteca, sus obras." *Revista de Historia de América* 19 (June 1945): 45–52.

Reyes, Alfonso. *Ultima Tule* [1942]. In *Obras completas de Alfonso Reyes*, vol. 11. Mexico City: Fondo de Cultura Económica, 1960.

Rial, José Antonio. *La destrucción de Hispanoamérica* (The Destruction of Hispanic America). Caracas: Monte Avila Editores, 1976.

Ringe, Donald A. *James Fenimore Cooper*. Boston: Twayne, 1962.

Robertson, William. *The History of America*. London: Strahan, Cadell, 1777.

Rodó, José Enrique. "Rubén Darío" [1899]. In *Obras completas de José Enrique Rodó*, edited by Emir Rodríguez Monegal: Aguilar, 1967.

Roselly de Lorges, Count Antoine Félix, *Histoire posthume de Christophe Colomb* (Posthumous History of Christopher Columbus). Paris: Librairie Académique Didier, 1885.

———. *Christophe Colomb: Histoire de sa vie et de ses voyages* (Christopher Columbus: History of His Life and His Voyages). 2 vol. Paris: Didier, 1856.

Roth, Cecil. *A History of the Marranos*. New York: Meridian, 1959.

————. "Who Was Columbus?" *Menorah Journal* 28 (October-December 1940): 12–34.

Rousseau, Jean-Jacques. *La Découvert du nouveau monde* (The Discovery of the New World). Paris, 1740.

Rush, Ralph L. *The Life of Ralph Waldo Emerson*. New York: Scribner's, 1949.

Ryan, Agnes. *Christopher Columbus in Poetry, History, and Art*. Chicago: Mayer & Miller, 1917.

Sale, Kirkpatrick. "A Dark Record." Letter to the editor of the *New York Times*, (25 July 1991).

————.*The Conquest of Paradise: Christopher Columbus and the Columbian Legacy*. New York: Knopf, 1990.

Sanguineti, Angelo. *La Canonizzazione de Cristoforo Colombo* (The Canonization of Christopher Columbus). Genoa: Sordo-Muti, 1875.

Schmidhuber, Guillermo. "La hispanidad y el personaje teatral de Cristóbal Colón" (The Hispanic World and Columbus as Dramatic Character). *Ideas '92* 5 (Fall 1989): 35–43.

Schmieder, Oscar. *Die Neue Welt: Mittel und Südamerika* (The New World: Central and South America). Heidelberg and Munich: Keyserische Verlagsbuchhandlung, 1963.

Schulman, Ivan A. *Génesis del modernismo: Martí, Nájera, Silva, Casal*. Mexico City and Seattle: El Colegio de México/Washington University Press, 1966.

————, and Manuel Pedro González. *Martí, Darío, y el modernismo* (Martí, Darío, and *Modernismo*). Madrid: Gredos, 1966.

Silva Castro, Raúl. *Antología crítica del modernismo* (*Modernismo*: A Critical Anthology). New York: Las Américas Publishing, 1963.

Smith, Henry Nash. *Virgin Land. The American West as Symbol and Myth*. Cambridge: Harvard University Press, 1950..

Stanley, Alessandra. "The Invasion of the *Niña*, the *Pinta*, and the *Santa María*." *New York Times*, 2 June 1991.

Stavans, Ilan. "En la tumba de W.W." (In the Tumb of W.W.) *Diario 16* (28 March 1992): 7.

————. "E Pluribus Unum" [review of Earl E. Fitz, *Rediscovering the New World: Inter-American Literature in a Comparative Context*]. *Review* 14 (1992): 137–153.

————. "Walt Whitman, Cristóbal Colón, Rubén Darío," *La Jornada Semanal* 150 (26 April 1992): 30–33.

————. "Dreams of Innocence." [review of Kirkpatrick Sale, *The Conquest of Paradise*]. *Hungry Mind* (Spring 1991): 6, 12.

————."Walt Whitman en persona" (Walt Whitman in Person) *La Nueva España* (10 May 1991): 10.

Suvin, Darko. *Metamorphoses of Science Fiction: On the Poetics and History of a Literary Genre*. New Haven: Yale University Press, 1979.

Taviani, Paolo Emilio. *Columbus: The Great Adventure: His Life, His Times, and His Voyages*. Translated by Luciano F. Farina and Marc A. Beckwith. New York: Orion Books, A Division of Crown, 1991.

————. *Cristoforo Colombo. La Genes della grande Scoperta*. 2 vols. Novara: Istituto Geografico de Agostin, 1974.

————. *Christopher Columbus: The Grand Design*. London: Orbis, 1985.

Test, George A. *James Fenimore Cooper: His Country and His Art*. Oneonta: State University of New York, 1985.

Thacher, James Boyd. *Christopher Columbus: His Life, His Work, His Remains, as Revealed by Original Printed and Manuscript Records Together with an Essay on Peter Martyr of Anghera and Bartolomé de Las Casas, the First Historians of America*. New York: Knickerbocker, 1903; 3-vol. ed., New York: G. P. Putman, 1903–04.

Todd, Charles B. *Life and Letters of Joel Barlow*. New York: G. P. Puttman, 1886.

Todorov, Tzvetan. *The Conquest of America* [1982]. Translated by Richard Howard. New York: Harper & Row, 1984.

Vargas Llosa, Mario. *A Writer's Reality*. Edited by Myron I. Lichtblau. Syracuse, N.Y.: Syracuse University Press, 1990.

Vela, David. "El mito de Cristobal Colón" (The Myth of Christopher Columbus). *Publicaciones de la Academia Guatemalteca* 4 (November 1935): 5–154.

Vignaud, Henry. "Columbus a Spaniard and a Jew?" *American Historical Review* 18 (1913): 505–12.

————. *A Critical Study of the Various Dates Assigned to the Birth of Christopher Columbus: The Real Date, 1551, with a Bibliography of the Question*. London: Stevens & Stiles, 1903.

Wagner, Henry Raup, with Helen Rand Parish. *The Life and Writings of Bartolomé de Las Casas*. Albuquerque: University of New Mexico Press, 1967.

Wassermann, Jacob. *Columbus: Don Quixote of the Ocean* [1929]. Translated by Eric Sutton. Boston: Little, Brown, 1930.

Wechsler, Robert. *Columbus à la Mode*. New York: Catbird Press, 1992.

Whitaker, Thomas R. *William Carlos Williams* [1968]. Boston: Twayne, 1989.

Wiesenthal, Simon. *Sails of Hope* [1972]. Translated by Richard and Clara Winston. New York: Macmillan, 1973. [*Segel der Hoffnung: Die Geheime Mission des Cristoph Columbus*. Olten: Walter, 1972.]

Wilford, John Noble. *The Mysterious History of Columbus: An Exploration of the Man, the Myth, the Legacy*. New York: Knopf, 1991.

Wills, Garry. "1492 vs. 1892 vs. 1992." *Time* (7 October 1991): 61.

————. "Man of the Year." *New York Review of Books* 38, no. 19 (21 November 1991): 12–18.

Wilson, Edmund. *The Shores of Light*. Evanston, Ill.: Northwestern University Press, 1985.

Winsor, Justin. *Christopher Columbus and How He Received and Imparted the Spirit of Discovery*. Boston: Houghton Mifflin, 1891.

Woodress, James. *A Yankee's Odyssey: The Life of Joel Barlow*. Philadelphia: J. B. Lippincott Co., 1958.

Young, Filson. *Christopher Columbus and the New World of His Discovery*, 3d ed. New York: Henry Holt, 1912.

Zunder, Theodore. *The Early Days of Joel Barlow*. New Haven: Yale University Press, 1934.

INDEX

THE AUTHOR

Ilan Stavans is a Mexican novelist and critic born in 1961. He holds a Ph.D. from Columbia University and teaches at Baruch College–The City University of New York. In Spanish, his books include the novel *Talia y el cielo* (1989, written in collaboration with Zuri Balkoff), which won the Latino Literature Prize; the collection of essays *Prontuario* (1991); and the volume of stories *La pianista manca* (1992). In English, he prepared the bilingual edition of Felipe Alfau's *Sentimental Songs/La poesía cursi*, and co-edited with Harold Augenbraum, *Growing up Latino: Memoirs and Stories* (1993). The recipient of many awards and grants by institutions such as the National Endowment for the Humanities and the New York State Council on the Arts, he lives in Manhattan.